GENDER INEQUALITIES IN TECH-DRIVEN RESEARCH AND INNOVATION

Living the Contradiction

Edited by
Gabriele Griffin

BRISTOL
UNIVERSITY
PRESS

First published in Great Britain in 2022 by

Bristol University Press
University of Bristol
1–9 Old Park Hill
Bristol
BS2 8BB
UK
t: +44 (0)117 374 6645
e: bup-info@bristol.ac.uk

Details of international sales and distribution partners are available at bristoluniversitypress.co.uk

British Library Cataloguing in Publication Data
A catalogue record for this book is available from the British Library

ISBN 978-1-5292-1947-0 hardcover
ISBN 978-1-5292-1948-7 OA ePub
ISBN 978-1-5292-1949-4 OA ePdf

Cover design: blu inc
Front cover image: Klaus Vedfelt – gettyimages.co.uk
Bristol University Press uses environmentally responsible print partners
Printed and bound in Great Britain by CPI Group (UK) Ltd, Croydon, CR0 4YY

Contents

List of Tables

Notes on Contributors

Carol Azungi Dralega is Associate Professor at NLA University College, Kristiansand, Norway. She holds a Doctorate in Media Studies from the University of Oslo (2008). Her research interests are in ICT/Media and discourses on Marginality, e-Inclusion, social justice and empowerment in policy and practice.

Hilde G. Corneliussen is Research Professor in Technology and Society at the Western Norway Research Institute (WNRI). Previously she worked at the University of Bergen for 18 years. Her main research topics include gender, identity and ICT from the perspective of inclusion and exclusion. She has been the PI of several research and innovation projects about girls and women in IT.

Ida Drange is Research Professor in the field of labour market studies, with special emphasis on diversity issues and labour market integration of highly educated immigrants. Her research encompasses gender equality in work life, immigrant career outcomes in relation to employment, job mobility, wage developments and occupational accreditation for migrating professionals. She has also done research on workplace democracy, trade unions and work environment factors. She is part of the NordiCore research group and her most recent publications feature in *Work & Occupations*, *Social Inclusion* and the *Nordic Journal of Working Life Studies*.

Gabriele Griffin is Professor of Gender Research at Uppsala University, Sweden, and Extraordinary Professor, Centre for Gender and Africa Studies at the University of the Free State, South Africa. She is coordinator of the Nordforsk-funded Centre of Excellence Nordwit (nordwit.com, 2017–22). She is also editor of the 'Research Methods in the Arts and Humanities' series (Edinburgh University Press). Her recent publications include *Bodily Interventions and Intimate Labour* (co-ed., Manchester University Press, 2020); *Body, Migration, Re/constructive Surgery: Making the Gendered Body in a Global World* (co-ed., Routledge, 2018); *Challenging the Myth of Gender Equality in*

Sweden (Bristol: Policy Press, 2016) and *Cross-Cultural Interviewing: Feminist Experiences and Reflections* (ed., Routledge, 2016).

Hanna-Mari Ikonen is a Lecturer at the University of Jyväskylä, Finland. Her research interests include different forms of entrepreneurial work and entrepreneurial mindsets. Her research has appeared, inter alia, in the *Journal of Youth Studies* and in *Gender and Education.*

Guro Korsnes Kristensen is Professor of Gender, Equality and Diversity Studies at the Department of Interdisciplinary Studies of Culture at the Norwegian University of Science and Technology. Her research areas are gender equality, gender balance, immigration and integration. She is the co-editor of *Comparative Perspectives on Gender Equality in Japan and Norway: Same but Different?* (Routledge, 2021).

Päivi Korvajärvi is Professor emerita in Gender Studies at Tampere University, Finland. She is one of the founding members of the Nordic Centre of Excellence Nordwit (2017–22). Her long-term research interest has been in gendering practices in work. She has also studied the gendered future expectations of young adults. Her recent co-authored articles are published in *Qualitative Research* (2019), the *European Journal of Cultural Studies* (2020) and *Feminist Encounters* (2021).

Malin Lindberg is Professor of Gender and Technology in the subject of Design at Luleå University of Technology, Sweden. She studies inclusive innovation and organization in the public, private and non-profit sectors, in terms of innovative solutions to societal and organizational challenges. Through a participatory research approach, societal actors are actively involved in her research, in order to engender both scientifically and societally relevant insights.

Rebecca W.B. Lund is Associate Professor (Docent) in Gender Studies, Tampere University, Finland. She currently works as a postdoctoral scholar and researcher at the Centre for Interdisciplinary Gender Research at the University of Oslo, Norway. Her research is focused on feminist methodology, epistemic injustice, emotions and gendered social relations in knowledge production and academia.

May-Linda Magnussen holds a PhD in sociology from the University of Oslo, Norway. She is Associate Professor at the Department of Sociology and Social Work at the University of Agder, Norway. Her research concerns gender and gender equality in the intersection between family and work life; migration, everyday life and welfare state; and gender in academia.

Ulf Mellström is Professor of Gender Studies at Karlstad University, Sweden. He studies gender and technology, masculinity, risk, crisis management, engineering, globalization and higher education. He situates his work within the three fields of social anthropology, gender studies, and science and technology studies, in particular feminist technology studies.

Siri Øyslebø Sørensen is Professor of Gender, Equality and Diversity Studies and Head of the Centre for Gender Research at the Department of Interdisciplinary Studies of Culture at the Norwegian University of Science and Technology. Her research interests include the making and implementation of gender equality policies, gender, diversity and power in organizations, career choices and media discourses on gender and feminism. Recently her work has focused on gender and diversity in academia. She is co-editor of *Bodies, Symbols and Organizational Practice: The Gendered Dynamics of Power* (Routledge, 2018).

Maria Pietilä works as Postdoctoral Researcher at the University of Eastern Finland. Her research interests include academic career systems, including questions of assessment and evaluation in academic careers, and gender equality in higher education. Her most recent co-authored articles are published in *Higher Education* (2021) *and Social Inclusion* (2021).

Liza Reisel is Research Director for the research group on Equality, Integration and Migration at the Institute for Social Research in Oslo, Norway. She is also Deputy Project Manager for the Nordic Centre of Excellence, Nordic Centre for Research on Gender Equality in Research and Innovation (NORDICORE). She has published extensively on inequalities in education, gender segregation in the labor market, equality and diversity legislation, education and labour market outcomes among children of immigrants, and health disparities.

Gilda Seddighi is a Senior Researcher in Technology and Society at the Western Norway Research Institute. She has a doctoral degree in Gender and Media Studies from the University of Bergen (2017). Her research interests are in representations of gender, and constructions of identity and opinion in digital media and in processes of digitalization.

Charlotte Silander is Associate Professor of Political Science at Linnaeus University, Sweden. Her current research focuses on gender equality policy and diversity policy in higher education. Her recent co-authored articles appear in *Social Inclusion* (2021) and *European Journal of Higher Education* (2021).

Trond Stalsberg Mydland is a social anthropologist who works as Research Director for Welfare Research at NORCE Norwegian Research Centre. His research is focused on welfare and development projects within democracy, the organization of public services, employee involvement, recovery strategies in mental health work and gender-based inequality.

Marja Vehviläinen is a Lecturer and Senior Researcher in Gender Studies at Tampere University, Finland. She is one of the founding members of the Nordic Centre of Excellence Nordwit (2017–22). She has researched gender, science and technology extensively. Her research also includes gendered agency in nature cultures and environment.

Paula Wennberg is a Project Manager at Luleå University of Technology, Sweden. She has a background in managing projects for gender inclusive growth and innovation in Sweden and internationally, with a particular focus on the IT industry. She is Project Manager of Gender Smart Arena, which forms part of Gender Contact Point.

Oili-Helena Ylijoki was Research Director of TaSTI, the Research Centre for Knowledge, Science, Technology and Innovation Studies, and Docent of Social Psychology at Tampere University, Finland. She is a Senior Research Fellow at TaSTI. Her research interests cover science studies, time studies and higher education studies. She has investigated, among others, disciplinary cultures, transformations of knowledge production, and academic identities and careers. She is a member of the Tampere team of the Nordic Centre of Excellence 'Beyond the Gender Paradox' (Nordwit).

Acknowledgements

This volume is the result of many hours spent talking and working with women and men engaged in research and innovation in academe, the public and the private sectors. Without these informants and collaborators our work would not have been possible, and we sincerely thank our interviewees and research participants who contributed so much to our research and stimulated our thinking.

We would also like to express our thanks to the various research funders who supported this work, most particularly Nordforsk (www.nordforsk.org/), who generously funded Nordwit (https://nordwit.com/), the Nordic Centre of Excellence on women in tech-driven careers (2017–22) located at Uppsala University. Nordwit was the basis for much of the research that is discussed in this volume. We particularly and warmly thank Siri Bjarnar, our scientific officer, and Jesper Werdelin Simonsen, the Executive Director at the Research Council of Norway who was programme director for the Nordforsk programme under which we were funded. We would also like to thank our Scientific Advisory Board set up by Nordforsk – Mary Ann Danowitz, Dean of the College of Education, NY State University; Marcela Linkova of the Centre for Gender and Science at the Institute of Sociology of the Czech Academy of Sciences; Elizabeth Pollitzer, Director of the Gender Equality Summit; Martina Schraudner, Director of the Fraunhofer Center for Responsible Research and Innovation – with whom we batted ideas about in more ways than one.

We also thank the Riksbanken Jubileumsfond (grant no. F19-1506:1) who generously co-funded an international workshop on 'Rethinking Research and Innovation: Does Gender Matter?' that we ran in February 2020 as the last offline event before COVID-19 locked us all down and transported our lives onto online platforms. We had wonderful discussions with colleagues such as Julia Nentwich (St Gallen, Switzerland), Yvonne Benschop (Radboud University, the Netherlands), Hilda Rømer Christensen (Copenhagen, Denmark), Clem Herman (Open University, UK), Liisa Husu (Örebro, Sweden), Susanne Andersson and Karin Berglund (Stockholm, Sweden), Katarina Pettersson (SLU, Uppsala, Sweden), Magdalena Petersson McIntyre and Zehra Sayed (Göteborg, Sweden) and Felizitas Sagebiel

(Wuppertal, Germany) who sharpened our thinking, and provided much stimulating food for thought.

We salute our sister Excellence Centre under the same Nordforsk programme, NORDICORE (www.samfunnsforskning.no/english/projects/nordicore.html), with whom we have collaborated and who, with Chapters 6 and 8 in this volume, are represented by Charlotte Silander et al and Siri Øyslebø Sørensen and Guro Korsnes Kristensen here. Their work has enriched ours, and we have learnt much from them. Plus: we have always been envious of your brilliant infographics – not reproduced here!

On behalf of all the contributors I would also like to thank our friends and colleagues in Sweden, Finland and Norway at the institutions where many of us contributors work: Uppsala University, Tampere University and the Western Norway Research Institute. You have collectively and individually been fantastic at supporting our work, discussing our ideas with us, providing solace, dinners, suggestions – and making our lives much more fun than they would have been without you! Particular thanks go to Elina Nilsson, our lovely administrator and scribe, who has worked hard with us for five years. You're ace!

All the contributors have given many papers on their work over the last three years. The places and events where we did this are too numerous to mention but we'd like to thank the audiences in all those locations, and including conferences such as Gender, Work and Organization and Work2021, that engaged with our work, offered thought-provoking input and shared glasses of wine.

Each contributor to this volume has their own list of people they would like to thank – too lengthy to include here – which often includes family, friends and partners who encouraged and supported the work on this volume through these COVID-19 times. A heartfelt thanks to all of you!

Finally, we would like to express our gratitude to the team at Policy Press who have overseen the process of this volume's production and facilitated its inception, and, of course, to the anonymous readers of the manuscript for their attentive reading and helpful suggestions.

1

Introduction

Gabriele Griffin

When my colleagues from Nordwit[1] and I first thought about this volume we had as its main title *Living the Contradiction*, with the contradiction referring to the fact that we live and work in what are considered to be the most gender-equal countries in the world – Finland, Norway and Sweden – while also being intensely aware that significant gender inequalities persist in all those countries (see Martinsson et al, 2016), including in research and innovation (R&I). This contradiction is also known as the 'Nordic gender paradox'. All our research on women working in tech-driven professions highlighted these contradictions, showing that women are caught between a strongly embedded public gender equality rhetoric and the fact that in emerging, highly technologized work contexts such as ICT and eHealth they constitute certain minorities despite numerous programmes and initiatives set up to increase women's participation in STEM (science, technology, engineering, and mathematics) domains (Stoet and Geary, 2018; Richardson et al, 2020). Tellingly, Nordic Statistics produces a table showing female and male participation in what they describe as 'female' and 'male dominated industries'. The very fact that industries can be described in these terms points to prevailing gender inequalities. In Nordic Statistics female-dominated industries include 'education, human health and social work activities, other service activities. Activities of households as employers, undifferentiated goods and services producing activities of households for own use', and male-dominated industries: 'agriculture, forestry and fishing, mining and quarrying, manufacturing, electricity, gas, steam and air conditioning supply, water supply, sewerage, waste management and remediation activities, construction, transportation and storage, information and communication' (Nordic Statistics, n.d.). For 2019 these tables broadly show that only 25 per cent or fewer of men work in female-dominated industries, and 25 per cent or fewer of women work in male-dominated industries. Like other statistical databases Nordic Statistics aggregate industries, employment sectors and, in higher education, disciplinary domains, and there are questions regarding the extent to which such statistics reflect people's actual lived work experiences. Those actual lived work experiences and their gendered dimensions as these pertain to R&I are what this volume sets out to explore. We argue that these gendered lived work experiences broadly fall under the heading 'living the contradiction'.

Focussing on this issue both inside and outside of the academy, this volume centres on the reported lived experiences of women working in tech-driven R&I arenas to understand how they negotiate this contradiction. The issue is all the more pertinent since the Nordic countries are internationally regarded as frontrunners and model states in both promoting equality and innovation (SHE Figures, 2018; European Innovation Scoreboard, 2019; Gender Equality Index, 2019). Yet women's experiences on the ground are, as this volume shows, in many ways at odds with the positions these indexes and statistics appear to support. This chapter briefly discusses gender, research and innovation, before providing a comparative section regarding the Nordic countries and their diverse positions in relation to gender equality issues. This comparison will include a discussion of how the Nordic countries as place and nation figure here. Finally, the Introduction will provide an outline of the structure of the rest of this volume.

Gender, research and innovation

R&I may be defined as socio-material practices involving multiple actors that produce new scientific knowledge and novel artefacts, processes or practices for societal use (Leyesdorff and Etzkowitz, 2003; Carayannis and Campbell, 2009). In this volume we focus in particular on the academy as a site of R&I, on relatively new and emerging employment fields such as biotechnology, Digital Humanities and ICT, and on women's careers and gender inequalities in these tech-driven work contexts. R&I both inside and outside of the academy is located within global orders such as capitalism and neoliberalism, as well as regional and national policy regimes. It is high on inter/national political agendas as developed economies become knowledge economies. Transnational organizations such as the European Union and the OECD have produced white papers, guidelines and reports (for example Joint Research Centre, 2013; OECD, 2016; NetWorld, 2020) on how R&I might be harnessed more effectively to meet the requirements of these economies and contemporary societies and cultures.

Simultaneously, there has been an increasing recognition that R&I are significantly gendered (see for example the GenderedInnovations project at Stanford or the EC-funded Efforti project).[2] These projects, and others (for example Valantine and Collins, 2015), clearly show not only how genderization occurs in R&I but also provide suggestions as to how this might be countered. Nonetheless, we still have a limited understanding of women's actual experiences of working in R&I within highly tech-driven contexts, and particularly in relation to the Nordic countries where equality is largely assumed to have been achieved and to be fully embedded.

As research into R&I has gained ground over the past 15 years or so, it has become clear that the genderization of R&I is a complex issue (for example Andersson et al, 2012; Lindberg, 2012; Kalpazidou Schmidt and Cacace, 2017), involving, in Charles Tilly's (1998) terms, exploitation, opportunity hoarding, emulation and adaptation. These mechanisms, but not just these, in varying and diverse combinations, establish and maintain gendered structures and practices in R&I which, however, do not necessarily follow a unitary path. Rather, they signal a variegated arena of complex interactivity that requires further investigation (see also Valantine and Collins, 2015). Why, for example, is it that even in the Nordic countries, so renowned for their public equality discourses and equality-related legislations, we still see the glass ceiling, the leaking pipeline and the scissors model of women's research careers when we talk about R&I? How do women negotiate in/equalities in the everyday in R&I? What have the shifts in labour market conditions such as changing funding regimes, moves towards the precarization of the labour force, the rise of neoliberal market economies and new forms of cultural conservatism done in relation to R&I? These are some of the questions this volume seeks to answer as it explores what the contributors consider to be gender paradoxes in R&I in the Nordic countries, that is, the contradiction between the high levels of institutionalized equality measures in the Nordic countries and the persistent gender inequalities that those working in R&I experience and report. To understand these paradoxes it is useful to consider the particularities of the Nordic countries in relation to gender equality.

The Nordic countries and gender equality: similarities and differences

Discursively the Nordic countries are frequently treated as one entity when, in fact, there are significant differences among them, including in terms of how they manage R&I (Pinheiro et al, 2019), and equality measures (Teigen and Skjeie, 2017). The phrase 'the Nordic countries' (Denmark, Finland, Iceland, Norway, Sweden, the Faro Islands, Greenland and Åland) suggests a block of similar countries. This emphasis is a response to a number of factors: geographical proximity; language similarities between Denmark, Norway and Sweden; the dominance of Protestantism; a history of similar political regimes, social democratically oriented, in the post-World War II period broadly lasting until the 1990s; a socio-economic welfare model; and a similar approach to international affairs as anti-militaristic, peace-building and compromise-ready (Browning, 2007). These similarities are reinforced by significant, extensive literatures on 'the Nordic welfare state' (for example Esping-Andersen, 1990; Kautto, 2010; Pedersen and Kuhnle, 2017) and 'Nordic exceptionalism' (for example Delhey and Newton, 2005; Browning, 2007; Loftsdóttir and Jensen, 2012; Martela et al, 2020). However, the supposed cohesiveness of the Nordic countries has increasingly been challenged, not least from the 1990s onwards, when these countries began to pull in somewhat different directions. Whereas Denmark, for example, had been a member of the European Union since 1973, Norway and Iceland became EEA/EFTA[3] states in 1994, and Finland and Sweden joined the European Union in 1995. This went together with a gradual embrace of neoliberal agendas such as deregulation, marketization and individualization, and a concomitant reshaping of the welfare state. In 2010 already Kautto suggested that 'Nordic distinctiveness is by no means as self-evident or as straightforward as it was two decades ago'. This also goes for the 'Nordic gender equality model' (2010: 600).

Spending on research and development as a percentage of GDP is somewhat different across the Nordics, with Finland and Sweden being relatively high spenders while Norway spends comparatively little (Table 1.1) but not as little as the UK, for example:

Table 1.1: R&D expenditure as a percentage of GDP, 2018

Country	DK	FI	NO	SE	UK	USA
R&D expenditure as a percentage of GDP	3.06	2.77	2.07	3.34	1.72	2.84

Source: World Bank (2019) https://data.worldbank.org/indicator/GB.XPD.RSDV.GD.ZS, accessed 27 May 2021.

In terms of the proportion (percentage) of female and male scientists and engineers among the total workforce, by sex, in 2017, Finland manifested the greatest gender gap by some considerable margin and Denmark the lowest (Table 1.2):

Table 1.2: Proportion (%) of female and male scientists and engineers among the total workforce, by sex, 2017

Country	DK		FI		NO		SE	
Sex	women	men	women	men	women	men	women	men
%	5.6	5.4	3.3	8.0	6.7	5.7	5.9	6.1

Source: adapted from SHE Figures (2018), Figure 3.3, p 40.

Teigen and Skjeie (2017) explore the 'Nordic gender equality model' and its supposed homogeneity in terms of *economic equity* and *democratic parity*

(2017: 126). Economic equity includes 'equal educational opportunities, equal pay for work of equal value, gender balance in family life, and gender-balanced participation in labour markets' (2017: 126). Democratic parity includes 'equal rights to vote, assemble and hold office … inclusive opportunity structures for civil society and gender balance in political decision making' (2017: 126). Teigen and Skjeie (2017) argue that the Nordic scores for democratic parity are more exceptional than those for economic parity (2017: 142) and as high scorers overall, the Nordic countries might be considered very similar but that, in fact, their underlying policies vary significantly (2017: 144). As the chapters in this volume reveal, according to the reported experiences of women in Finland (FI), Norway (NO) and Sweden (SE) working in R&I, inequalities of different kinds are still a norm. These include horizontal and vertical segregation in both education and in the workplace, the persistence of the gender pay gap and the unequal distribution of household and care tasks. These persistent inequalities (Griffin and Vehvilainen, 2021) are evident in relevant international statistics in most areas of R&I. Thus according to the SHE Figures (2018) the proportion (percentage) of women among doctoral graduates by broad field of study in 2016 was as shown in Table 1.3:

Table 1.3: Proportion (%) of women among doctoral graduates by broad field of study, 2016

Country	Education	Arts & Humanities	Natural Sciences, Maths & Statistics	Information & Communication Technologies (ICT)	Health & Welfare
EU-28	68	54	46	21	60
DK	-	53	37	-	63
FI	74	59	49	18	63
NO	64	58	40	15	61
SE	73	55	41	24	61

Source: adapted from SHE Figures (2018), Table 2.2, p 23.

Table 1.3 shows that there are quite significant differences between the different Nordic countries in the proportion of women among doctoral graduates by broad field of study, involving a 10 per cent difference between Finland and Norway for education, for example, and 9 per cent difference between Sweden and Norway regarding ICT. The Swedish percentage for ICT is the same as the UK (not shown here, but 24 per cent), and the Finnish one at 18 per cent is only one percentage point above the Polish one which was 17 per cent. Based upon these statistics, one could therefore postulate quite different similarities and differences across European countries than the phrase 'the Nordic countries' suggests.

The gender wage gap also shows differences across the Nordics. Boschini and Gunnarsson (2018) argue that:

> Despite men's and women's almost equally high labour force participation and women's, on average, higher educational levels, the median gender wage gap among full-time employed has changed only marginally since 1991. … It was 7.8 per cent in Denmark (2012), 18.7 per cent in Finland (2012), 7.0 per cent in Norway (2013) and 15.1 per cent in Sweden (2012) according to OECD. (2018: 105)

In other words, there are significant discrepancies regarding the gender wage gap among the Nordic countries, with more than 10 percentage points difference between those countries with the lowest wage gap (Denmark, Finland) and those with the highest (Norway, Sweden). Here, again, the Nordics do not emerge as a unitary block but rather as countries with individual particularities. This is also the case when one considers researcher numbers in the government and business sectors (Table 1.4):

Table 1.4: Researchers in the government and business sectors, 2015 (headcount)

Country	Government sector		Business sector	
	women	men	women	men
DK	1,284	1,301	7,254	22,394
FI	2,160	2,728	4,849	23,128
NO	2,960	3,411	4,838	16,368
SE	5,574	6,657	11,287	41,081

Source: adapted from SHE Figures (2018), Annex 3.2, p 55 and Annex 3.3, p 56.

The differences in number across the four Nordic countries evident in Table 1.4 cannot be explained through relative population size for example (DK = 5,792,202; FI = 5,540,720; NO = 5,421,241; SE = 10,099,265),[4] or relative size of the sectors. Table 1.4 shows that the number of female researchers in the public sector in Denmark is significantly lower than in Finland and Norway where the population is roughly the same size. It also shows that the number of female researchers working in the government sector is almost equal to that of men in Denmark, but less equal in Finland, Norway or Sweden. The gender gap regarding female researchers in the business sector is huge compared to the government sector at roughly 25 per cent or fewer of female researchers in that sector. Again, significant discrepancies can be observed for Finland compared to Norway, but also in terms of numbers of female researchers in the business sector in Denmark compared to those in Finland and Norway.

When it comes to precarious working contracts (see also Standing, 2011), women researchers fare consistently worse than male researchers, again with significant discrepancies across the Nordic countries (Table 1.5):

Table 1.5: Proportion of researchers in the higher education sector working under 'precarious' working contracts, by sex, 2016

	DK	FI	NO	SE
Women	4.4	12.6	8.2	10.2
Men	3.2	6.9	5	6.1

Source: adapted from SHE Figures (2018), Figure 5.2, p 99.

Thus while the gender gap regarding precarious contracts is relatively small in Denmark, in Finland almost twice as many women as men have precarious working contracts, and the gender gap is also significantly larger in Sweden than in Denmark. Further, there are sizeable differences regarding the parental leave schemes across the Nordic countries (Table 1.6):

Table 1.6: Parental leave in the Nordic countries

	DK	FI	NO	SE
Number of weeks	52	48	49	69
Number of weeks reserved for fathers	0	6	10	8

Source: adapted from Teigen and Skjeie (2017), Table 5, p 141.

Table 1.6 shows significant differences in the amount of time allocated to parental leave. There is a 17-week difference in parental leave allocation between Denmark and Sweden, and there are also important differences in the number of parental leave weeks reserved for fathers. Since fathers' participation in childcare is key to women's ability to have a career in R&I (see Chapter 9 by Seddighi and Corneliussen, this volume), these differences matter.

What all the figures cited earlier tell us is that any finer-grained analysis of gender equality issues in R&I across the supposedly very similar Nordic countries will reveal significant differences among them (Åseskog, 2018). But rather than assess the relativity of these differences and similarities, it might be more pertinent to ask for what purposes these discourses of similarity or difference are mobilized. One could argue that the public assertion of achieved gender equality serves to silence dissenting voices and absolves relevant bodies and organizations from addressing gender equality issues in the Nordic countries. One could further argue that the homogenization of the Nordic countries under that very umbrella term serves to obscure significant differences (see Larsen et al, 2021) that the individual countries involved might need to address. Conversely, one could also suggest that highlighting the differences between the Nordic countries and the range of gender inequalities that continue to prevail (Griffin and Vehvilainen, 2021) is an incitement for action and change. Any emphasis on differences or similarities between the Nordic countries is thus a strategic and political decision, based on the purpose the comparison is meant to serve.

Institutionally the Nordic countries have cemented their similarities through joint bodies such as the Nordic Council of Ministers. Given the geographic location and proximity of the countries, their relative size both of territory and of population (see Table 1.7), the linguistic affinities between Danish, Norwegian and Swedish, and the Nordic countries' social-democratic welfare state histories, it makes sense to emphasize the similarities and to foster close allegiances among them. The Nordic countries occupy comparatively large geographical spaces while having small populations as becomes evident in their population per square kilometre ratio (see Table 1.7). Sweden, for instance, is geographically roughly twice the size of the UK but has a population of less than one sixth of the UK's. This also means that there are few large cities and that large tracts of each country except for Denmark are uninhabited or very sparsely inhabited. This impacts on issues such as social cohesion and trust, but also on interdependence among the Nordic countries.

Table 1.7: Size of geographic territory (in km^2) and population in 2020 by Nordic country (UK added as comparator)

	Denmark	**Iceland**	**Finland**	**Norway**	**Sweden**	**UK**
Size of territory in km^2	42,916	103,000	338,145	323,802	450,295	242,900
Total population	5,792,202	341,243	5,540,720	5,421,241	10,099,265	68,192,697
Population density per km^2	137	3	18	15	25	281

Source: adapted from www.worldometers.info/world-population/population-by-country/, accessed 12 May 2021.

Countries with small populations benefit and suffer from the fact that members of specific subsections of the population such as those working in Digital Humanities or biotechnology all tend to know each other. Such familiarity fosters trust and social cohesion but it can also produce subtle mechanisms of in- and exclusion (Husu, 2001, 2005) such as become evident in some of the chapters in this volume (for example Chapters 5 and 11). The COVID-19 pandemic has cast this situation into a new global light, not least regarding R&I. The pandemic has highlighted the tensions between globalization and localization, two major forces that are structuring inter- and transnational interaction against a longer-term backdrop of rising populism, right-wing politics and neo-nationalism that is anti-global except where the circulation of capital is concerned. The pandemic, but also climate change, for example, as global phenomena require global cooperation to address them. Here sharing knowledge regarding the virus, for example, constituted a push towards globalized collaboration in R&I, but the manufacture and especially the distribution of the anti-viral vaccines reinforced nationalistic tendencies as countries and indeed in some instances regions within countries 'looked after their own', despite the setting up of Covax,[5] a worldwide distribution system of anti-viral drugs by the World Health Organization. The Nordic countries were no exception in this, responding differently to the pandemic in terms of degrees and timing of restrictive measures and so on. Place and belongingness have thus come to matter in new and unexpected ways, including in the Nordic countries, which, despite their generally close cooperation, closed borders against each other's citizens, for example, in order to stem the spread of infection. Travel abroad, there as elsewhere, was discouraged and in 2021 many people did not consider holidays abroad. We already have significant research showing how COVID-19 has reinforced existing gender inequalities among women and men (for example Alon et al, 2020; Collins et al, 2021). One concern must be that the pandemic provides license to entrench gender inequalities further, as political and economic priorities displace certain inequalities from policy and governmental agendas. This needs to be guarded against in these times of challenge and change.

Structure of the volume

All the chapters in this volume are based on original empirical qualitative data, collected between 2017 and 2020. Many of these, but not all, derive from research carried out under the auspices of the Nordforsk-funded Excellence Centre Nordwit (nordwit.com). They all engage with the issue of gender inequalities in tech-driven R&I from the perspective of those who work in that context, in other words, from below, and centre on findings from three Nordic countries: Finland, Norway and Sweden. These countries, as discussed earlier, have many similarities, particularly historically, not least their public emphasis on gender equality, and their relatively high investment in R&I as a percentage of GDP (Table 1.8):

Table 1.8: R&D expenditure as % of GDP

Country	DK	FI	NO	SE	USA	UK
R&D expenditure	2.9	3.1	1.7	3.1	2.7	1.6

Source: http://uis.unesco.org/apps/visualisations/research-and-development-spending/, accessed 26 May 2021.

However, the Nordics are also countries that have become increasingly drawn into the orbit of neoliberal policies and dispositions (for example Berg et al, 2016; Kamali and Jönsson, 2018; Nygren et al, 2018). Some would argue (for example Browning, 2007; Kautto, 2010) that this is what has begun to create subtle differences among these countries, their policies and modi operandi. Others have suggested for some considerable time that conceptual frames such as 'woman-friendly states', applied to 'the Nordic countries', 'downplay differences between the five Nordic countries' and that there are 'important differences in the form of women's mobilization, their inclusion in political parties as well as the extent of institutionalization of gender equality' in these Nordic countries (Borchorst and Siim, 2002: 92). The chapters in this volume explore those similarities and differences in dialogue with each other, in the understanding that, to quote a well-established feminist line, knowledge is situated (Haraway, 1988), and that gender and R&I, as entangled constructs in particular contexts, are also situated, even as they operate at local, national and international levels simultaneously.

Gabriele Griffin's chapter on the precariousness of R&I in academe sets the tone for much of the work in this volume which highlights the ambivalences that accompany women's and to some extent men's (see also Hearn, 2017) reported working experiences in R&I in contemporary academe (see also Murgia and Poggio, 2019). She draws on interviews with Digital Humanities practitioners in Finland, Norway and Sweden to argue that emerging inter- and multidisciplinary knowledge domains which constitute epistemic innovations operate in 'unsettledness'. This term describes R&I as such which is all about the new, change and the transformative. It also applies to those working in new knowledge domains which are frequently established in atypical higher education formations such as centres, labs or forums that exist outside the main conventional decision-making structures of academe and are hence marginalized. Drawing on Charles Tilly's (1998) depiction of inequality mechanisms, in particular opportunity hoarding and exploitation, but also on Henry Etzkowitz and Carol Kemelgor's (1998) elaboration of the role of centres in universities, Griffin illustrates how conditions of unsettledness which extend to the provisional contractual situation of many Digital Humanities practitioners enable gendered inequalities to flourish in contexts where there is – public equality discourses notwithstanding – little room for redress. Thus R&I institutions such as universities both invite and disavow innovation, for instance through how they both desire innovation as long as it is accompanied by external funding, and disavow it by not supporting it in terms of their recruitment and promotion criteria where interdisciplinarity, for instance in publications terms, can be an active disadvantage. Universities emerge as not agile here, and as insecure sources of employment, pushing women who often embrace innovation opportunities, either out of their jobs or into service appointments which fail to do justice to their expertise, knowledge and competences.

This topic is also taken up by Oili-Helena Ylijoki in her chapter on navigating the career paradoxes of women researchers in biotechnology. Biotechnology, like Digital Humanities, is a new kid on the R&I block, and in academe. And like in Digital Humanities, the researchers are predominantly female. Indeed, Ylijoki's case study, a biotechnology centre at a Finnish university, originally had *only* female researchers. As an emerging knowledge domain biotechnology has no track record of institutional embeddedness, professional associations or other obvious support structures. It is hence the object of institutional and educational policy decision-making in ways that challenge its efficacy. Ylijoki discusses how the multiple mergers which this centre underwent as part of a national Finnish higher education restructuring strategy to create bigger units, led to its dissolution, with half its female staff leaving to seek work in the private sector and the other half continuing under constraining working conditions in which they found it almost impossible to gain institutional recognition in the form of permanent jobs and promotions to professorships despite bringing in more money than some of their colleagues from other, much more established, related disciplines such as medicine. Ylijoki identifies three career imaginaries that shape these women's views of their professional lives: i) the tenure track position, introduced into Finland (but not into other Nordic countries) in 2010, which is open to younger scholars on the basis of their 'promise' and which leads to a permanent professorship but is only achieved by very few, hence not a realistic prospect for most; ii) academic entrepreneurs who exist from project to project on insecure temporary employment even if they are highly successful in terms of generating external funding; and iii) leaving academe to gain more secure and less stressful employment in the private sector. The paradox in all this is that biotechnology when it emerged was regarded as having great potential to generate transformative scientific results, opportunities for commercialization and academy-industry links, and its institutionalization was accompanied by great hype. Academe clearly desired it, but unrealistic expectations of the instantaneity of its transformational and income-generating potential coupled with structural changes in higher education challenged the biotechnology centre's viability, and its absorption into ever larger male-dominated units within the university dissolved its potential, leaving the women in the unit floundering and unable to see their career futures in anything other than bleak terms.

Against such bleakness Hilde G. Corneliussen and Gilda Seddighi's chapter shows that women find ways into ICT even when the odds are stacked against them, not only because ICT is considered to be male dominated but also because they are not encouraged into ICT at the point of entering higher education or because they are interested in something else at that stage. Corneliussen and Seddighi focus on ICT work in Norway. They found that women migrated to ICT through three different, circuitous routes. One was by doing a second degree in an ICT field later on in life after the women had already completed a first degree (this is, of course, a more likely route in countries where education is free, rather than where one has to pay fees as in the UK). The second occurred as a function of the technologization of non-tech contexts. And the third came about as a result of the need for non-tech specialisms within ICT fields. Importantly, women such as the ones interviewed for this chapter are not captured in OECD and other databases documenting ICT domains because these databases often take only the first higher education degree into account – which in these women's cases was in non-ICT subjects – and because we have as yet no effective ways of measuring either shifts in occupational parameters as a function of increasing digitalization, or of tracking career moves across domains. The low numbers of women in ICT that are conventionally reported may therefore be somewhat misleading in terms of actual numbers of women engaged in ICT-focussed research and innovation.

In the same way that we know little about women finding their way into ICT through circuitous routes, we also have little research to date that addresses how changing research funding regimes impact differentially on women and men although it is established that gendered biases in research funding occur (Ranga et al, 2012; Van der Lee and Ellemers, 2015). Vehviläinen et al's chapter provides useful insights into this phenomenon. They chart experiences of an initial great welcome followed by a narrative of decline as a function of changing research funding regimes in relation to women working in biotechnology, a new R&I area in contemporary Finnish academe. They outline Finland's shifts in research funding, the result of changing economic fortunes and in particular the spectacular rise and decline of one company and private research funder, Nokia. Here the disproportionate influence of one company on the finances of a country with a small population become evident. But Vehviläinen et al's account also demonstrates that in times of economic contraction women fare significantly worse than men, being excluded from research opportunities, particularly where these collide with family responsibilities and childbearing issues. The women's inability to resist their exclusion from R&I as funding shrank is painful to behold; it speaks to the difficulty of changing the underlying cultures of gender inequality which are held at bay during times of plenty but surface in almost unchanged ways in times of austerity, even in supposedly gender equal countries.

Charlotte Silander et al's chapter discusses the effectiveness of different equality measures in redressing prevailing gender inequalities in Finland, Norway and Sweden. It covers the period 2000–18 and compares the relative effectiveness of *organizational measures* such as having gender equality plans and *targeted measures* directed specifically at women in STEM universities. They reveal interesting differences between the countries: while all of them use organizational equality measures, Finland did much less regarding targeted measures. However, the findings show that targeted measures, some of which might be construed as positive action, are more effective in achieving change than organizational measures. The paradox and problem is that targeted measures that could be construed as positive action are not permissible under EU law and hence the two countries that used them the most, Norway and Sweden, had to discontinue them (see also Skjeie et al, 2019: 443–4).

The effectiveness of such measures is also under scrutiny in May-Linda Magnussen et al's chapter, which provides very concrete evidence of what such targeted measures might mean. Here a specific measure, preliminary evaluations of more junior female academics in a technology university in Norway, is under scrutiny. The preliminary evaluations concerned the women's curricula vitae (CV) and their readiness to be promoted to professor. The chapter finds that women who underwent such evaluations by and large felt motivated to work towards a professorship. For some this was because they felt recognized and made visible through the process of the evaluation itself – they were being paid attention. For others it was about gaining a better understanding of what was required in CV terms, and negotiating more research time to improve their outputs. Magnussen et al, however, point out that such recognition came at a cost. They argue that the women were effectively invited to emulate male-centred academic cultures, that is, become more competitive, more narrowly focussed, say 'no' to anything that was not CV-supportive, focus on number one (that is, themselves) and so on; in other words, they were neoliberalized and indeed, invited to adapt themselves to the masculinized work environment that the neoliberal academy has promoted (Hearn, 2017). The authors rightly ask if this is the kind of R&I environment we want to foster (see also Morley and Lund, 2020).

Siri Øyslebø Sørensen and Guro Korsnes Kristensen's chapter shows how much that work environment has already become rooted in early career researchers' imaginaries regarding their futures in academe. The Norwegian postdocs they interviewed saw the academic environment as highly competitive and extremely demanding, leaving little room for 'having a life'.

In this they clearly resembled the Finnish academics whom Oili-Helena Ylijoki discussed in her chapter in this volume. However, unlike in Finland where tenure track positions have become a new norm, such positions are not available in Norway, thereby changing the futures early career researchers can imagine. A professorship which would change the Norwegian postdocs' status from temporary to permanent employment was seen as a way out of the precarity that accompanied their present status, but it was not something they regarded as possible to 'choose' as such. This contradicts the neoliberal rhetoric of 'choice' that has come to dominate many work-related discourses.

'Choice' also played a very limited role in their initial decision to undertake postdoc positions. Being supported by more senior academics, having luck, and serendipity loomed larger than any notion of choice in their imaginaries, with the added gendered, not necessarily expected dimension that women were much more upfront about that support than men who tended to downplay it. Differences in gendered perceptions also played an interesting role in how the entanglement of career and family was narrated. Men talked about their partners as equally committed to their careers as they were, while the women talked more in terms of their own agency in managing family and work. Interestingly, male interviewees suggested that the question of having a family was as pertinent for them as for women, thus pointing to potential new alliances between younger men and their partners regarding this issue.

For the Norwegian postdocs becoming a professor was regarded as desirable because it led out of precarious work situations, it lent authority and it seemed the inevitable goal of pursuing an academic career, but it was also viewed as hugely demanding and incompatible with having a work-life balance. That issue of the work-life balance is also taken up in Gilda Seddighi and Hilde G. Corneliussen's chapter regarding the challenges women working in ICT research and innovation in Norway in the governmental and business sectors face as they try to reconcile work and family life in an age when flexible working has been heralded as the means to enable women to spend more time with family, and to have both a career and a family. However, and first, the generous childcare policies that are a hallmark of Norway proved insufficient to the needs of these women who were required to draw on their individual personal resources regarding childcare to enable them to pursue their career. In the context of the dual-earner model that is prevalent in the Nordic countries, Norwegian women working in ICT had to rely on partners with different work patterns than their own, in particular predictable standard-office-hour work times, not too much travel or commuting and the flexibility to be home early to manage childcare issues. Second, flexibility in these women's account of their careers meant working *more*, rather than less, and often evenings and weekends to 'make up for' time spent with children. The 'greedy' work cultures that prevail in

ICT R&I were difficult to negotiate for women, and even as they worked there full-time, and indeed more, some felt like that they had opted out from a career because they gave their time to family.

One answer to such difficulty might, of course, be to save time by going online (though COVID-19 has shown that this has many gendered implications also – see Alon et al, 2020; Collins et al, 2021; Hupkau and Petrongolo, 2020). Malin Lindberg et al's chapter on co-creative platforms deals with the question of how gender research can be used effectively across academe and industry or business/enterprise through just such platforms, in this instance two located in Sweden. Co-creative platforms in themselves constitute an innovation, and Lindberg et al's work explores how gender research can inform – through a co-creative, collaborative endeavour between academe and business – innovative equality practices in businesses. Their study reveals that these platforms engage researchers and stakeholders in innovation processes of joint identification, exploration and solution of societal and organizational challenges, as is common in social innovation. Both struggle, however, to bridge the critical agenda of the researchers and the constructive agendas of the stakeholders. Lindberg et al emphasize the potential of gender research to improve organizational competitiveness, innovativeness and attractiveness, on the one hand, while advancing academic knowledge on mechanisms for organizational and societal transformation, on the other. However, they also indicate some of the vicissitudes of collaborating across sectors, ranging from incompatibilities of timetables which made the arrangement of meetings difficult to managers' disbelief regarding some of the research findings. Cross-sectoral collaboration, a much vaunted *desideratum* in contemporary academe, proves more demanding than anticipated.

The volume finishes with a text on a little explored subject, the relationship between ICT R&I and geographical location. We tend to think of R&I as occurring largely in urban conglomerations but technologization has changed work opportunities in rural regions as businesses and government bodies have relocated there, both to support local and regional development and in search of cost effectiveness. This is important in the Nordic countries which have huge rural areas that are sparsely populated and where out-migration by women is more common than out-migration by men (SSB, 2018). For women, as Hilde G. Corneliussen et al show, the changing workscape in rural regions produces interesting job opportunities that might not be available to them in urban areas. In the Norwegian context, on which this chapter concentrates, these opportunities coincide with women's desire to live in areas where they grew up, to spend more time with family and to enjoy the benefits that living in a rural environment offers such as outdoor activities which are highly popular in the Nordic countries, such as hiking in the summer and skiing in the winter. Corneliussen et al found that scarcity of human resources in under-populated areas in Norway and the technologization of companies and the public sector afforded women who were either keen to move to the countryside anyway or who already had family connections there meant that women had opportunities to get jobs and utilize or develop their ICT expertise while at the same time cutting down on commuting and improving their work-life balance. However, for migrant women with no prior family connections isolation in the countryside could also become a problem, and all women had to grapple with the fact that overall there were far fewer workplaces to choose from than in urban arenas. Nonetheless Corneliussen et al's work counteracts the prevailing assumption that women in ICT research and innovation are inevitably low in numbers and cannot find a way of reconciling work and life. The countryside emerges as a space of qualified opportunity for women in ICT.

Gender inequalities in R&I continue to prevail (see Striebing et al, 2020), even in the Nordic countries. This much is clear. However, there are also signs of gradual change. According to the SHE Figures (2018) 'the proportion of tertiary educated women and men working as professionals or technicians are almost equal at the EU-28 level' (2018: 40). 'Women are also more likely than men to work in knowledge-intensive activities' (2018: 42) and 'While women are under-represented as authors in research publications, they are slowly closing the gap' (2018: 142). The funding success rates for women and men show that in Denmark and Finland overall women have greater success rates than men; in Norway they are almost equal; and only in Sweden do men have higher funding success rates (SHE Figures, 2018: 173). These indicators may signal that women in R&I are gradually adapting to the neoliberal workscape they inhabit without this necessarily changing the work cultures they have to navigate, or it may suggest an overall shift in work environments affecting both women and men. One thing is for sure: living the contradiction is not sustainable.

Notes

1. Nordwit is a Nordforsk-funded Excellence Centre (2017–22) focussing on women in tech-driven careers (see www.nordwit.com).
2. For details of the GenderedInnovations project see https://genderedinnovations.stanford.edu; for the Efforti project see www.efforti.eu, both accessed 15 April 2021.
3. EEA: European Economic Area; EFTA: European Free Trade Association.
4. Figures from www.worldometers.info/world-population/population-by-country/, accessed 24 May 2021.
5. See www.who.int/initiatives/act-accelerator/covax, accessed 26 May 2021.

References

Alon, T.M., Doepke, M., Olmstead-Rumsey, J. and Tertilt, M. (2020) *The Impact of COVID-19 on Gender Equality* (No. w26947), Cambridge, MA: National Bureau of Economic Research. Available at: www.nber.org/system/files/working_papers/w26947/w26947.pdf, accessed 20 January 2022.

Andersson, S., Berglund, K., Gunnarsson, E. and Sundin, E. (eds) (2012) *Promoting Innovation: Policies, Practices, and Procedure*, Stockholm: Vinnova.

Åseskog, B. (2018) 'National machinery for gender equality in Sweden and other Nordic countries', in S.M. Rai (ed) *Mainstreaming Gender, Democratizing the State?*, Manchester: Manchester University Press, pp 146–66.

Berg, L.D., Huijbens, E.H. and Larsen, H.G. (2016) 'Producing anxiety in the neoliberal university', *The Canadian Geographer/le géographe canadien*, 60(2): 168–80.

Borchorst, A. and Siim, B. (2002) 'The women-friendly welfare states revisited', *NORA: Nordic Journal of Feminist and Gender Research*, 10(2): 90–8.

Boschini, A. and Gunnarsson, K. (2018) 'Gendered trends in income inequality', in R. Aaberge et al (eds) *Increasing Income Inequality in the Nordics: Nordic Economic Policy Review 2018*, Copenhagen: Nordic Council of Ministers, pp 100–27.

Browning, C.S. (2007) 'Branding Nordicity: models, identity and the decline of exceptionalism', *Cooperation and Conflict*, 42(1): 27–51.

Carayannis, E.G. and Campbell, D.F. (2009) '"Mode 3" and "quadruple helix": toward a 21st century fractal innovation ecosystem', *International Journal of Technology Management*, 46(3–4): 201–34.

Collins, C., Landivar, L.C., Ruppanner, L. and Scarborough, W.J. (2021) 'COVID-19 and the gender gap in work hours', *Gender, Work & Organization*, 28: 101–12.

Delhey, J. and Newton, K. (2005) 'Predicting cross-national levels of social trust: global pattern or Nordic exceptionalism?', *European Sociological Review*, 21(4): 311–27.

Esping-Andersen, G. (1990) *Three Worlds of Welfare Capitalism*, Cambridge: Polity Press.

Etzkowitz, H. and Kemelgor, C. (1998) 'The role of research centres in the collectivization of academic science', *Minerva*, 36(3): 271–88.

European Innovation Scoreboard (2019) European Commission, Directorate-General for Internal Market, Industry, Entrepreneurship and SMEs, Brussels: Publications Office. Available at: https://data.europa.eu/doi/10.2873/342097, accessed 19 January 2022.

Gender Equality Index (2019) European Institute for Gender Equality. Available at: https://eige.europa.eu/gender-equality-index/2019, accessed 19 January 2022.

Griffin, G. and Vehvilainen, M. (2021) 'The persistence of gender struggles in Nordic research and innovation', *Feminist Encounters*, 5(2): art. 28.

Haraway, D. (1988) 'Situated knowledges: the science question in feminism and the privilege of partial perspective', *Feminist Studies*, 14(3): 575–99.

Hearn, J. (2017) 'Neoliberal universities, patriarchies, masculinities, and myself: transnational-personal reflections on and from the global north', *Gender a výzkum*, 18(1): 16–41. Available at: https://nordics.info/show/artikel/podcast-identity-politics-in-a-post-global-nordic-societies/, accessed 25 May 2021.

Hupkau, C. and Petrongolo, B. (2020) 'Work, care and gender during the COVID-19 crisis', *Fiscal Studies*, 41(3): 623–51.

Husu, L. (2001) 'Sexism, support and survival in academia: academic women and hidden discrimination in Finland', Department of Social Psychology, University of Helsinki. Available at: www.researchgate.net/publication/274192317_Sexism_support_and_survival_in_academia, accessed 2 July 2020.

Husu, L. (2005) 'Women's work- and family-related discrimination and support in academia', *Advances in Gender Research*, 9: 1–40.

Joint Research Centre (2013) *Drivers of Change: The Main Drivers of Change Affecting the Research and Innovation Landscape and Their Implications for EU Policy*, Brussels: Publications Office. Available at: https://data.europa.eu/doi/10.2791/97082, accessed 19 January 2022.

Kalpazidou Schmidt, E. and Cacace, M. (2017) 'Addressing gender inequality in science: the multifaceted challenge of assessing impact', *Research Evaluation*, 26(2): 102–14.

Kamali, M. and Jönsson, J.H. (eds) (2018) *Neoliberalism, Nordic Welfare States and Social Work: Current and Future Challenges*, London: Routledge.

Karpestam, P. and Håkansson, P.G. (2021) 'Rural boys, urban girls? The mystery of the diminishing urban–rural gender gap in Sweden', *Journal of Rural Studies*, 86: 282–97.

Kautto, M. (2010) 'The Nordic countries', in F.G. Castles, S. Leibfried, J. Lewis, H. Obinger and C. Pierson (eds) *The Oxford Handbook of the Welfare State*, Oxford: Oxford University Press, pp 586–600.

Larsen, E., Moss, S.A. and Skjelsbaek, I. (2021) *Gender Equality and Nation Branding in the Nordic Region*, Abingdon: Routledge.

Leydesdorff, L. and Etzkowitz, H. (2003) 'Can "the public" be considered as a fourth helix in university–industry–government relations? Report on the Fourth Triple Helix Conference, 2002', *Science and Public Policy*, 30(1): 55–61.

Lindberg, M. (2012) 'A striking pattern: co-construction of innovation, men and masculinity in Sweden's innovation policy', in S. Andersson, K. Berglund, E. Gunnarsson and E. Sundin (eds) *Promoting Innovation: Policies, Practices, and Procedure*, Stockholm: Vinnova, pp 47–67.

Loftsdóttir, K. and Jensen, L. (2012) 'Nordic exceptionalism and the Nordic "others"', in K. Loftsdóttir and L. Jensen (eds) *Whiteness and Postcolonialism in the Nordic Region: Exceptionalism, Migrant Others and National Identities*, London: Routledge, pp 1–12.

Martela, F., Greve, B., Rothstein, B. and Saari, J. (2020) 'The Nordic exceptionalism: what explains why the Nordic Countries are constantly among the happiest in the world', in J.F. Helliwell, R. Layard, J.D. Sachs and J.E. De Neve (eds) *World Happiness Report*, pp 128–45. Available at: https://worldhappiness.report, accessed 13 May 2021.

Martinsson, L., Griffin, G. and Giritli-Nygren, K. (eds) (2016) *Challenging the Myth of Gender Equality in Sweden*, Bristol: Policy Press.

Morley, L. and Lund, R.W. (2020) 'The affective economy of feminist leadership in Finnish universities: class-based knowledge for navigating neoliberalism and neuroliberalism', *Discourse: Studies in the Cultural Politics of Education*, 42(1): 1–17.

Murgia, A. and Poggio, B. (eds) (2019) *Gender and Precarious Research Careers: A Comparative Analysis*, London: Routledge.

NetWorld (2020) *Strategic Research and Innovation Agenda 2021–27*. Available at: www.networldeurope.eu/wp-content/uploads/2018/11/networld2020-5gia-sria-version-2.0.pdf?x70854, accessed 19 January 2022.

Nordic Statistics (n.d.) *LABO06: Labour Market Segregation by Gender Domination, Reporting Country, Unit, Sex and Time*. Available at: https://pxweb.nordicstatistics.org/pxweb/en/Nordic%20Statistics/Nordic%20Statistics__Nordic%20Gender%20Equality%20Indicators__Labour%20market/LABO06.px/?rxid=4bd7ba15-3c4a-4793-8711-6db1fc878223, accessed 19 January 2022.

Nygren, K.G., Martinsson, L. and Mulinari, D. (2018) 'Gender equality and beyond: at the crossroads of neoliberalism, anti-gender movements, "European" values, and normative reiterations in the Nordic model', *Social Inclusion*, 6(4): 1–7.

OECD (2016) *Innovating Education and Educating for Innovation*. Paris: OECD Publishing. Available at: http://dx.doi.org/10.1787/9789264265097-en, accessed 19 January 2022.

Pedersen, A.W. and Kuhnle, S. (2017) 'The Nordic welfare state model', in O. Knutsen (ed) *The Nordic Models in Political Science: Challenged, But Still Viable?*, Bergen: Fagbokforlaget, pp 249–72.

Pinheiro, R., Geschwind, L., Foss Hansen, H. and Pulkkinen, K. (eds) (2019) *Reforms, Organizational Change and Performance in Higher Education: A Comparative Account from the Nordic Countries*, Cham: Springer Nature.

Ranga, M., Gupta, N. and Etzkowitz, H. (2012) *Gender Effects in Research Funding*, Bonn: Deutsche Forschungsgemeinschaft.

Richardson, S.S., Reiches, M.W., Bruch, J., Boulicault, M., Noll, N.E. and Shattuck-Heidorn, H. (2020) 'Is there a gender-equality paradox in science, technology, engineering, and math (STEM)? Commentary on the study by Stoet and Geary (2018)', *Psychological Science*, 31(3): 338–41.

SHE Figures (2018) Brussels: European Commission. Available at: https://op.europa.eu/en/publication-detail/-/publication/9540ffa1-4478-11e9-a8ed-01aa75ed71a1, accessed 19 January 2022.

Skjeie, H., Holst, C. and Teigen, M. (2019) 'Splendid isolation? On how a non-member is affected by – and affects – EU gender equality policy', in M. Dustin, N. Ferreira and S. Millns (eds) *Gender and Queer Perspectives on Brexit*, Cham: Palgrave/Macmillan, pp 439–62.

SSB (2018) *Men and Women in Norway*, Norway Statistics. Available at: www.ssb.no/en/befolkning/artikler-og-publikasjoner/_attachment/347081?_ts=1632b8bcba0, accessed 21 May 2021.

SSB (2018) *Women and Men in Sweden*, Örebrö: Statistics Sweden. Available at: www.scb.se/contentassets/4550eaae793b46309da2aad796972cca/le0201_2017b18_br_x10br1801eng.pdf, accessed 22 May 2021.

Standing, G. (2011) *The Precariat: A New, Dangerous Class*, London: Bloomsbury.

Stoet, G. and Geary, D.C. (2018) 'The gender-equality paradox in science, technology, engineering, and mathematics education', *Psychological Science*, 29(4): 581–93.

Striebing, C., Schmidt, E.K., Palmén, R., Holzinger, F. and Nagy, B. (2020) 'Women [sic] underrepresentation in R&I: a sector program assessment of the contribution of gender equality policies in research and innovation', *Evaluation and Program Planning*, 79: 101749.

Teigen, M. and Skjeie, H. (2017) 'The Nordic gender equality model', in O. Knutsen (ed) *The Nordic Models in Political Science: Challenged, But Still Viable?*, Bergen: Fagbokforlaget, pp 125–47.

Tilly, C. (1998) *Durable Inequality*, Berkeley: University of California Press.

Valantine, H.A. and Collins, F.S. (2015) 'National Institutes of Health addresses the science of diversity', *Proceedings of the National Academy of Sciences*, 112(40): 12240–2.

Van der Lee, R. and Ellemers, N. (2015) 'Gender contributes to personal research funding success in The Netherlands', *Proceedings of the National Academy of Sciences*, 112(40): 12349–53.

World Bank (2019) Available at: https://data.worldbank.org/indicator/SP.URB.TOTL.IN.ZS, accessed 12 May 2021.

2

Research and Innovation in the Academy: A Precarious Business

Gabriele Griffin

Introduction

Research and innovation (R&I) in academe is a precarious business. Considered highly desirable by policymakers at local, national and international levels (Veugelers et al, 2012), it is nonetheless fraught with difficulties (Treussard and Arnott, 2017; Kuzma and Roberts, 2018). This chapter explores these difficulties as they arise in the context of Digital Humanities in academe in three Nordic countries (Finland, Norway, Sweden). It asks how women and men working in Digital Humanities fare in this emerging area of work. Digital Humanities (DH) is a knowledge production domain that conjoins humanities disciplines, conventionally associated with a strong female presence in terms of student and staff numbers, and technology, an arena more commonly associated with a strong male presence (OECD, 2019). DH is also a domain that depends extensively on collaboration (Deegan and McCarthy, 2012) since its inter- and multi-disciplinarity, minimally already encoded in the conjoining of technology and humanities, requires interaction between humanities scholars and technology experts (Griffin and Hayler, 2018), often from several disciplines. This collaboration is in itself already demanding (Griffin et al, 2013a, 2013b), partly because it defies the 'lone scholar' tradition that has been common in the humanities, and partly because very different, and differently demanding, knowledge arenas are brought together.

To date, and in contrast to the US (Zorich, 2008) and to some extent the UK, DH in the Nordic countries exists mainly in centres, labs, fora and other such formations within the university – formations that are largely atypical for higher education institutions that still function mainly along the divisions of faculties and departments. This atypicality in itself has consequences regarding the (relative) precarity of R&I in academe as that manifests itself in DH. It is part of the precarizing culture and practices that pervade much of contemporary employment (Berardi, 2009; Standing, 2011). In this chapter I explore these precarities and their gendered effects and consequences for those who work within DH. Theoretically, I frame this chapter in terms of the four durable inequality mechanisms identified by Charles Tilly (1998): exploitation, opportunity hoarding, emulation and adaptation. Of these, and based on my data, I focus in particular on two mechanisms: opportunity hoarding and emulation. But I begin by discussing the literature on R&I in academe in its relation to DH, and Tilly's four mechanisms, before describing my research methods, the participants, my data and their analysis. I shall then discuss three issues that emerged in the interview data as factors that produce precarity for research and innovation in academe, before analyzing their implications.

Digital Humanities as research and innovation in academe

DH as a knowledge domain has a fairly recent history in academe, dating back to the 1980s and 1990s (Kirschenbaum, 2012). It co-emerged with the arrival of new information and communication technologies in universities (Duhaney, 2005; Levin et al, 2012), which invited the digitalization of data and their digital exploration. Originally concerned with the creation of digital versions of analogue data (for example in computational linguistics and of library collections), it quickly expanded, aided by the rapidly increasing affordances of digital tools, to encompass the creation, curation and analysis of materials both analogue and born digital across a significant range of humanities disciplines. In the Nordic countries, as much as in many other countries which embraced this higher education innovation, DH was institutionally configured as research groups, labs, centres or forums. These formations are in many ways atypical for higher education institutions (HEIs) and their decision-making structures (Griffin, 2019) which tend to continue to operate largely through faculties and departments. However, these atypical HEI formations were also part of the diversification of university subdivisions that occurred largely in the 1980s and 1990s, partly in recognition of the increasing 'importance of academic research for technology, innovation and economic growth' (Veugelers, 2014: 3) and changing funding regimes in higher education.

R&I in academe have been viewed as key drivers for economic growth for some considerable time (Etzkowitz and Leydesdorff, 2000). In recognition of this, HEIs have transformed in the past 30 years or so, even though 'the history and legacy of universities can make them resistant to change' (Blass and Hayward, 2014). Part of this transformation has been the accelerated establishment of research centres of different kinds within universities (Etzkowitz and Kemelgor, 1998). These centres share certain characteristics which render them precarious. Etzkowitz and Kemelgor argue that centres 'represent less of an institutional commitment than departments: they need no permanent staff' (1998: 272). As a university tactic 'in [the] academic struggle for funds' (1998: 274), 'centres are temporary bodies that may close if funds run out' (1998: 277). Altogether, this signals the 'transferring [of] risks and insecurity onto workers and their families' (Standing, 2011: 1), which Guy Standing diagnoses as a key aspect of the neoliberal labour market and of the emergence of the precariat. It, in a nutshell, describes the situation DH has found itself in in many European countries including the Nordic ones in the past 25 years or so. It heralds the precarization and unsettled work conditions which afflict much cognitive work in contemporary academe. Academic institutions, of course, and ironically perhaps, seek to safeguard their own existence through this process of the precarization of the staff. The traits described earlier make these centres part of the 'endless transition' which Etzkowitz and Leydesdorff diagnose as being a key characteristic of contemporary academe's place in the R&I nexus, described by them as the triple helix of university-industry-government relations.[1] As they also suggest, not only is there an unsettled dynamic among the helixes but also within each one, unsettledness is part of its specificity. While unsettledness may be described as the necessary corollary of, or synonym for, innovation, transformation and change, it has consequences for those who work in conditions of unsettledness, and for those who seek to innovate under those conditions, whether as institutions, funders or researchers. These consequences will be explored later.

Unsettledness and Charles Tilly's inequality mechanisms

The unsettledness of HEIs as research and innovation hubs, and their peripheralization of DH in atypical institutional formations occur in a context where 'inequality regimes' prevail (Acker, 2006). Charles Tilly (1998: 10) has identified four mechanisms which sustain these regimes: exploitation, opportunity hoarding, emulation and adaptation. These mechanisms are based on distinctions being made between categorical pairs (for example woman, man; professor, student) that are constructed as standing in an asymmetrical relation to each other. That asymmetrical relation produces inequalities. Exploitation involves the use and benefit of resources from which those who help to produce them are excluded. Opportunity hoarding refers to people having access to and using resources within their own network that they simultaneously deny others whom they regard as outside their network. Emulation involves the reproduction of existing models of institutions and practices which reproduce the inequality mechanisms already inherent in them. Finally, adaptation references the adjustment of oneself, one's situation, one's environment to existing norms, practices and structures such that one reproduces their particularities and biases in the new context. These mechanisms thus (re)produce durable inequality. It is worth noting that Tilly's inequality mechanisms describe relations between people working in institutions rather than institutional mechanisms as such. In that sense they lead back to individuals. However, as will become clear later, much of the opportunity hoarding and emulation that occurs in R&I contexts is undertaken on behalf of institutions which condone and support those mechanisms. There is hence an institutional and structural component to the persistence of these inequality mechanisms. Of these inequality mechanisms, two in particular – emulation and opportunity hoarding – manifested themselves in my data.

Tilly's inequality mechanisms continue to have salience in contemporary academe (Griffin and Vehvilainen, 2021). Their explanatory force becomes evident when one considers the experiences detailed by my interviewees, DH practitioners working in HEIs in Finland, Norway and Sweden. I shall now turn to these and describe the research process, participants, data collection and analysis, before turning to the discussion of my data.

Methodology and data analysis

Between 2017 and 2018 the author conducted one-on-one, semi-structured interviews in English with 30 DH practitioners, 17 women and 13 men, from Finland, Norway and Sweden. The interviewees' ages ranged from 29 to 62. The interviewees were purposively selected by searching university and research funder websites; the main criterion was that the participants should work in or with DH. Both women and men were interviewed to get a sense of how they experienced their working conditions and the latter's genderization. Thus women and men generally agreed that those mainly working with technology, for example as programmers or technicians, were usually men, and this proved to be the case in my sample. Of the 23 interviewees who were, broadly speaking, academics, 14 were women and nine were men – the majority were therefore women. Since DH is still in a state of disciplinary unsettledness, and involves collaborations across knowledge domains, many job descriptions emerged when the interviewees were asked what their current job was. The descriptions included professor, associate professor, assistant professor, temporary lecturer, researcher, postdoc, PhD student, technician, programmer, director of studies, course coordinator, director of a DH centre, collaboration manager and others. Some had more than one job description, being, for instance, both a director of a DH centre and a professor, or a programmer and a researcher. This is partly because a number of them had multiple jobs, being for example split 50/50 across different posts (Griffin, 2022).

Most interviews were conducted face to face but some were done online, related to participant availability. They were given information sheets about the project and asked to sign consent forms allowing the use of their anonymized interview data in subsequent publications. All interviewees were pseudonymized, and their institutions and other identifying traits eliminated from the transcribed interviews. The interviews lasted between 43 and 70 minutes. They were audio-recorded and transcribed, then uploaded into NVivo 11 Pro for thematic analysis (Braun and Clarke, 2006). That analysis, done in the form of close repeated readings of the interviews and coding according to emerging inductive and deductive themes, produced a range of themes such as 'interdisciplinarity', 'mentoring', 'male mentor', 'leaving job', 'going into industry', 'supportive institution', 'support for DH', 'career blocking' and so on. These were then re-read and grouped together according to larger themes such as 'support', 'career progression', 'working conditions'. Re-reading those themes revealed how institutional structures and practices in their entanglement with gender produced precarities for DH practitioners that had important consequences for their working lives. These will be explored next through three issues that were typical for DH as an emerging field.

Issue 1: Uncertain support – the case of the work that was closed down

DH as a knowledge domain has both female and male staff but with a fairly conventional gendered divide: the researchers are often women, the 'techies' tend to be men, a situation that was confirmed across the board by my interviewees. Terras (2012) describes this bipolar situation in terms of women tending to function as the 'other' in this environment since some of them may lack the technical education and know-how to translate their research ideas into 'doable' DH projects. As one, Britta, told me: "Without the technicians, the two men who helped us, nothing could have been developed." And as another female interviewee told me: "The very early days, I suppose it was male-dominated, you know, throughout, there were very few women who were interested in this side of, this kind of research" (Aava). Even in 2018 when I interviewed her, she said, only "20 per cent in our faculty are female professors". Another female interviewee put it like this: "It's a bunch of guys, they are adorable, but you know, it's a little bit like the Silicon Valley show. The administration is a girl, you know, and that's it" (Nina).

Several of the interviewees who came into this environment as young female doctoral students or postdocs reported significant difficulties with the male professors leading these research environments in which the women felt frequently unsupported and sidelined. As one woman said: "I didn't get any support at all, I mean the support I got was that I was invited to be part of the project, but I was very much left on my own … it was terrible, [those] years were not good in any way, I think it was kind of devastating because I was lost" (Lena). Another interviewee described being bullied by her male professor when she was doing her PhD, and while she ultimately resisted this behaviour, it did make her leave the university "disillusioned" and work in private sector research for a number of years. Another woman described how lack of support from the senior male professor meant that her work was closed down, meaning that she was deprived of opportunities to apply for further funding in her DH research area when her money ran out to the point where she had to look for work elsewhere.

Her experience occurred at the interface of gender, seniority and the embedding of a new discipline, DH, into academe. The professor in question, a linguist, had "hired one to the group who was more into DH in order to make it more experimental". However, "when we actually tried to work with it, he [the professor] got afraid because of reviewing or yes, you know, publishing and so on". In the interviewee's view those who started to "get scared" were men "who wanted to polish their careers in a more traditional way". Here we have evidence of Tilly's inequality mechanism of emulation where people, in this instance men, seek to profile themselves professionally by emulating traditional ways of promoting their careers, here through the publishing of conventional research articles. This is not unreasonable given that careers in academe depend significantly on researchers' publication profile as a key criterion for their advancement (Balsmeier and Pellens 2014). The professor in question "didn't want to endorse further ideas … he didn't believe in our results, so he got very conservative along the way" (Lena). Etzkowitz and Kemelgor (1998: 282) refer to professors' ability to limit what researchers can do. But in this instance the informant saw what happened as part of a wider question of the legitimacy of DH as an innovation in the institution. As she suggested, "that's part of what people in Digital Humanities … like always see as like their biggest problem, convincing people that this is valid, it works … very often they feel people don't believe in them or think it's real research" (Britta).

Treussard and Arnott (2017) talk of 'bubbles in academe' and the issue of how one knows when to (dis)invest in an innovation. DH as an innovation in academe had to, and continues to have to, establish its legitimacy in the university and, as part of that, suggesting that DH is 'just like other disciplines' is a powerful but also potentially highly conservative mechanism that invites emulation and hence the reproduction of existing biases, including those of gender. It also does not encourage the university to recognize change but rather invites it to maintain the status quo. Britta, the interviewee referred to earlier, was eventually forced to move into an administrative role within the university to secure her livelihood since her DH work was closed down.

All this was in stark contrast to many of the interviewed men's experiences. They expressed a great sense of support from male colleagues who had encouraged them into jobs and careers – the classic boys' network –, even if their academic credentials did not meet the job requirements at the time they started that job (Griffin, 2022). As Jens, for example, said:

> 'I always felt supported and always felt that I got, you know, I've been helped into being promoted, why I have been able to stay in academia for this long after doing my PhD is that I have been invited to be part on several research projects … and this has really helped my career, and it's all because of these male project leaders, and they have been very supportive in that sense.'

Here there was a clear sense of Tilly's opportunity hoarding in that men supported other men to enter into university careers within DH. However, as indicated, this was mostly not the case for the women, many of whom on the contrary talked about being actively discouraged from pursuing their interests or career aspirations.

Issue 2: The vicissitudes of interdisciplinarity

Since DH requires collaboration across radically different knowledge domains, work within the field gets caught up in the 'mangle of practice' (Pickering, 1995). This entails unsettledness as a condition of collaborative practice. It emerged in the example of Britta earlier, in her professor's anxiety about the reception and acceptance of more experimental DH work within the field of linguistics. Britta also revealed that "every year you can apply for research time based on publication and stuff, and other stuff as well, but developing tools or making new research corpuses or whatever it is that you do in DH is not part of that reading". This lack of institutional recognition of DH work had contributed to the lack of support she experienced at micro level from her professor who grappled with the fact that new paradigms of research often have a hard time achieving institutional recognition. As she described it:

> 'The [male] professor was quite sceptical … he hired one to the group who was more into digital humanities in order to make it more experimental but when it came to be or when we actually tried to work with it, he got afraid because of reviewing, or, yes, you know, publishing and so on. So that halted things … he didn't want to endorse further ideas of that and got really … he didn't believe in our results, so he got very conservative along the way.'

This problem of recognition was already evident at the point of recruitment. As a male interviewee put it:

> 'people talk about interdisciplinarity … you know, as something that should be … supported but then in fact, in quite a few cases, when decisions, for example, teaching are made, or on hiring people, quite a few people tend to focus on this kind of a disciplinary background that they can say, well, this person who has a degree in, a BA from here, an MA from here, and a PhD from here, so let's take that person.' (Anders)

Although there is slippage here from the question of disciplinarity to that of the alma mater (in the repeated 'from here'), the implication is clear: deviation is not welcome. Institutional practices such as recruitment processes which insist on monodisciplinarity as a condition for employment through the expectation that one's publications are all clearly within a specific discipline or disciplinary field thus try to force adaptation to existing norms by requiring individuals to submit to the prevailing demand to be monodisciplinary in one's profile. Unsurprisingly, another interviewee, Britta, like Anders, asserted that she could not compete career-wise with others because she had done too many different things to be identified with a single discipline.

Anna, however, yet another interviewee, said of herself: "I am a researcher in not any particular field, but I have a field, an interdisciplinary field, that I feel I belong to." This stance was fairly unusual. The more common response from both female and male DH practitioners was to disavow any identification with DH and instead to assert an academic affinity with the discipline in which they had been trained (Griffin, 2019), for example linguistics, history or anthropology. Jan summed this problem up as follows: "multi-disciplinarity is one challenge, also the novelty of the whole field … there is as yet no long tradition of research in the field of digital humanities". The opportunities that the unsettledness of a new knowledge domain produce are missed when absence of tradition becomes a criterion for excluding practitioners in new domains from full participation in the university.

It is worth noting that across my interviewees there was consistent and unselfconscious slippage across the phrases trans-, multi-, post- and interdisciplinarity. The DH practitioners were much less concerned with defining these terms than with exploring how working across disciplines in an emerging field impacted on their work experiences. I use the term interdisciplinarity here since the imbrication of humanities with technologies is one of the hallmarks of DH but in the awareness that a huge literature and debate attends terms to do with trans-, multi-, post- and interdisciplinarity (for example Klein Thompson, 1990; Strathern, 2004; Moran, 2010).

An interdisciplinary disposition can go back a long way. Five women in particular in my sample had very divergent disciplinary backgrounds which began at school where they were good at both natural sciences and languages for example. The assumption that different knowledge domains require different and potentially mutually exclusive kinds of aptitudes, and that some subjects are 'serious' while others are not, is widespread and feeds into the anti-interdisciplinary stance that is pervasive in education institutions to this day. One of my interviewees, for instance, had been keen on rhythmic gymnastics and dance at school, which she wanted to study but her parents' view that she 'should have a decent first degree first' prompted her to go from Norway to France to take a degree in engineering. She returned to dance much later but, missing certain mental rigours of engineering, then went into human-computer interaction (HCI) to combine her interests in human movement with the affordances of HCI. Encouraged by a mentor she set up her own company to develop particular hard- and softwares but that company eventually went bankrupt because, from her particular perspective, her innovation was ahead of the curve, and it was not understood. At the time of the interview employed in academe in an innovation collaboration manager capacity, she said of herself: "I have this very complex background … I don't have this, you know, like ideal path. … I don't have this deep niche knowledge within a specific field … so it's not easy to benchmark me against other candidates, for example. I think it's been difficult to create a good CV" (Berit). Another interviewee, Elsa, studied technical physics but then found "maybe physics was not that interesting … so I was more interested in partying and also language courses" which in turn became her springboard into corpus linguistics.

Interdisciplinary backgrounds, often forged between high school and university, served as useful starting points for becoming involved in DH, not least because as an emerging discipline it is not hampered by the norms and conventions that attend more established disciplines. Eleven female and nine male interviewees talked about their divergent backgrounds, usually combining interests in arts, humanities or social science domains with interests in science, technology, engineering or mathematics (STEM). They would say things such as "my history is a bit curled and swirly" (Anders), or "Somehow I'm not disciplinary any more. … I could even use the term post-disciplinary" (Harriet), or "I've for a long time thought of myself as being in a sort of interzone that's not defined as traditional, from a traditional disciplinary standpoint" (Knut). These non-disciplinary educational and professional histories and self-definitions propelled my interviewees into DH where practitioners, according to one interviewee, had "one thing in common, and that is that they are not, they are not afraid of being outside their comfort zone" (Marta).

But this very openness also meant that they bucked institutional trends. As Olof put it: "there was a dream that people could take some part in different departments … [but] it has turned out it has in practice been very difficult having things going on in between different departments". Here divergence from conventional structures and disciplinary divisions created obstacles in realizing the potential of interdisciplinarity. It led some to returning to the conventional disciplines they had left behind. The unsettledness that interdisciplinarity entails could not sustain them in the positions they had assumed, not least because it was not amenable to emulation of conventional disciplinary structures as these manifest themselves in the organizational structures of the university.

Issue 3: Caught in [sic] the Scylla of project work and the Charybdis of unsettled funding

The establishment of DH in Nordic universities coincided with increasing pressure to gain external funding in a context where the professional norm in the Nordic (and some other European) countries was that following on from one's PhD, one would go through an often quite extended period of many years of working as a postdoc on projects before securing a permanent position (OECD, 2021). Permanent positions in Nordic universities are usually tied to teaching-related funding which universities receive as a block grant. Those on permanent teaching contracts can buy themselves out of (some of) that teaching by obtaining research funding. However, there are also significant numbers of academics who work as researchers, existing solely on externally gained competitive funding, in other words, under precarious work conditions. And, increasingly, many academics are on so-called permanent contracts but their employment is nonetheless subject to them bringing in external funding. As Michel, working in a Norwegian university and half employed in a DH archive, half in a traditional department, described it: "my position … was always depending on a sort of funding. I mean it was called permanent … but it was dependent on attracting external funds, but here then the archives got a real permanent position." This complicated scenario, with 'real' and not really permanent contracts generates instability and suggests the casualization of staff, with a diversification of contracts, which evacuates these contracts' meaning since 'permanent', for instance, does not de facto mean permanent any more. It leads to exploitation by universities of their staff where, as Etzkowitz and Kemelgor (1998) argued, institutions show limited, some might say no, commitment to their staff whom they try to put into expendable positions through the contracts they issue. Such expendability, however, comes at a price: staff who do not feel valued do not feel loyal to their institution in turn, and will readily depart for 'greener sites'. Unsettledness in the form of temporary contracts thus exerts a price, in particular the loss of highly qualified staff, often at inopportune moments such as in the middle of a project (Griffin, 2022).

Project work is by its very nature time-delimited and hence precarious. It foreshortens the horizon of possibility to the duration of the project. In many contexts, junior researchers also cannot apply for project funding in their own right but are dependent on being invited into a project by a more senior researcher making an application. This means that their employment depends on having the right connections and personal networks rather than on academic competence alone. Lena described this as follows:

> 'like your employment at university, everything is about securing funding and the only way to do this is through external funding and like, knowing people … applying for money yourself … is difficult as long as you're a junior researcher … the only option seems to be to know the right people and get invited to be part of their projects because otherwise you would lose your position, no matter how you got it'.

This situation lends itself to the preferentialism associated with old boys' networks that constitute, in Charles Tilly's terms, a form of opportunity hoarding since it allows senior staff to shoe juniors of their own ilk into positions. Unsurprisingly one female interviewee told me: "from my old graduate school … there's at the moment six people with permanent jobs, five of them are men". These men, Nina said, "were instantly given positions in their networks. Permanent".

Project work is in that sense a social enterprise (Griffin et al, 2013b), a tricky business when one works in an emerging field. Aarne, one of my interviewees told me, "when I was writing my thesis I was kind of alone in my department, there was no kind of like-minded supervisors around". Such lack of connection had knock-on effects. Berit said: "when I finished my PhD … I didn't have any funding for continuing it, and I hadn't been so proactive in trying to find it either, and part of that was because I didn't really know the academic system". Lack of mentoring reflected in ignorance about the academic system here led to temporary unemployment. Britta, too, commented on this lack of mentoring, saying that the PhD students she started with "were quite lost" and that "almost nobody in [her Humanities discipline] got finished with their PhD because they did not know how to do it". Britta's experience is not unique; completion rates across the Nordic countries for PhDs are poor. In Sweden, for example, only 23 per cent of 2009 female PhD entrants had completed their degree after five years; in Norway only 35.1 per cent of 2014 female PhD entrants had completed their degree after five years (Sadurskis, 2018; Statistics Norway, 2020). More women than men reported such lack of mentoring and lack of initiation into research and innovation funding regimes, which often continued into postdoc positions. Britta, for example, talked of a PhD student who "always met resistance from professors and so on … so she had to do everything herself, and find mentorship within peers and her own hierarchy, so to speak". She said that "in the humanities, they've never been organized with mentorships". This meant that the doctoral students "were quite lost, almost nobody in art history got finished with their PhD because they didn't know how to do it or where to go". Lena described a terrible work situation with the male professor leading the DH project she worked in and "not feeling supported in what I did. … I never got any substantial feedback from him, he never asked to read anything that I wrote … it was so badly organized and being like at the start of your career, I think it made me feel kind of helpless". Nina also said, "I didn't feel I had that kind of support."

The unsettledness of R&I funding, conjoined with institutional inertia to intervene, effectively creates unproductive environments. As Lena described it: "It was terrible … because everything was quite unsure during a long time because we didn't know if we would lose our funding or what would happen, we didn't have proper leadership in the lab. … I don't think a lot of people felt very well during that period … a lot of people also quit during this process." Lengthy periods of uncertainty without key appointments were not uncommon. As Nicole told me: "we were like three years without [a professor] after [female Norwegian colleague] left before they let us advertise positions". Nicole attributed this to the emergent nature of DH: "it speaks volumes I think about their sort of like 'oh, I don't know, is it a real subject?' I think they've still … not been quite sure if it is a real discipline or not, you know?"

One thing that institutions and to some extent researchers in DH had not bargained for is that DH itself is very different from conventional Humanities subjects in that it no longer relies on just a "well sharpened pencil", as Petra put it, but involves technological infrastructure, itself in many ways an innovation which institutions find difficult to handle. Academics and institutions can apply to research council infrastructure funds or private foundations to acquire technological equipment such as eye-movement tracking equipment, 'cave' environments (with surround screens), or floor screens but these then have to be serviced and maintained and became obsolete very quickly as technologies move on. Nina had several stories related to this. She told me: "the floor screen we have, it's been leaking for three years and nobody is fixing it because it is more expensive, and then we don't use it for anything other than showing people things". She also said: "we have invested in two massive angled screens. Nobody knows why they were angled … we need a coder to run them, and they have a life expectancy that will cost a lot of kronor to fix." The prohibitive cost of fixing things also spelt the death knell for cave technology at another university: "the caves in [Danish university]. Fantastic when they came out. For two years. And then too many expenses and they could not keep it up" (Nina). Nina's view was that universities, in contrast to private industry, failed to understand technological infrastructure in the Humanities as a process that needed long-term iterative investment on multiple fronts to maintain it and use it. However, often only one or two researchers work with that technology, making it an expensive resource. Humanities as the Cinderella of academe in terms of infrastructure investment has radically changed with the arrival of digital methods and tools but this has yet to become fully acknowledged by higher education institutions.

The pattern for funding for DH more generally was either entirely external, or a mix of some limited university funding and external grants, all on time-limited terms. Inevitably when, as was the case in Norway, "national funding disappeared, the centre was reduced" (Olof). Sven told me that: "some project money was about to end … we had redundancies, so we had to, what do you say, lay off or fire people". This process affected women more than men because they were the majority of the researchers. So while the technicians were retained, according to Sven "to do with the funding", the researchers were let go. To forestall a recurrence of this situation, Sven said, "we put a lot of effort into applying for money". But in the age of competitive research funding "it's never easy to get money" (Sven). Another interviewee, Knut, described having no continuing money to maintain the database he had been funded to set up, saying, "even kind of some basic maintenance things right now are a problem".

For emergent R&I, universities are not a safe source of employment. As Dirk put it: "they pay our salaries and if they don't do that any more, they don't". His centre was funded by the Faculty, "so that means three years and then we have to apply for a new period, and it's not a lot of money". This is in a context where research councils may announce strategic funding on a particular topic but, as one programme manager in Finland put it to me, "it rarely happens that an academic programme … receive another programme more or less directly in the same field". In other words, strategic priorities are changed after three or five years, signalling the end of the related funding, unless one can squeeze one's project in under another heading.

The majority of my interviewees talked extensively about the precarities that arose from such short-term, insecure funding. As Lena said of her situation: "I mean the future seems quite insecure. … I have a position right now and I know I have funding for a couple of more years, but after that I don't know what happens." Nils pointed to the contradictions in his institution's attitudes towards this situation: "everybody knows this [bringing in external funding] is the conditions for being here … in academia that's also a major condition, competing about financing, but you are not supposed to talk about it that way. You do a lot but you also try to uphold some kind of idea that you are actually part of this organization for different reasons, you know?" This recognition and simultaneous disavowel of the realities of academic employment in R&I, reflected in Michel's description that the archive he worked in was "owned by the university but not part of the university", testifies to the university's uncertain relation to the changes in its practices and procedures, and staff's difficulties in negotiating these. Unable to continue just to emulate previous practices and unable to fully absorb the new conditions, the university emerges as a greedy institution, ready to exploit its labour force while unwilling to accept responsibility for the consequences of these shifts.

Discussion and conclusion: The price of unsettledness and precarity

R&I in academe, of which DH is one manifestation, have to contend with the unsettledness that changing precarized labour market conditions entail, and which the imperatives of innovation – change and transformation – demand. However, as the earlier discussions show, that unsettledness comes at a price. The institutional organization of R&I into centres heralds their provisional nature, since centres as atypical – even if proliferating – formations do not signal institutional commitment to their continuance or the permanent employment of their staff. As emerging epistemological and methodological fields such as DH seek to establish themselves, part of an increasing drive to foster interdisciplinarity, they are invited to be part of the university while also remaining apart from it. In so far as they are invited in, they are also invited to emulate the organizational practices into which they are inserted which encourage them to reproduce the biases and particularities already inherent in the organization. This is especially evident in terms of how these centres are asked to legitimize themselves (for example through standard measures such as publications), which, however, can be difficult to do if the practices the new knowledge domain entails, such as digitizing collections or producing born-digital scholarly work, are not recognized in conventional research assessments or when staff are recruited.

Emerging interdisciplinary knowledge domains offer opportunities for those with a divergent education history who defy the mono-disciplinary imperative that governs much conventional academic work, and in this study both women and men with divergent backgrounds responded to those opportunities. These knowledge domains invite researchers who are content to be outside their comfort zone and curious beyond the boundaries of a single discipline. However, they also condemn these staff to hover on the edge of academe, with uncertain employment prospects because of that very interdisciplinarity, and, through the prevailing funding and project culture, in perpetual pursuit of the next project or grant. The acquisition of such grants which benefits the university in terms of its research profile is done at great cost to the researcher, since time to prepare applications is not usually part of any grant allocation process, and there is no guarantee that they will be duly included in new project work even if it is based on their ideas (see also Chapter 7 in this volume). One might argue that this constitutes an institutional form of exploitation in Tilly's terms. Especially for women who may take time out to have a family this is a threat to their career. Women in this study in particular could find themselves excluded, already at doctoral and postgraduate level, from the opportunities to get jobs extended to their male peers, a classic version of Tilly's (1998) opportunity hoarding among men where senior males would invite juniors into projects and jobs that set these young men up for their academic career.

Universities' lack of commitment to the R&I they encourage was also evident in the materially compromised working conditions that the interviewees spoke of. Institutions expect new formations within them to emulate their existing context. However, that context, for instance the low-tech history that accompanies humanities disciplines, is inadequate to the R&I that contemporary new knowledge domains such as DH bring with them. The inadequacy of much of the technology provision that DH centres or labs had – inadequate because inadequate thinking and resource provision had gone into the fact that these technologies need to be serviced, maintained, and that they also become obsolete – retards possibilities for innovation and new research to take place. Especially in the case of women, some of whom had clearly been ahead of the curve with their work, it led to them abandoning the work they did and moving into administrative or other posts within the university. This implies a concomitant loss of expertise and knowledge to the university, with highly trained staff moving out of R&I into secure administrative posts that, however, contribute only to the bureaucratic processes of the institution and not to its R&I. The point here is that emulation and adaptation are mechanisms to reproduce existing structures, but these mechanisms are inadequate to the contemporary demands of our changing academe.

The agility demanded of those working in R&I needs to be matched by institutions becoming more agile. In 'Agile methods for agile universities' Michael Twidale and David Nichols (2013) discuss institutional manifestos to foster agility, based on underlying principles and values. Agility, however, does not mean expendability, or a heedless embrace of unsettledness as a permanent condition. It demands a considered disposition which acknowledges the complexities of changing knowledge domains and combines a proper assessment of what is needed with appropriate care for those working at the forefront of research and innovation.

Note

1 This model has been extended into the quadruple helix to encompass society as well (Carayannis and Rakhmatullin, 2014), but the fundamental notion of a continual dynamic, and hence unstable, relation between these components has not been changed by that addition.

References

Acker, J. (2006) 'Inequality regimes: gender, class, and race in organizations', *Gender and Society*, 20(4): 441–64.

Balsmeier, B. and Pellens, M. (2014) 'Who makes, who breaks: which scientists stay in academe?', *Economics Letters*, 122(2): 229–32.

Berardi, F.B. (2009) *Precarious Rhapsody: Semiocapitalism and the Pathologies of the Post-Alpha Generation*, Wivenhoe: Minor Compositions.

Blass, E. and Hayward, P. (2014) 'Innovation in higher education: will there be a role for "the academe/university" in 2025?', *European Journal of Futures Research*, 2(41): 1–9. DOI: 10.1007/s40309-014-0041-x.

Braun, V. and Clarke, V. (2006) 'Using thematic analysis in psychology', *Qualitative Research in Psychology*, 3(2): 77–101.

Carayannis, E.G. and Rakhmatullin, R. (2014) 'The quadruple/quintuple innovation and beyond', *Journal of the Knowledge Economy*, 5(2): 212–39.

Deegan, M. and McCarthy, W. (eds) (2012) *Collaborative Research in the Digital Humanities*, Farnham: Ashgate.

Duhaney, D.C. (2005) 'Technology and higher education: challenges in the halls of academe', *International Journal of Instructional Media*, 32(1): 7–15.

Etzkowitz, H. and Kemelgor, C. (1998) 'The role of research centres in the collectivization of academic science', *Minerva*, 36(3): 271–88.

Etzkowitz, H. and Leydesdorff, L. (2000) 'The dynamics of innovation: from national systems and "mode 2" to a triple helix of university–industry–government relations', *Research Policy*, 29: 109–23.

Griffin, G. (2019) 'Intersectionalized professional identities and gender in the digital humanities in the Nordic countries', *Work, Employment and Society*, 33(6): 966–82.

Griffin, G. (2022) 'The "Work–Work Balance" in higher education: between over-work, falling short and the pleasures of multiplicity', *Studies in Higher Education*. Available at: www.tandfonline.com/doi/full/10.1080/03075079.2021.2020750, accessed 20 January 2022.

Griffin, G. and Hayler, M. (2018) 'Collaboration in digital humanities research: persisting silences', *Digital Humanities Quarterly*, 12(1): 1–33.

Griffin, G. and Vehvilainen, M. (2021) 'The persistence of gender struggles in Nordic research and innovation', *Feminist Encounters*, 5(2): art. 28.

Griffin, G., Bränström-Öhman, A. and Kalman, H. (eds) (2013a) *The Emotional Politics of Research Collaboration*, New York: Routledge.

Griffin, G., Lundgren, B. and Hamberg, K. (eds) (2013b) *The Social Politics of Research Collaboration*, New York: Routledge.

Kirschenbaum, M. (2012) 'What is digital humanities and what's it doing in English departments?', in M.K. Gold (ed) *Debates in the Digital Humanities*, Minneapolis: University of Minnesota Press, pp 3–11.

Klein Thompson, J. (1990) *Interdisciplinarity: History, Theory, and Practice*, Detroit: Wayne State University.

Kuzma, J. and Roberts, P. (2018) 'Cataloguing the barriers facing RRI in innovation pathways: a response to the dilemma of societal alignment', *Journal of Responsible Innovation*, 5(3): 338–46.

Levin, S.G., Stephan, P.E. and Winkler A.E. (2012) 'Innovation in academe: the diffusion of information technologies', *Applied Economics*, 44(14): 1765–82.

Moran, J. (2010) *Interdisciplinarity*, London: Routledge.

Murgia, A. and Poggio, B. (eds) (2019) *Gender and Precarious Research Careers: A Comparative Analysis*, London: Routledge.

OECD (2019) *Education at a Glance 2019: OECD Indicators*, Paris: OECD Publishing. DOI: 10.1787/f8d7880d-en.

OECD (2021) *Reducing the Precarity of Academic Research Careers*, OECD Science, Technology and Industry Policy Papers No 113, Paris: OECD Publishing.

Pickering, A. (1995) *The Mangle of Practice: Time, Agency and Science*, Chicago: University of Chicago Press.

Sadurskis, A. (ed) (2018) *Higher Education in Sweden Status Report 2018*, Stockholm: Swedish Higher Education Authority.

Standing, G. (2011) *The Precariat: A New, Dangerous Class*, London: Bloomsbury.

Statistics Norway (2020) 'Completion rates of students in higher education', StatBank source Table 11299. Available at: www.ssb.no/en/utdanning/statistikker/hugjen/aar, accessed 2 April 2021.

Strathern, M. (2004) *Commons and Borderlands: Working Papers on Interdisciplinarity, Accountability and the Flow of Knowledge*, Wantage: Sean Kingston Publishing.

Terras, M. (2012) 'Being the other: interdisciplinary work in computational science and the humanities', in M. Deegan and W. McCarthy (eds) *Collaborative Research in the Digital Humanities*, Farnham: Ashgate, pp 213–40.

Tilly, C. (1998) *Durable Inequality*, Berkeley: University of California Press.

Treussard, J. and Arnott, R.D. (2017) 'I was blind, but now I see: bubbles in academe' (1 June). Available at: https://papers.ssrn.com/sol3/papers.cfm?abstract_id=3040947, accessed 3 March 2021.

Twidale, M.B. and Nichols, D.M. (2013) 'Agile methods for agile universities', in T. Besley (ed) *Re-imagining the Creative University for the 21st Century*, Leiden: Brill Sense, pp 27–48.

Veugelers, R. (2014) *The Contribution of Academic Research to Innovation and Growth*, WWWforEurope, Working Paper No. 71, Vienna: WWWforEurope.

Veugelers, R., Callaert, J., Song, X. and Looy, B.V. (2012) 'The participation of universities in technology development: do creation and use coincide? An empirical investigation on the level of national innovation systems', *Economics of Innovation and New Technology*, 21(5–6): 445–72.

Zorich, D.M. (2008) *A Survey of Digital Humanities Centers in the United States*, Washington: Council on Library and Information Resources. Available at: www.clir.org/wp-content/uploads/sites/6/pub143.pdf, accessed 15 July 2018.

3

Navigating Career Imaginaries in Academia: A View from Women Researchers in Biotechnology

Oili-Helena Ylijoki

Introduction

In the current managerial university context, academic career building has become increasingly competitive, selective and demanding. Growing dependence on external funding, metrics-based performance assessments and intensifying managerial control over academic work have shaped the ways in which academic career building is understood and evaluated. Several studies have pointed to an increasing fragmentation and polarization of academic staff into winners and losers (Musselin, 2005; Ylijoki and Ursin, 2013; Murgia and Poggio, 2019). There are elite groups of academics with abundant resources and space for autonomy and academic freedom (for example Henningsson et al, 2018) alongside a growing mass of fixed-term academics on insecure and uncertain employment, the majority of whom are women (Murgia and Poggio, 2019). Apart from the individual level, this polarization takes place across various disciplinary fields that are located differently in terms of science-policy priorities and possibilities of engaging in academic capitalism (Slaughter and Leslie, 1997). Many STEM fields, in particular, are often regarded as winners because their research culture and mode of operation fit well with the current priorities: they have a long history of collaboration with industry that generates research funding, patents, spin-offs and economic impact, and their publication patterns and research organization in project teams produces results that are favoured in metrics-based performance assessments.

This chapter investigates women researchers' career building in one STEM field, biotechnology. Since this is a new and interdisciplinary field freighted with great expectations of commercial and practical utility, one might think that career building in this kind of policy priority area would be especially rewarding and easy. However, by looking more deeply at the experiences of women researchers in one specific university context in Finland, the chapter shows a much more complicated picture, involving strikingly circumscribed and limited career imaginaries on the part of the research participants. These imaginaries, in turn, shape the ways in which people make sense of what is possible and what is impossible, how goals can be reached and what obstacles are to be expected.

Career imaginaries are shaped not only by specific epistemic and institutional contexts, but also by general national academic career models. In the Finnish higher education system, academic career building has traditionally been based on what Musselin (2005) calls the tournament model, in which many candidates apply for an open post against heavy competition. In this model, academic career paths are particularly uncertain, risky and selective. Getting a permanent position, especially a professorship, require waiting for an open position to emerge as well as the long-term accumulation of merits. This means that achieving a professorship typically occurs in a rather late career phase, often when candidates are already in their 50s. However, this has gradually changed since 2010 when the tenure track system was introduced in Finland (Pekkola et al, 2020). Universities have implemented the system in different ways but common to all is that those recruited into the tenure track progress from a fixed-term appointment to a tenured full professorship if they pass their performance assessment (Herbert and Tienari, 2013; Pietilä, 2015, 2019). Although candidates need to be already-established scholars, their future potential has become an important selection criterion as tenure track recruitments usually take place at a rather early career phase (Pekkola et al, 2020). This increasingly leaves room for subjective and unreflexive elements in the assessments, including ones related to subtle gender biases (van den Brink and Benschop, 2011; Herschberg et al, 2019).

In the following, I examine how women researchers in one Finnish biotechnology unit envision their career futures in the current managerial university context. I first present my data and the analytical lens to interpret them. Next, I describe the future horizon of the biotechnology unit in which researchers' career building takes place, thereby setting it in the broader epistemic and institutional context. Then, I move to individual experiences and distinguish three career imaginaries – the tenure track, academic entrepreneurship and leaving academia – to discuss the prospects and restrictions they impose on researchers. I end by reflecting on the complexities and narrow visions of academic career building.

Data and method

This chapter is based on a study of one biotechnology unit located at a research-intensive and multi-faculty university in Finland. The unit was established in the early 2000s as a small independent research centre of the university. Since then, it has undergone a series of organizational fusions, first integrating sequentially with two research institutes, and then merging with the Faculty of Medicine. In this process, the unit's history illustrates well the recent Finnish higher education policy, in which structural development and mergers between and within universities have been priorities, aiming to strengthen the dynamics, effectiveness and competitiveness of universities (Ylijoki, 2014b). From the beginning, the primary goal of the biotechnology unit was to create new commercial and clinical solutions in the health care sector. The unit's research involves interdisciplinary laboratory science, combining biosciences and engineering. Unlike technology more generally, biotechnology is a female-dominated field. In this unit, too, almost all the researchers were women.

The empirical material in this chapter comprises focussed interviews with 16 women researchers who all have a close connection to the biotechnology unit. At the time of the interviews, one half of the interviewees were working at the unit, while the other half had worked there before but had recently moved to work outside of academia in private, public and third-sector organizations such as pharmaceutical companies, start-ups and hospitals. The interviewees' ages, and correspondingly the lengths of their career histories, differed: five interviewees were born in the 1960s, five in the 1970s and six in the 1980s. By and large, those who had left academia were younger and those who had stayed represented the older generation; only one interviewee born in the 1980s was still working at the unit. Of those who remained in academia, three were professors (all belonging to the oldest generation), one was a project researcher and the rest were research group leaders. All interviewees were qualified researchers with PhDs. Their disciplinary backgrounds varied. Some of the younger researchers had studied and gained a doctorate in biotechnology, but the majority came from other fields, such as biochemistry, genetics, molecular biology, material technology and medicine. All but two interviewees had children and all had partners.

The interviews were open and informal in nature, allowing the interviewees to talk freely about their work experiences. The themes discussed included work history, career support and obstacles, the role of gender, future goals and work-life balance. The interviews which lasted one to two hours were recorded and transcribed verbatim. All quotes presented in this chapter are translations from Finnish into English and the names are pseudonymized.

The interviews were analyzed through a temporal lens (Ylijoki, 2014a), by exploring the future horizons embedded in the ways in which the interviewees made sense of career building in academia. The point of departure was that career building is not solely a personal pursuit based on individual choice but is deeply rooted in culturally and socially available career scripts and narratives (Cohen and Mallon, 2001; Duberley et al, 2006). These both facilitate and constrain individuals in their career construction. The focus of the analysis is on future imaginaries that shape and mould present understandings of what it means, and what it takes, to have an academic career in biotechnology. The specific research questions were: i) How many and what kinds of career horizons were there?; ii) What kind of temporality was embedded in the career horizons?; and iii) How did the researchers navigate among different career imaginaries?

Future horizons of biotechnology: from hype to harsh reality

> 'This was really a sexy topic at that point [2000s], we will produce human spare parts and things like that. ... People said wow, are you really doing these things? I felt so proud of being part of this kind of research. It got so much respect and media visibility. ... When I started, we still had this hype that we will be able to cure the whole world. Then the reality struck, perhaps these human spare parts will not be available within ten years. We had big plans but, at some point, we needed to start to give up. ... The situation changed; we turned into a normal university laboratory.' (Anita)

In the aforementioned quote, Anita describes the changes that took place at the biotechnology unit in terms of a declining storyline. This narrative arc was shared across the interview material. According to this trajectory, the unit started with great hype that gradually faded away, transforming radically the future horizon of the research work. The beginning of the unit is a good example of an economy of technoscientific promises (Felt, 2009), which offers grand visions of fast science making accelerating progress with immense commercial and practical success in the future. The unit was expected to create not only rapid scientific breakthroughs but also powerful dynamics that would lead to economic growth and innovative solutions for overcoming diseases. This future horizon was appealing both inside and outside of academia. The unit got much media visibility nationally and received abundant funding from various sources 'as money followed money'. This horizon represents what Adam and Groves (2007) call the present future: the future is seen as empty, open and subjugated to human will. It is an unlimited terrain, full of possibilities, which can be seized for the benefit of the present.

However, this horizon gradually transformed due to various obstacles. The open horizon turned into the future present (Adam and Groves, 2007), a contested and limited future which de facto was already latent in the present. Epistemic constraints emerged when the promises of an accelerating scientific pace were not fulfilled. Fast science turned out to be slow science because the laboratory experiments involved much waiting time that could not be sped up by human will. Thus, although the research work was, in many respects, successful, it involved much 'epistemic uncertainty' (Fochler and Sigl, 2018). Likewise, converting scientific results into commercial products was a long-term process, strongly regulated by the authorities and requiring time-consuming testing. Therefore, the vision of great commercial and clinical success moved into the dim and distant future. This was accompanied by financial obstacles, which were further aggravated by a general decline in research funding in Finland (see Chapter 5, this volume).

The narrowing of the future horizon was also related to the institutional context of career building. The unit started as a small, all-female, independent centre but then underwent several mergers that turned a close community of women researchers with "a crazy drive" into a component of increasingly large formations within the university structure. As a consequence, the size of the work environment "increased exponentially". This substantially changed social relations and the general atmosphere. Anita, one of the interviewees, described these changes as follows:

> 'We had such nice people there and such a great spirit. … We didn't have any kind of hierarchy; we were all best friends. We spent a lot of free time together and we had such lovely crayfish parties. It was so relaxed. It really was a fantastic work community. … But of course, when the size grew, you couldn't know all the people. People were of different ages, different kinds of people came, and the spirit of the core group broke up.' (Anita)

The mergers had an important impact on the prevailing research culture, values and management practices of the unit. While the unit was very outward-looking and business-oriented in the beginning, with a fancy office "almost like in start-ups", after the mergers it needed to adapt to traditional faculty-based university structures and modes of action. More than that, the mergers meant declining autonomy in decision-making. In particular, the last merger with medicine created tensions and a sense of marginalization. Sara, who worked as a research group leader, described this relationship as "a state of war" as she related the difficulties she had experienced:

> 'When the merger took place and we were not professors, we were not seen as being as good as they. And the funding that we brought in was not as good as their funding from the Academy. But if you bring in 100,000 Euros in a year and I bring 300,000 Euros, how can you say

> that you are better than I am, and how can you get more benefits than I, and I'm not allowed to sit at the same PIs table. And we all happened to be women and none of us had the status of a professor.' (Sara)

The interviews suggested that, in this changing institutional context, the future horizons of biotechnology were circumscribed by the power of medicine, in several senses. Biotechnology was an interdisciplinary and entrepreneurially oriented newcomer in academia, with only very few permanent positions, while medicine had a strong disciplinary status, a long history in academia and a mass of professorships. Consequently, the institutional position of biotechnology was weak and vulnerable, as manifested by the repeated mergers. Further, biotechnology was not a professionally oriented field with strong linkages to a given professional group in society to provide backup support. In clear contrast to this, medicine had powerful institutional standing in the university structures and influential professional support from medical doctors outside. On top of this, the biotechnology unit was a female-dominated field with a history of a close-knit community spirit without hierarchies, whereas medicine at the professoriate level was male-dominated and its overall work culture reflected the spirit of hospital hierarchies, as the relations between the university and university hospitals were intense and deep-rooted.

All these distinctions between the two fields worked to the disadvantage of biotechnology and put it in a subordinate position to medicine. At the individual level, visions of the future narrowed, at worst leading to experiences of not being acknowledged and valued as a colleague, as in Mia's account: "There are those men who have arranged everything beforehand. This makes me feel that I'm a smaller and smaller mosquito in their eyes, that is to say, I am nothing at all" (Mia). The tensions and uneven power relations shaped the ways in which career futures were envisioned. Instead of an open career future full of possibilities, the future appeared restricted and limited by persistent and long-lasting structures, cultural barriers, and "Neanderthal rules" which made career prospects in this biotechnology unit blank. For instance, Tanja, having experiences of being disregarded by the medical professors in power, felt that there was no future for her at the unit and was seriously considering leaving – which, in the end, she did not do:

> 'It was a really tough situation. I even thought of leaving altogether, I won't accept this. I could have transferred my research to [another university]. And my team already had work contracts here, so they would have been forced to pay salaries to the team. It would have been a real mess for them, I could have taken all my money with me. At that point I really was considering leaving, there was no sense in this.' (Tanja)

Career imaginaries

In their career building, researchers draw upon socially and culturally available career scripts and narratives. National career models and the specific local conditions shape the understandings of what kinds of prospects for academic career building are imaginable and what is required to become a successful academic. Basically, the prevailing career imaginaries among the participants of this study entailed only three visions of what was possible: to become a professor, mostly via the tenure track route; to work as a research group leader dependent on external research funding for both one's group and oneself; and to move away from academia. Instead of a free, unlimited and open future, these career imaginaries provide a predefined and circumscribed view of what is possible. Next, I shall explore each of these three imaginaries in turn.

Tenure track positions

According to the interviewees, in their current university context the tenure track represented the most valued and recognized way to build an academic career. It led to a permanent position as a professor at the top of the career hierarchy, offering career safety and success. The competition for a tenure track position is, however, intense, and only very few succeed. Therefore, this career vision was experienced as out-of-reach by most of the interviewees. Correspondingly, securing permanent employment in academia was seen as overly difficult. Leena, who was one of the three professors who had gained their positions before the rise of the tenure track system, painted a gloomy picture of the employment prospects for early-career researchers:

> 'The university is the worst employer in the world while the hospital, there is always a need of medical doctors. ... If I think of my own research group, it is easy to get funding as long as you're doing your doctoral dissertation but, when you finish, what then? The university has nothing to offer. ... A research career is really bleak.' (Leena)

Apart from being highly selective, tenure track positions are embedded in a rigid and standardized vision of academic career building. The latter involves a linear and vertical career trajectory with predefined, steady progression to a professorship. In this, it contradicts the notion of a boundaryless career (Arthur and Rousseau, 1996), which understands career advancement in present-day flat organizations as horizontal enlargement and enrichment of duties and competences rather than as vertical progress. Contrary to this, the tenure track position always rises upwards, entailing only the options up or out. This sustains the traditional imaginary of the academic profession, with professors holding power and influence at the top of the career ladder. Among the interviewees, this hierarchical image did not resonate particularly well, as the unit's history had been one of cherished equality and community spirit.

Furthermore, this vision of the tenure track allows no deviations or boundary crossings. Although career moves between different sectors, especially between academia and industry, are strongly advocated in policy discourses, the tenure track works against these. To keep oneself competitive, one must avoid wasting time with false steps outside the scientific circle since, in the final analysis, only scientific merits count in tenure track evaluations. The common understanding among the interviewees was that what really mattered were publications in high-impact journals and the amount of external research funding from prestigious sources one could get. Again, this did not sit well with the research culture adopted in biotechnology since, as they explained, "research is not just research, but we always have an idea of commercial products" and "benefits for others". From this perspective, the tenure track vision entailed a narrow image of what it means to be a successful academic (see Pietilä, 2019).

The tenure track vision also entailed a specific kind of temporality called 'anticipatory acceleration' (Müller, 2014). This refers to the speed-up in the pace of work for the sake of gaining a reward in the future. Since the competition for tenure track positions is fierce, researchers need to work harder and harder to testify to their excellence and overcome their competitors. And, if they are successful in this, they cannot but keep up the accelerated tempo to ensure that they meet the rising standards of their final assessment and are granted a permanent position as full professor. Thus, the imaginary of the tenure track intensifies the notion of academic work as an increasingly high-speed activity requiring total commitment, superhuman performance and hyper-productivity (see Ylijoki, 2013; Murgia and Poggio, 2019; Pietilä, 2019). This image was emphasized, for instance, by Emilia, who said that "if you want to continue in the research world you have to give it your whole life".

Tenure track positions are also important institutional investments in the future, involving struggles for resources and research priorities. Having investigated the tenure track system in Finland, Pietilä (2015) concludes that the system is utilized as a strategic instrument and a control mechanism by university management to steer future activities into the desired direction. Faced with tensions with medicine in their work environment, the interviewees in this study said that they needed to be watchful and keep an eye on how "the game is played" to protect their interests. Since the potential of academics plays an important role in tenure track recruitments, this career vision becomes particularly risky and prone to biases (see Herschberg et al, 2019). Liisa, working as PI without a permanent position, offered a gloomy view:

> 'Tenure tracks provide just more space for different games and also for discrimination because you don't need to say any more that okay, we take the most qualified. That's why it is completely and totally in the control of those who are on the recruitment committee to decide who is selected.' (Liisa)

At the time of the interviews, only one research participant had secured a tenure track position. She had been very determined, watched out for an appropriate position to open up and, when an opportunity came, "managed to snatch it up". Yet, she was still concerned about the risk that her position might be cut because of institutional micro-politics. In this sense, the imaginary of the tenure track was freighted with heavy competition not only among individuals but also among disciplinary fields and research areas. In this competition, the researchers in biotechnology felt that they had unequal conditions compared to the researchers in medicine because, among other things, disciplinary merits tended to count more than interdisciplinary ones in academic recruitment.

All in all, although the tenure track vision had alluring elements and was associated with success and prestige, it represented a normative ideal which most interviewees found difficult to identify with. It was seen as very competitive, individualistic, demanding and available only to very few people – not an obvious path for their own career futures. Heidi, for instance, distanced herself from the tenure track image of a successful researcher and hoped to find some other way to build her academic career – at the time of the interview still without success:

> 'Although I don't aim to become a professor or anything like that but even so I could produce high-quality research, I hope. ... But the university has really nothing to offer my kind of researcher, the path you should take is somehow so clear-cut, there is no place for my kind of researcher.' (Heidi)

Academic entrepreneurship

The majority of the interviewees who worked in the biotechnology unit were research group leaders employed on temporary contracts. They acted as principal investigators of externally funded research projects and were responsible for fund-raising both for their group and for themselves. In this sense, they were academic entrepreneurs leading quasi-firms within academia. Entrepreneurial activities are part and parcel of present-day academia since the university system at all levels engages in academic capitalism (Slaughter and Leslie, 1997) and depends on external funding. Yet, there are significant differences among different categories of academic staff. Although established professors and tenure track academics also need to be successful in fund-raising for their research groups, their own salaries are covered by the university. In contrast, academic entrepreneurs work at their own risk and need to attract funding for themselves, which makes their vision of their career future uncertain and vulnerable.

What is more, a temporary position is not a brief entry-level phase before permanent employment but rather, an enduring situation, as growing numbers of academics, especially women, work for years or decades on a series of fixed-term contracts (Murgia and Poggio, 2019). This was the case in this study, too. All the research group leaders without permanent employment were born in the 1960s and 1970s and had more than 30 years of temporary research work in the university. Thus, the career trajectory of an academic entrepreneur is circular and horizontal, moving from contract to contract, with no promises of future upward mobility on the career ladder.

The uncertainty and insecurity embedded in academic entrepreneurship makes this imaginary look like a rocky road. In the first place, it is a question of money and livelihood. While working on temporary employment, one cannot know whether there will be a next project and a next contract, which the interviewees experienced as stressful. They described fund-raising as "really awfully difficult" due to tight competition and the amount of time and energy it took. Further, over time salary became an issue. For instance, Maria said that she had begun to think about the financial side and wanted to earn some money at some point, and Pirjo remarked that she had not received any salary increase for a long time but needed to get her salary on an upward trajectory in the future.

Being stuck in the same position over a long period of time also impacted on the interviewees' emotional relations to their career futures. Although circuitous and horizontal career trajectories have become increasingly common, the linear career progression to professorship is still largely regarded as a sign of success and high-level merit in academic culture. Therefore, the lack of linear advancement upwards easily carries a certain professional, and even social, stigma. Among the interviewees, this was related to comparisons with those who had managed to get a tenure track position. Comparisons with the neighbouring discipline in particular, that of medicine, led to a sense of unjust and unequal treatment in recruitment to tenure track positions. Pirjo emphasized that she did not need to worry about funding because she had been very successful in that respect and was convinced that "money would bring money" in the future. However, she was frustrated because she felt that she should have received a tenure track position and that not having it did not look good in her own and in others' eyes, hampering her work situation:

> 'It begins to look absurd. My colleagues in Finland keep saying, "Oh, don't you have it yet [a tenure track position]?" … It begins to look

> so absurd. Those colleagues who have got tenure do the same kind of work, they have exactly the same job description and, in fact, I have brought in the biggest amount of money. It will be rather absurd if I don't get it next time.' (Pirjo)

Even though the tenure track includes aspects that did not accord with the interviewees' career building preferences, this model had a strong normative power, shaping their understandings and self-conceptions. The award of a tenure track position signalled long-term commitment by the university to these scholars and their work, which was thereby acknowledged and valued, whereas the academic entrepreneurs tended to feel that they were not appreciated and, instead, left to their own devices (see van der Weijden et al, 2016). Although they brought in significant sums of money, the local work environment did not offer recognition or encouragement regarding future career prospects in return. As Nora said:

> 'The university has not provided me much more than to allow me to be here; it is the Academy of Finland that has given me the funding. I received a significant grant and with this funding I was able to realize my dream. ... There was no space, nothing. I managed to get new laboratory space, buy new instruments, and get new people. I recruited them and educated them and developed the methods. And we created great systems and our research has really progressed. ... The university has had nothing against this, but they have given nothing to me.' (Nora)

The future horizon of academic entrepreneurship seemed, thus, constrained and unsettled, further complicated by struggles with the neighbouring discipline and its top professors who seemed to downplay their biotechnology co-workers' work and merits. When such a situation has prevailed for a long time and there seems to be no possibility of change in the future, work motivation can diminish and "a nihilistic feeling" can easily take over. Yet, the temporarily employed researchers were not submissive and desperate victims. For instance, Pirjo said that she was not "the kind of person who digs a hole and cries that I want to spend the rest of my life here". She had decided to give the university two more years to offer her better work conditions, and if this did not occur, she would be ready to move away. Nora explained her feelings and future plans in a similar manner:

> 'I have possibilities to do international, really interesting, and really important research, but somehow it is awfully difficult to commit to it if you don't have any position. It is hard to do this as a half-freelancer who rakes in money but has no official position anywhere. In a way, it has slowed me down and affected my career advancement and obstructed

> my research. I wonder how long I really want to go on if it continues to be very hard and there is no position in sight. … I need to start to think about creative solutions outside of academia in that case.' (Nora)

Leaving academia

Half of the interviewees in this study had worked in the biotechnology unit but had recently moved outside of academia. A couple of them had never seriously considered an academic career but stayed for some time after their PhD, when their group leader had invited them to continue in an ongoing project. Others had more fluid and complex career intentions both towards and away from academia (see Wood et al, 2020), but, finally, they either decided to, or had to, leave. Common to all was that the imaginaries of academic career prospects had turned out to be too narrow, too risky and too demanding for them. Katja summarized her feelings in a way that was typical for the interviewees:

> 'I had seen how competitive all funding is after the dissertation, and everyone preaches that you must go abroad for at least one year if you ever want to get any money from anywhere. And then you must have excellent ideas and establish your own research group at once. And I wondered if I'd be able to do that, and I started to think what do I want to do with my life and what is important to me? At that point, I got the idea of applying to [elsewhere]. I will have a firm source of income and yet interesting work. If you want to continue in the research world, it requires so much, and especially as a woman, you really have no time for anything else. And I certainly want to see my friends and my family and take a holiday with a clear conscience.' (Katja)

Among the interviewees, there was a widely shared understanding that "the university is a place mainly for those who want to become professors". Without a professorship as a goal, it seemed rather pointless to stay. The career path to a professorship, in turn, was envisioned as exceptionally exhausting and challenging, requiring living with financial insecurity, coming to terms with serious competition, working hard for long hours, creating brilliant research ideas and having competencies beyond compare (see Laudel and Gläser, 2007). It was, therefore, not for "an ordinary person". Academic career building was also viewed as focussing merely on the accumulation of scientific merits and on writing publications. For many, this was not enough, as they preferred more direct and quicker impacts that would benefit the health care system and patients. In consequence, these interviewees had concluded that the career future offered by the university did not coincide with their own preferences.

Yet, there were also those who would have wanted to continue in academia but had to leave because they were not successful in getting grants. In these cases, leaving was a painful experience, recalled in a tragic tone of voice. Emma said that, after moving away, "it lasted for a long time, a couple of years, that I felt pain". Mia had similar feelings. She had been part of the biotechnology unit almost from the start and experienced it as akin to her home. Despite this long-term commitment, she had ended up in a situation where she had no funding for herself and was therefore forced to leave. This was a nadir experience, which made her lose her vision of the future:

> 'All those plans that we had made together, they were suddenly taken from me. It was a hard moment. I became unemployed, I didn't have any idea of what the future would be, and I had a small child. … It was hard to leave that work community and leave everything behind. They were all my projects, and now I'm totally out of it. And I remember how I felt when I was removed from our WhatsApp group, a feeling of shame.' (Mia)

Irrespective of the reasons for moving outside academia, leaving was always an outcome of a variety of factors (Wood et al, 2020) and related to the interviewees' overall life situation and the future horizon involved in it (see McAlpine and Emmioglu, 2015). All interviewees had commitments in their private lives, and most of them had families and children. Hence, the future visions of their private lives were entangled with career decisions, albeit in different ways. Some utilized a "family first" strategy, some gave priority to career considerations, but nobody planned their career future in a social vacuum. For instance, the importance of financial security was emphasized, as it ensured "that we will manage even if one of us becomes unemployed". Likewise, getting a better work-life balance became crucial when one had "the sweetest child in the world at home" and wanted to devote time to her. Going abroad for a longer period, defined as necessary in academic career advancement by the interviewees, became unfeasible when one's partner refused to come along because "he had just spent four years as a postdoc in the US". And for some, the crucial thing was that one's working-class "eight-to-four environment" with a home-centred lifestyle could not be reconciled with the university's culture of long hours. These kinds of mismatches between one's private life and the visions of academic career pushed some interviewees out of academia.

All the interviewees who had left academia have, since, succeeded in finding good jobs in a variety of areas. However, leaving was challenging because there were hardly any other career imaginaries than the academic one available in their local environment. As the field was new and did not educate people for a specific profession, the researchers simply did not know what kinds of jobs they could apply for and where their qualifications would be sufficient and relevant. In this sense, the future was fuzzy and veiled for many, and they had to carve it out themselves. Hence, pioneers became important. For instance, one researcher's recruitment by an international pharmaceutical company paved the way for a couple of others to follow this route. Overall, the interviewees were satisfied with the employment they had gained, but even so they kept their career horizons open and were ready to move again in the future.

All in all, these interviews reflected very narrow visions of career building in academia, basically excluding options other than the vertical progression to the top of the career ladder. The university was viewed as a 'greedy organization' (Currie et al, 2000; Thun, 2020) which requires personal sacrifices but is not willing to give career security and support in return. This image became all the gloomier due to local conflicts with the merger partner, shaping the everyday life of the smaller unit. As a result, although the interviewees were motivated to undertake research work, in the end their visions of an academic career were not personally appealing enough, which ultimately made it easy to leave.

Discussion

This small-scale qualitative study of one biotechnology unit at one Finnish university shows the complexity and manifold tensions of academic career building in the current neoliberal higher education context. Although biotechnology as a research field matches the policy priorities of major scientific, societal and commercial expectations, the lived experiences of women researchers were far from straightforward success stories. Instead, their career visions were strongly shaped by the intersections of gender, disciplinary hierarchies and university institutional structures which worked to their disadvantage. After several mergers, their career building took place in the shadow of the bigger, more influential and male-dominated merger party, medicine, which created extra challenges for them in the already highly competitive and risky university environment. Yet, the researchers were no victims of the structural barriers but, rather, skilful actors who crafted personally meaningful careers both inside and outside academia.

In the career imaginaries identified in this study, professorship and tenure track structures had a key role. Although introduced only in 2010 in Finland, the tenure track model has shaped the ways in which a successful and valued academic career is made sense of. By 2019, it was already the most common way to recruit professors in Finland (Pekkola et al, 2020), creating elitism and polarization between those who are on this track and the vast majority working outside of it (Herbert and Tienari, 2013; Pietilä, 2019). The tenure track system puts those senior researchers, who in this study are called academic entrepreneurs, in an awkward situation: they are, de facto, too qualified and established for the tenure track since these positions are usually targeted at rather early career academics. This darkens their prospects for career progression. Moreover, the tenure track model is deeply rooted in the meritocratic ideal that the best and brightest be recruited to top positions. Yet, this ideal has been repeatedly challenged by showing subtle and un-reflective biases, such as gendered pre-selection patterns and selection criteria as well as blindness to the life situations of candidates (van den Brink and Benschop, 2011; Acker et al, 2012; Nikunen, 2014; Nielsen, 2016; Herschberg et al, 2019; Pietilä, 2019; Thun, 2020).

Based on this study, it is evident that the socially available stock of imaginaries and narratives of academic career building are strikingly circumscribed and limited, involving only three possibilities: tenure track, academic entrepreneurship or leaving academia altogether. There seem to be no alternatives in the current university context that is 'inescapably competitive, individualistic and oriented to exchange value not use value' (Clegg, 2010: 359). Clegg calls for imagining higher education otherwise. On a similar note, Escobar (2020) extends this call to include the whole of society. He argues that the real, the possible and the political are all connected and, therefore, 'it is precisely because other possibles have been turned into "impossibles" that we find it so difficult to imagine other realities' (Escobar 2020: 3). Against this there-is-no-alternative rhetoric, he advocates the politics of the possible, or a way of thinking that another possible is possible – not least in academia.

Acknowledgements

The research was done in a Nordforsk funded Centre of Excellence Nordwit. I thank Tiina Suopajärvi and Minna Leinonen who conducted the interviews and Tiina Suopajärvi for contributing substantially to the initial analysis of this study. I also thank all members of Nordwit for their valuable comments on the first draft of this chapter.

References

Acker, S., Webber, M. and Smyth, E. (2012) 'Tenure troubles and equity matters in Canadian academe', *British Journal of Sociology of Education*, 33(5): 743–61.

Adam, B. and Groves, N. (2007) *Future Matters*, Leiden: Brill.

Arthur, M.B. and Rousseau, D.M. (1996) *The Boundaryless Career: A New Employment Principle for a New Organizational Era*, New York: Oxford University Press.

Clegg, S. (2010) 'Time future: the dominant discourse of higher education', *Time & Society*, 19(3): 345–64.

Cohen, L. and Mallon, M. (2001) 'My brilliant career? Using stories as a methodological tool in careers research', *International Studies of Management and Organization*, 31(3): 48–68.

Currie, J., Harris, P. and Thiele, B. (2000) 'Sacrifices in greedy university: are they gendered?', *Gender and Education*, 12(3): 269–91.

Duberley, J., Cohen, L. and Mallon, M. (2006) 'Constructing scientific careers: change, continuity and context', *Organization Studies*, 27(8): 1131–51.

Escobar, A. (2020) *Pluriversal Politics*, Durham, MA: Duke University Press.

Felt, U. (ed) (2009) *Knowing and Living in Academic Research*, Prague: Institute of Sociology of the Academy of Sciences of the Czech Republic.

Fochler, M. and Sigl, L. (2018) 'Anticipatory uncertainty: how academic and industry researchers in the life sciences experience and manage the uncertainties of the research process differently', *Science as Culture*, 27(3): 349–74.

Henningsson, M., Jörnesten, A. and Geschwind, L. (2018) 'Translating tenure track into Swedish: tensions when implementing an academic career system', *Studies in Higher Education*, 43(7): 1215–26.

Herbert, A. and Tienari, J. (2013) 'Transplanting tenure and (re)construction of academic freedoms', *Studies in Higher Education*, 38(2): 157–73.

Herschberg, C., Benschop, Y. and van den Brink, M. (2019) 'The peril of potential', in A. Murgia and B. Poggio (eds) *Gender and Precarious Research Careers*, London: Routledge, pp 111–42.

Laudel, G. and Gläser, J. (2007) 'From apprentice to colleague: the metamorphosis of early career researchers', *Higher Education*, 55(3): 811–41.

McAlpine, L. and Emmioglu, E. (2015) 'Navigating careers: perceptions of science doctoral students, post-PhD researchers and pre-tenure academics', *Studies in Higher Education*, 40(10): 1770–875.

Müller, R. (2014) 'Racing for what? Anticipation and acceleration in the work and career practices of academic life science postdocs', *Forum: Qualitative Social Research*, 15(3). DOI: 10.17169/fqs-15.3.2245.

Murgia, A. and Poggio, B. (eds) (2019) *Gender and Precarious Research Careers*, London: Routledge.

Musselin, C. (2005) 'European academic labor market in transition', *Higher Education*, 49(1–2): 135–54.

Nielsen, M. (2016) 'Limits to meritocracy? Gender in academic recruitment and promotion processes', *Science and Public Policy*, 43(3): 386–99.

Nikunen, M. (2014) 'The entrepreneurial university, family and gender: changes and demands faced by fixed-term workers', *Gender and Education*, 26(2):119–34.

Pekkola, E., Siekkinen, T., Kujala, E.-N. and Kanniainen, J.-P. (2020) *Professoreiden rekrytoinnit*, Helsinki: Professoriliitto.

Pietilä, M. (2015) 'Tenure track career system as a strategic instrument for academic leaders', *European Journal of Higher Education*, 5(4): 371–87.

Pietilä, M. (2019) 'Incentivising academics: experiences and expectations of the tenure track in Finland', *Studies in Higher Education*, 44(6): 932–45.

Slaughter, S. and Leslie, L. (1997) *Academic Capitalism*, Baltimore: Johns Hopkins University Press.

Thun, C. (2020) 'Excellent and gender equal? Academic motherhood and "gender blindness" in Norwegian academia', *Gender, Work & Organization*, 27(2): 166–80.

van den Brink, M. and Benschop, Y. (2011) 'Gender practices in the construction of academic excellence: sheep with five legs', *Organization*, 19(4): 507–24.

van der Weijden, I., Teelken, C., de Boer, M. and Drost, M. (2016) 'Career satisfaction of postdoctoral researchers in relation to their expectations for the future', *Higher Education*, 72(1): 25–40.

Wood, C.V., Jones, R.F., Remich, R.G., Caliendo, A.E., Langford, N.C., Keller, J.L., Campbell, P.B. and McGee, R. (2020) 'The national longitudinal study of young life scientists: career differentiation among a diverse group of biomedical PhD students', *PLOS ONE*, 15(6): e0234259. DOI: 10.1371/journal.pone.0234259.

Ylijoki, O.-H. (2013) 'Boundary work between work and life in the high-speed university', *Studies in Higher Education*, 38(2): 242–55.

Ylijoki, O.-H. (2014a) 'A temporal approach to higher education research', in J. Huisman and M. Tight (eds) *Theory and Method in Higher Education Research II*, Bingley: Emerald Publishing, pp 141–60.

Ylijoki, O.-H. (2014b) 'University under structural reform: a micro-level perspective', *Minerva*, 52(1): 55–75.

Ylijoki, O.-H. and Ursin, J. (2013) 'The construction of academic identities in the changes of Finnish higher education', *Studies in Higher Education*, 38(8): 1135–49.

4

Unconventional Routes into ICT Work: Learning from Women's Own Solutions for Working around Gendered Barriers

Hilde G. Corneliussen and Gilda Seddighi

Introduction

Diversity in the development of digital products and services is recognized as vital for the benefit of a diverse society (Losh and Wernimont, 2019) and is a goal across Europe (Barbieri et al, 2020). A continuously low proportion of women in ICT challenges this goal. About one in five ICT experts in Norway is a woman (Simonsen and Corneliussen, 2020), and a similar trend is visible in most European countries (Eurostat, 2019). Research has documented that gender stereotypes produce images of ICT as a male field (Master et al, 2016). A recent study from Norway suggests that girls need external influence in order to choose an education so closely associated with boys and men (Corneliussen, 2021). Most girls leave high school with no intention of pursuing a career in ICT. Some of these, however, find their way to ICT education and work at a later point, and it is these women's narratives we analyze here, as we ask: what motivates women's alternative and late entries into fields of ICT? The analysis builds on qualitative interviews with women working with ICT-driven research, development and innovation in Norway. None of these women had chosen ICT when leaving high school. Thus, pursuing a career in ICT represented a career change into ICT that they had not had in mind when entering higher education.

The narratives of the women in our study give a unique insight into how ICT has become a more visible, relevant, even necessary field to engage with, as disciplines and professions are changing through processes of digitalization. This study shows that when facing such processes, women adjust their education and career path to include ICT. The analysis illustrates three unconventional routes leading these women into ICT work: first, a delayed entry into ICT education; second, a natural progression into ICT due to digitalization of non-technological disciplines; and third, pursuing opportunities, as non-technological competences are needed in ICT-driven research, development and innovation.

Initiatives to recruit girls to ICT education often assume that the optimal way for this is to make girls copy features associated with masculine relations to ICT, for instance by sparking girls' interest in tinkering and playing with technology, assumed to be important gateways to ICT education (McKinsey & Company and Pivotal Ventures, 2018). Most studies of women's recruitment to ICT focus on women following a conventional route where the decision to pursue ICT happens before high school, or upon shifting from high school to higher education. Our analysis of women's unconventional routes expands and adds to this literature by identifying how other interests and motivations work as door openers for women to choose ICT also at later stages than the beginning of their time at university. With a theoretical framework from Feminist Technology Studies (FTS) and theories about predictors of academic choices, the analysis illustrates how the women's narratives draw pictures of alternative and unconventional routes leading them through a gendered landscape of ICT disciplines and professions, contributing new ways of co-constructing gender and ICT.

Women's entry points into ICT education and work: a literature review

There are many studies of girls' and women's under-representation in fields of ICT, suggesting a complex problem that has changed over time and place (Cohoon and Aspray, 2006; Misa, 2010; Charles and Thébaud, 2018). Despite variations, it is widely recognized that gendered norms, discourses and stereotypes affect young people's choices of education in ways that reproduce the gender imbalance in ICT (OECD, 2016; UNESCO, 2017; Frieze and Quesenberry, 2019) because gender stereotypes work to limit their educational choices (NOU, 2019: 19).

Studies of young people's motivation to pursue a career in ICT have often focussed on when and how *interest in* ICT develops, for instance indicating the teens as a period when stereotypical perceptions of disciplines grow stronger (Talks et al, 2019). Many youths lose interest in science, technology, engineering, and mathematics (STEM). This affects girls more than boys, leaving a short gap to capture girls' interest in ICT (Microsoft Corporation, 2017). This interest itself is, however, coded masculine. Thus, the many 'road bumps' and 'potholes' in women's paths towards ICT (Branch, 2016) make active support, mentoring and encouragement more significant for girls than for boys (Corneliussen, 2021). This makes parents, teachers and educators important for girls' educational choices (Eccles, 2015; Tænketanken DEA, 2019), but the former themselves are of course influenced by gender stereotypes, with an observed result being weak attempts to recruit girls to ICT (Corneliussen and Prøitz, 2016). A Danish study found that 70 per cent of parents believed that boys are more interested in ICT than girls; less than 1 per cent of parents imagined girls to be more interested than boys (Tænketanken DEA, 2019).

Despite gendered patterns in education, gender remains a little discussed issue in Norwegian schools (Mathiesen et al, 2010), including in questions relating to girls' (lack of) participation in ICT subjects (Corneliussen and Tveranger, 2018). Gender stereotypes combined with young people's lack of knowledge about ICT disciplines also have a more negative effect on girls than boys, making it less likely for girls to move from high school to higher ICT education (Talks et al, 2019). A recent study from Norway shows that many women enter ICT as a second education, which according to Corneliussen (2021), represents a 'penalty round for women' who due to gender stereotypes had not perceived ICT as a relevant or welcoming discipline at high school and therefore had chosen other disciplines. This, however, led the women to discover and get to know ICT in new ways that made it more relevant and available to them, for instance, because they could identify a non-technical interest or competence as an entry point and 'a platform in ICT that they identify as "safe and familiar" without competing with the male image' of computing (Corneliussen, 2021: 57).

Other studies have also identified women being recruited to ICT later and through other arenas than school, for instance through coding boot camps (Lyon and Green, 2020). Lyon and Green found that this came too late for many women to change to ICT, and Vainionpää et al claim that 'senior high school is the last opportunity to influence girls' major and career choice' (2019: 1). While these studies clearly highlight an important and often missed opportunity to recruit women through schools (Seibel and Veilleux, 2019), they also point to the importance of increasing our knowledge not only of what motivates high school girls to choose ICT, but also to identify what makes women approach alternative routes to ICT competence and work. One optimistic strand of research in the late 1990s and early 2000s suggested that women were wanted and needed in the development of ICT, based on assumptions of women representing a type of hybrid work profile that incorporates feminine characteristics (Plant, 1997; Woodfield, 2000). While there might be different interests and motivations behind girls' and boys' educational attainments (Microsoft Corporation, 2017; Master and Meltzoff, 2020), the differences between women and men working in ICT and engineering are not so large (Faulkner, 2001) and what women and men care about in ICT work is also rather similar (Holtzblatt and Marsden, 2018). Expanding on the field of research revisited here, this chapter contributes to studies of women's recruitment into ICT education and work with an analysis of how women's alternative routes into this are shaped by gendered barriers and how they identify entry points less affected by masculine stereotypes.

Theoretical framework

Gender is a reflection of socially constructed differences between women and men, developed through cultural discourses and negotiated in many arenas (Connell, 2005). Technology is one of the fields strongly affected by gendered structures, and a growing field of research has since the 1980s explored the relationship between gender and technology (Wajcman, 2004). An illustrative example is the classic study of the gendered transformation of the microwave oven that was first imagined as a high-tech device and promoted for men alongside other products often bought by men. However, when the microwave was reframed to target women, it was also redesigned and presented as low-tech device for domestic work often used by women (Cockburn and Ormrod, 1993). This seminal study illustrates how technology as well as users of technology are gendered in ways that make the one reflect the other. This as well as other contributions in the field of feminist technology studies demonstrate that the gendering of technology is a cultural process, based on social and cultural choices and considerations (Grint and Gill, 1995; Oldenziel et al, 2003). Furthermore, social constructivist theories emphasize that gender and technology can be understood as mutually affecting each other, co-constructed and reflected in the images of who works with technology (Cockburn, 1992). This tradition contributes to our understanding of the gendering of ICT, for instance identifying that a major challenge for recruiting women to ICT is caused by its masculine image, making it appear less welcoming to girls than boys (Cheryan et al, 2013; Charles and Thébaud, 2018). Gendered images of and stereotypes about ICT have different effects on girls' and boys' ability to associate themselves with the field (NOU, 2019: 19).

While it is challenging to determine what has affected one particular individual's educational choices, it is even more challenging to determine this for all women as Dee points out (2021). The aim of identifying how men and women make educational choices that result in patterns of gender difference has, however, generated a growing body of research. Some of the most popular motivational theoretical frameworks have roots in psychology such as self-efficacy theory (Bandura, 1977), emphasizing that the way we understand ourselves and our own abilities affect study choices (Dee, 2021). Eccles developed this line of theories with the expectancy-value perspective, suggesting that individuals make their choices based on a combination of how well they expect to manage a task and the value they associate with the task (Eccles, 2009). Master and Meltzoff (2020) add to this by including research emphasizing how stereotypes affect students' sense of belonging. They develop a theoretical model describing how students (for example women) who face negative stereotypes regarding their identity in STEM, integrate these stereotypes into their self-representation in ways that influence their interest and engagement in STEM. The main difference between the original expectancy-value theory and Master and Meltzoff's model is that the first proposes that the subjective task value including interest, together with ability belief, are the most important predictors of students' choices (Eccles, 2011), while Master and Meltzoff suggest that interest is an outcome, based on research showing that 'ability beliefs are more likely to predict interest over time than the reverse', and that 'interest has distinct motivational properties, including the predisposition to re-engage with a domain over time' (2020: 160).

Although we have not engaged in a psychological study of the concepts mentioned earlier, some of the concepts from these theories are still relevant for our study as they emphasize how academic choices are affected by cultural stereotypes, interest, women's trust in their abilities, or 'ability belief', and a sense of belonging, all of which are elements that we can identify in the narratives of the women we have interviewed. One difference, however, is that these theories are mainly developed with the conventional route into STEM in mind. Our analysis engages with these concepts as a guide to exploring how these factors are valid for women who navigate unconventional routes into ICT education and work.

Methodological framework

Qualitative interviews with women in ICT work

This chapter reports on a Nordwit case study where we interviewed women working with ICT in western Norway. They were recruited through research funders, incubators and other organizations in fields of ICT research and innovation. Since we wanted to explore women's experiences in ICT work from a variety of occupational fields and workplaces, we included women working in the public and the private sector as well as women in academia. In total 28 women, aged between 24 and 59, were interviewed. They all had university degrees (one BA, 18 MAs and nine PhDs). The 28 women's disciplinary backgrounds reflect the fact that ICT work is not specific to ICT-educated specialists; only 15 of the 28 women had a degree in a discipline allied to computer science or information science, while the others had graduated in fields such as social sciences, humanities, natural science, health care, law, or economics. As the aim of this chapter is to explore unconventional routes leading women to ICT work, we do not discuss the 11 women who had followed a conventional route from high school to higher ICT education and focus instead on the remaining 17 women. The interviews involved a professional-life history perspective and included questions about education, occupational history and experiences in workplaces, and relationship to technology. The interviews followed an interview guide while also aiming to give the women space for reflection (Kvale and Brinkmann, 2009). When discussing individual women, we have in some cases omitted the exact discipline and position to secure their anonymity. The study was approved by the Norwegian Centre for Research Data.

Grounded theory approach

The interviews were analyzed using a grounded theory approach, suitable for developing new perspectives and understandings (Strauss and Corbin, 1998). We read and manually coded the transcribed interviews before extracting the codes, organizing them in groups and developing categories (Charmaz, 2006). In the next phase, we explored the women's work histories as 'routes to ICT work', including the analytical categories resulting from the coding: 'educational choices', 'finding a place' and 'belonging'. While emphasizing that the women's voices should give meaning to the categories and experiences that we analyzed, we continued to refine these categories through reading and discussing sections of the interviews, comparing findings in the categories, and comparing our findings with similar studies. Thus, we were not only asking analytical questions of the interview material, but simultaneously engaged in comparative readings, exploring how the patterns we found related to research from other western countries. Through this analytical process we identified four routes leading to ICT work among the interviewed women. One of these was the traditional route leading from high school to ICT education and work. This route has been studied in many projects. We were instead interested in the other three, less studied routes. We focus on these in the following section.

Three unconventional routes into ICT education and work

The three routes into ICT work analyzed here are probably not the only unconventional routes into ICT work, and nor are they entirely exclusive. However, they contribute to highlighting how the field of ICT is still gendered in ways that create barriers for young women to pursue the conventional route into ICT, while simultaneously documenting alternative motivations for women moving into the core processes of ICT research, development and innovation. Table 4.1 gives an overview of some of the main features of the routes we identified, illustrating how they depart from

Table 4.1: Women's unconventional entry routes into ICT work

	Route 1: delayed entry into ICT education	**Route 2: digitalization of (non-technical) disciplines**	**Route 3: non-technological professions engaged in ICT research and innovation**
Education	First degree in a non-technical discipline Second degree in ICT	Education in disciplines traditionally not recognized as technical	Education in non-technical discipline
Reason for choosing ICT	Support for future work	Necessary or natural change due to digitalization of chosen discipline	New opportunities in digitalization for non-tech professions
Way of acquiring ICT competence	Degree in higher ICT education	Development in original discipline with higher ICT education or workplace-based upskilling of ICT competence	Formal ICT courses and workplace-based upskilling of ICT competence
Current position	ICT expert	ICT as expert area within original (non-tech) profession	Occupied in original profession in area of digitalization
Current work tasks	Designing, programming, implementing new technology, management	Designing, programming, implementing new technology, management	Designing, implementing new technology, management

Source: the authors.

formal education. The first route includes a university degree in ICT as a second education after changing direction. The second route involves ICT training as well but as a form of competence development growing out of a discipline traditionally *not* recognized as technological. The third route builds on a non-technological education while also involving mainly workplace-based, formal and informal ICT training. All the women were at some level involved in designing, building or implementing new technology. However, the first and second group were more involved in technical work such as programming, while the third group was more involved in design and management. The reasons for moving into ICT, however, had similarities across the routes, as we shall see when we start to unpack the routes.

We start by illustrating the main features of these routes, with an emphasis on when and how the women entered fields of ICT, before we engage with some of the key concepts discussed in the theoretical framework: interest, ability belief and sense of belonging.

A delayed entry into ICT education (route 1)

Four women had originally chosen a non-technical education, before they changed to an ICT discipline, illustrating a *delayed* entry into ICT education. Like the conventional route, this route too involved a university degree in ICT, but was shaped (and gendered) by how the women had *not* chosen ICT but rather a non-technical discipline in the first place. Three of the women described the transition as coincidental. One of them had started with a degree in economics, but wanted to add something more "practical" and took a course in ICT that resulted in a change of direction:

> 'The plan was to become an economist, I think. I'm not sure I had a plan, really. At least I knew I would take [subjects like] administration, organization and economics, and then I liked economics a lot, so that's what I wanted to continue with. But then I also thought that I needed some IT because it is practical. Then I started in information science, and that was a good experience … and suddenly I had a Bachelor degree in IT. … The combination was a bit coincidental. It wasn't according to a plan from the start.' (Ann)

Ann's first entry into ICT was a strategic move related to future work opportunities. She admits that initially she was not at all interested in technology. She started working as a programmer after finishing her Bachelor degree, realizing she really liked the job:

> 'We started to build a data warehouse, and then I felt that I was in the right place, because then I got the combination of the analytical side

> of economics plus that you could work a bit with technology. It is not the geeky type of technology. It is a very practical use of technology. That appealed a lot to me.' (Ann)

She returned to university to do a Master's degree in IT, and at the time of the interview she was responsible for developing a data warehouse from scratch, doing everything from designing and programming, to implementing and teaching the users. She described this as "great fun". Simultaneously she illustrated the gendered landscape of ICT by emphasizing the limits of her relationship with technology:

> 'I think my strength is that I am analytic and see connections and manage to get things to fit together and the use of it, more than being an expert or very good in programming. I'm not there at all. … For me, technology is a means to accomplish something. … So I'm not so into technology as such.' (Ann)

Bree was another woman who took a delayed route into ICT but had already been interested in it at high school. Her father advised her against choosing ICT and she accepted his argument that she was not really interested in it: "So I did not take any mathematics, because I was going to learn to talk to people and to understand society, that was what I wanted." At university she had wanted to study ICT, but then realized she was not eligible for this, having followed her father's advice. Cut off from ICT, she finished a Bachelor degree in social science, before she once again thought about ICT. This time she found an opening while contemplating what kind of jobs a degree in social science would lead to:

> 'What job prospects do you have when you take that kind of [social science education]? … Then I realized that there were many job announcements asking for a combination of technology and social sciences, so I thought, okay maybe I should choose ICT to combine with the social sciences I already have.' (Bree)

The turning point occurred when she realized that combining her degree in social science with ICT could be a door opener to interesting jobs. She was finally able to defy her father's advice, but at the cost of starting all over again with a new Bachelor degree. Bree's narrative illustrates her growing interest in technology including a geeky delight in programming:

> 'When I started to study IT I got a better understanding of what it really was and how it works and then it was more like … it is a nice course, it's great fun with things that you solve, and programming is

> a bit like solving the crosswords on the last page of the newspaper. It is like, finally you crack the code! And then it works, and you are satisfied.' (Bree)

After her Master's degree she had worked mostly as a programmer and systems architect; at the time of the interview she was developing new digital solutions for a private company.

Like the other women who took a delayed route into ICT, Bree too described this move as coincidental, not part of her original plan, and not a response to an interest in ICT per se, but rather a response to the sense that ICT training would provide useful competence for her future career. Though these women expressed doubt about their interest at first, when learning more about ICT they found themselves in 'the right place' within highly technical work processes in ICT development and innovation. Bree also defined limits for her relationship to ICT with reference to a discourse of programming as an activity often pursued by men in their leisure time, saying: "I'm not programming at home in my spare time or use a lot of time like that on technology" (Bree).

Digitalization of (non-technical) disciplines (route 2)

The women described earlier had a delayed entry point into ICT education. In the next group, too, there were ten women who decided to study ICT as part of their formal education. However, the driving force for these women was not a *change* from one field to ICT disciplines, but rather expanding their ICT competence along with increasing digitalization within their chosen profession in fields traditionally not recognized as technological such as nursing, pedagogy, biology and chemistry. Recognizing ICT competence as increasingly vital in their profession, these women made adjustments to develop and update their competence in ICT, even returning to university. While for some this meant a change of direction, others experienced it as a natural progression.

Health care is one of the sectors with a rapidly growing demand for digitalization. Two interviewees were working with technology in the health care sector. One, originally a nurse, was now responsible for digitalization processes including innovation and implementation of new digital solutions in the public health care sector. Her interest in ICT was stirred when she realized that her organization was like "Bambi on ice" regarding technology. Developing technology-driven health care services was "a huge transition" that she wanted to be part of:

> 'There was a missing link between the job I was going to do [nursing] and the IT department. There was no communication at all and no

> dialogue. Because I did not understand what they said, and they did not understand what we were saying. And then all of us just thought that all the others were idiots.' (Cora)

Cora returned to university to study for a Master's degree in health informatics, encouraged by people in the organization telling her that she would 'fit' that: "I started at the university in a health informatics programme, because there were some holes that I felt I could contribute to, which had to do with understanding technology and collaboration between technology and people – those who are in fact using it" (Cora). She saw herself as a translator in the process of "digital transformation": a total change in how to plan and provide health care services redefined as e-health. Nurses like her needed to learn more about ICT, but equally importantly, the ICT experts also needed to develop knowledge about health care: "The boundaries for those who work with technology have changed and it is no longer enough that they only know the platform and the technical side. They need to understand the effect of the system [in health care services] in order to solve a problem" (Cora). This highlights the conditions for her intermediary position between the tech personnel and the health care personnel, and between technology and human beings. This role was vital because "technology is nothing if the people who are supposed to use it cannot use it, because that is where you find the real benefit" (Cora). The two work cultures meeting in her work were not frictionless but she had developed a "thick skin" and a strategy for letting things cool down as she navigated the gendered workspace between health care and ICT:

> 'I'm doing better and better because I am respected in the IT department. They can see that I have knowledge. And if I feel that they look upon me as stupid, I do not care about that, I just continue after a short break and then I go back into the situation. But it is still as if they want to be in charge of their own areas, in particular these men.' (Cora)

Cora's narrative illustrates how her career changed direction due to her *active choice* to be part of the new e-health. Dani, on the other hand, regarded her move into ICT as a *natural progression*. Dani had started in chemistry and made choices during her Bachelor and Master's degrees that gradually led her to a PhD in cybernetics. We asked her about that choice:

> 'Well, in fact I chose chemistry. When I finished [high school] I didn't even know what cybernetics was. And I am not sure that I would have chosen it even if I had known. … The most important thing is that you see as you go along, whether you like the subject or not, and

then make choices based on that. So, I started with chemistry but then I chose the subjects with less chemistry, more towards control systems. Therefore, it was a natural transition into cybernetics for me.' (Dani)

At the time of the interview Dani was working in research, developing and testing technological process control systems. She worked in a highly male-dominated field, and despite initial doubts about her educational choices she found the combination of chemistry and cybernetics a "good fit" for her, one she "enjoyed a lot", and she was "very happy" about her current work. However, Dani also made sure to identify her limits: "There are more boys and men who sit and spend their leisure time on things like that [programming]. But we [women] use it, and we are interested in it in a work-related setting, but when I go home, I leave it behind at work" (Dani). Dani made a clear and gendered distinction between work and leisure here, with ICT being firmly located in her work environment.

Non-technological professions engaged in ICT research and innovation (route 3)

The third route into ICT was also taken by women with a background in a non-technical profession. However, in contrast to route 2, it was not their own profession that was being digitalized, but rather new opportunities arose for these women's non-technological professions in processes of digitalization. Their original career choices, such as administration and management, economy and law, became a gateway to working with ICT and digitalization. There was also a trend among these women of being promoted into ICT work. Many of them had developed their career to the point of high management positions in workplaces where technology and digitalization were at the core of the organizations' operations, and where they recognized that non-technological professions also had important roles to play. One of these women, Ella, illustrated both the integration of non-technological competences into digitalization, and taking on a leading role. Her background was in an "old-fashioned" and not at all technical discipline. After many years of "traditional" work in this profession, a coincidence provided a job opportunity in developing a framework for digital products and services. She recognized this as a change of direction into a field she did not know much about, when she recalled deciding to join the company: "I chose [company], even though I didn't really understand much of what they were doing. I tried to read stuff to understand more. In the beginning I felt like a very 'analogue person'. … I had to learn about technology, and it took a lot of time" (Ella). Technology and digitalization represented a new world that she found "very exciting". She contributed to national as well as international digital innovation: "we had to build a methodology and our own tools. … We had to start with blank pages back then and we have built some of it, but we still have more to do". She is considered a digital pioneer in the field. Recalling the start she said: "there were no answers, so when we were doing this, we had nowhere to look. No one had done it before, so we have invented this ourselves". After nearly a decade in this work she no longer saw herself as an "analogue person": "now I feel that I am very technological, that I know a lot about technology, … because [my work] has to do both with the code and with design and content, and now I know a lot about all of that" (Ella). Not taking the time to stop and acquire a formal education in ICT, she had developed her ICT competence on the job and she experienced her work identity as "more on the technological side" than within her non-tech profession. She did not consider herself an ICT expert, but for her, the fabric of digitalization was also not just technological:

> 'One of the reasons we have succeeded is that we don't think about technology as a separate field … it is a tool that needs to work in-between, for instance me and you, or for something else, but at least there are people at all ends. And to emphasize this perspective is important; that it is not just to build components that are supposed to talk to each other and do stuff, but making it work in a holistic perspective and asking what you want from it.' (Ella)

Ella was one of five women in our sample who from a non-technological education had become deeply involved in processes of research and innovation with ICT and digitalization at their core. These new opportunities to work with technology reflected the development of new digitalized workspaces, products and services where multi-disciplinary competences are required. Different from the previous women, these women did not formally update their education, but instead engaged in learning processes on the job. Their lack of formal competence did not stop them; indeed, one of the women in this group is recognized nationally as one of the most important people in technology development in Norway.

Discussion: interest, ability belief and a sense of belonging

Drawing on social constructivist theories within feminist technology studies emphasizing the co-construction of technology and gender (Cockburn, 1992) and relying on theories of cultural stereotypes, interest, ability belief and a sense of belonging, we have illustrated the entry points of the three unconventional routes that led our interviewees to working within ICT and digitalization. Different from the conventional route from high school to university, the unconventional routes include examples of women changing their educational direction entirely (route 1), pursuing ICT competence in disciplines in transition due to digitalization (route 2), and becoming involved in ICT because non-technological professions are drawn into processes of digitalization (route 3). Although the 17 women were not recruited to ICT at high school, this did not prevent their later entry into ICT or pursuing opportunities in new fields of digitalization. We shall now unpack how these routes and the women's narratives fit into some of the key elements of the theories about recruitment to ICT, such as interest, ability belief and sense of belonging.

Starting with the question of interest, Master and Meltzoff (2020) found that interest was a vital driver for recruiting students to a field because interest would make you return to that field. Bree illustrated this as she described several points where she had considered choosing ICT, suggesting that her interest in ICT made her more aware of opportunities related to the field. However, she did not refer to interest when describing why she finally decided to leave social science and start over in ICT. Instead, she described her change of direction as a strategic choice to secure interesting jobs in the future, similar to Ann's motivation to choose ICT. However, while Bree described interest in terms of a geeky pleasure in programming, some of the others, like Ann, did not recognize ICT as interesting. This indicates that when considering women who were not recruited through the conventional route, *interest is not enough to make women enter fields of ICT*, but it also suggests that *lack of interest is not the main barrier to women's entry into ICT*.

Ability belief (cf. Master and Meltzoff, 2020) seems to be a much more potent explanation for these women's actual decisions to move into ICT. Bree repeatedly considered ICT as a potential career, but it was not until she could connect ICT to her already established competence and ability belief in social science that she made the relevant move into ICT. This illustrates a characteristic she shared with the other 16 women: they all had a non-technological discipline or profession as a starting point for their engagement with ICT. As Bree's story illustrates, her already established competence in social sciences provided a *safe platform* from which to move into ICT. The women's unconventional entry points suggest that they experienced less competition with masculine coded fields of ICT when they could establish their ability belief in a field less characterized by masculine stereotypes, or even within professions dominated by women such as health care.

It seems that it is mainly at the entry point that the 'safe platform' makes a difference in relation to ability belief and interest, both of which are challenged by gender stereotypes. After developing their competence in fields of ICT, the women gradually established their sense of belonging into those fields. Cora, for instance, became the support person for both health care and IT personnel in her organization, and Ella's work identity increasingly rested both on her original profession and her new competence in a field of digitalization. The importance of these starting-points or platforms in the women's narratives illustrates how their ability belief as well as their sense of belonging increasingly rested on a *combination* of ICT with their first chosen non-technological discipline. Although they worked with designing, programming, developing and implementing ICT systems, it was the power of producing and controlling technical systems in the context of other fields that made the women feel that they were "in the right place", like Ann discovering she could work with both programming and economics, Bree working on business development through producing information systems, and Cora improving health care services through technology.

The women changed, some of them quite literally, by leaving one field and entering ICT; others by developing their competence in ICT in a direction that they had not intended when they first entered university. Some of the women pointed out how this differentiated them from colleagues who had not acquired ICT competence. They described new configurations of ICT work where they saw themselves filling holes between the tech-people and, for instance, health care workers, who did not speak the same language. They illustrated also how ICT had changed: since none of them came through the conventional and direct route to ICT, they had added other competences to ICT research, development and innovation, suggesting that they represented hybrid work profiles. This hybridity was built on professionally acquired competence that added to and expanded their understanding of technology. This should not be mistaken for the type of hybrid work profiles supposedly built on feminine features, as discussed in earlier research (Plant, 1997).

Unconventional entry routes into ICT are not reserved for women, but the women's narratives illustrate how they experienced this as navigating a gendered landscape. This was most clearly articulated when they described their limited interest in ICT, with references to different expectations regarding men's and women's relationships to technology: unlike their male colleagues, the women left the technology behind at work.

Conclusion: documenting a failure or proposing a solution?

After decades of research, we know quite a lot about factors excluding women from ICT, but we are still short of effective solutions for recruiting women. Most studies exploring the challenges of recruiting women to ICT focus on conventional routes with career decisions made at high school. Solutions often aim to produce changes in the same context: targeting girls' interest in ICT, aiming to support their ability beliefs, and making them feel welcome (Master and Meltzoff, 2020). In this chapter we have explored a much less studied phenomenon, which is women pursuing less conventional routes into ICT education and ICT work, suggesting that they find other ways of dealing with the existing gendered barriers. Reflecting the masculine stereotyping of ICT, the first route illustrates barriers excluding even women who are interested in ICT. The women's solution follows after a delay, the gendered 'penalty round' shaped by women's experience of barriers to choosing ICT at high school and university that initially sent them into other fields (Corneliussen, 2021). While this delay has a cost, for instance for Bree who literally had to pay for two Bachelor degrees, it also gave the women a platform in a non-technical field. This provided an entry point into ICT education and work that was not equally riddled with gendered stereotypes. Learning more about ICT and how they could combine ICT with their previous discipline, the women experienced being "in the right place".

We agree with theories suggesting that gender stereotypes about ICT are likely to affect women's interest as well as ability belief in the field (Eccles, 2015; Master and Meltzoff, 2020). However, the women analyzed here differ from the main target groups behind these theories, making questions of interest and ability belief in ICT less relevant. In fact, our analysis shows that interest in ICT is *neither enough, nor a requirement*, for women to choose ICT. It is important to emphasize that our findings do not suggest that women are not interested in ICT, nor that encouraging such interest is irrelevant. However, for this group of women who had not been recruited at an earlier point, it was when they realized that ICT was important for business development, that ICT and social science could go hand in hand and that technology was necessary for delivering good health care services, that they became enthusiastic. They still had a major part of their professional identity, including interest and ability belief, invested in their original non-technological profession, but this did not prevent them from embracing ICT, developing their competence and finding a sense of professional belonging. Our analysis suggests that the 'safe and familiar' platform in a non-technological field is one key to understanding how the women developed a hybrid work identity combining non-technological fields with ICT in ways that avoided direct competition with the masculinized notion of ICT experts (Corneliussen, 2021).

Our study supports findings such as Master and Meltzoff's (2020) suggestion that ability belief is important for supporting women's entry into male-dominated fields like ICT. However, different from expectancy-value theories that suggest that ability belief and interest reside in the discipline in question, the women pursuing unconventional routes to ICT described their interest, ability belief and sense of belonging as linked to their investment in a non-technological discipline. They successfully solved the main challenge implied in Master and Meltzoff's model, which is to identify ways of motivating students (for example women) facing negative stereotypes regarding STEM (for example ICT). However, the women we met found their own ways of solving this: by ignoring their discursive 'lack of fit' with stereotypes of ICT and defining their fit based on a hybrid competence model. A conclusion to draw from this is that ICT is not the only relevant starting point for choosing ICT, and that other fields of interest can provide less masculine coded entry points for individuals who do not associate themselves with this type of masculinity.

Are these women illustrating solutions to recruiting women into ICT, or do they rather represent failed opportunities? Our analysis suggests both. Some represented failure by pointing out that they could have been recruited earlier, while others rather rejected that view, such as Dani who doubted that she would have chosen ICT earlier even if she had known more about it. Thus, while learning from failures of recruiting women through the conventional route, we should also look at unconventional routes as solutions with a potential for bringing a more diverse group into ICT work. Our study supports the often-repeated advice to develop the message about 'who belongs' in ICT to also include women (Cheryan et al, 2015; Master and Meltzoff, 2020), though this is also mainly limited to the conventional route. To capture a wider group of women including those who feel diverted away from the conventional route, we need to expand the message to include the vital role of ICT across a vast range of disciplines, industries and sectors not previously considered technological, including fields dominated by women.

References

Bandura, A. (1977) 'Self-efficacy: toward a unifying theory of behavioral change', *Psychological Review*, 84(2): 191–215.

Barbieri, D., Caisl, J., Karu, M., Lanfredi, G., Mollard, B., Peciukonis, V., La Hoz, M.B.P., Reingardė, J. and Salanauskaitė, L. (2020) *Gender Equality Index 2020: Digitalisation and the Future of Work*, Luxembourg: EIGE: European Institute for Gender Equality.

Branch, E.H. (ed) (2016) *Pathways, Potholes, and the Persistence of Women in Science: Reconsidering the Pipeline*, Lanham MD: Lexington Books.

Charles, M. and Thébaud, S. (2018) *Gender and STEM: Understanding Segregation in Science, Technology, Engineering and Mathematics (Special Issue of Social Sciences)*, Basel, Switzerland: MDPI.

Charmaz, K. (2006) *Constructing Grounded Theory: A Practical Guide through Qualitative Research*, London: Sage.

Cheryan, S., Master, A. and Meltzoff, A.N. (2015) 'Cultural stereotypes as gatekeepers: increasing girls' interest in computer science and engineering by diversifying stereotypes', *Frontiers in Psychology*, 6(49): 1–8.

Cheryan, S., Plaut, V.C., Handron, C. and Hudson, L. (2013) 'The stereotypical computer scientist: gendered media representations as a barrier to inclusion for women', *Sex Roles*, 69(1–2): 58–71.

Cockburn, C. (1992) 'The circuit of technology: gender, identity and power', in R. Silverstone and Hirsch, E. (eds) *Consuming Technologies: Media and Information in Domestic Spaces*, London: Routledge, pp 32–47.

Cockburn, C. and Ormrod, S. (1993) *Gender and Technology in the Making*, Thousand Oaks, CA: Sage.

Cohoon, J.M. and Aspray, W. (eds) (2006) *Women and Information Technology: Research on Underrepresentation*, Cambridge, MA: MIT Press.

Connell, R.W. (2005) 'Change among the gatekeepers: men, masculinities, and gender equality in the global arena', *Signs: Journal of Women in Culture and Society*, 30(3): 1801–25.

Corneliussen, H.G. (2021) 'Women empowering themselves to fit in ICT', in E. Lechman (ed) *Technology and Women's Empowerment*, London: Routledge, pp 46–62.

Corneliussen, H.G. and Prøitz, L. (2016) 'Kids code in a rural village in Norway: could code clubs be a new arena for increasing girls' digital interest and competence?', *Information, Communication & Society*, 19(1): 95–110.

Corneliussen, H.G. and Tveranger, F. (2018) 'Programming in secondary schools in Norway: a wasted opportunity for inclusion', *Proceedings of Gender&IT'18, Heilbronn, Germany, May 2018*, New York: ACM, pp 172–82.

Dee, H. (2021) 'Computing in schools', in G. Arnold, H. Dee, C. Herman, S. Moore, A. Palmer and S. Shah (eds) *Women in Tech:* A *Practical Guide* to *Increasing Gender Diversity* and *Inclusion*, Swindon: BCS Learning & Development Limited, pp 24–47.

Eccles, J. (2009) 'Who am I and what am I going to do with my life? Personal and collective identities as motivators of action', *Educational Psychologist*, 44(2): 78–89.

Eccles, J. (2011) 'Gendered educational and occupational choices: applying the Eccles et al model of achievement-related choices', *International Journal of Behavioral Development*, 35(3): 195–201.

Eccles, J. (2015) 'Gendered socialization of STEM interests in the family', *Journal of Gender, Science and Technology*, 7(2): 116–32.

Eurostat (2019) *ICT Specialists in Employment: Statistics Explained*. Available at: https://ec.europa.eu/eurostat/statistics-explained/index.php/ICT_specialists_in_employment, accessed 10 May 2021.

Faulkner, W. (2001) 'The technology question in feminism: a view from feminist technology studies', *Women's Studies International Forum*, 24(1): 79–95.

Frieze, C. and Quesenberry, J.L. (2019) *Cracking the Digital Ceiling: Women in Computing around the World*, Cambridge: Cambridge University Press.

Grint, K. and Gill, R. (eds) (1995) *The Gender-Technology Relation: Contemporary Theory and Research*, London: Taylor & Francis.

Holtzblatt, K. and Marsden, N. (2018) 'Retaining women in technology: uncovering and measuring key dimensions of daily work experiences', *Proceedings from the 2018 IEEE International Conference on Engineering, Technology and Innovation (ICE/ITMC)*, pp 148–55.

Kvale, S. and Brinkmann, S. (2009) *Det kvalitative forskningsintervju*, Oslo: Gyldendal akademisk.

Losh, E. and Wernimont, J. (2019) *Bodies of Information: Intersectional Feminism and the Digital Humanities*, Minneapolis: University of Minnesota Press.

Lyon, L.A. and Green, E. (2020) 'Women in coding boot camps: an alternative pathway to computing jobs', *Computer Science Education*, 30(1): 102–23.

Master, A. and Meltzoff, A.N. (2020) 'Cultural stereotypes and sense of belonging contribute to gender gaps in STEM', *International of Gender, Science and Technology*, 12(1): 152–98.

Master, A., Cheryan, S. and Meltzoff, A.N. (2016) 'Computing whether she belongs: stereotypes undermine girls' interest and sense of belonging in computer science', *Journal of Educational Psychology*, 108(3): 424–37.

Mathiesen, I.H., Buland, T. and Bungum, B. (2010) *Kjønn i skolens rådgivning– et glemt tema*, Trondheim: SINTEF-rapport Teknologi og samfunn.

McKinsey & Company and Pivotal Ventures (2018) *Rebooting Representation: Using CSR and Philanthropy to Close the Gender Gap in Tech.* Available at: www.rebootrepresentation.org/report-highlights/, accessed 10 May 2021.

Microsoft Corporation (2017) *Why Europe's Girls Aren't Studying STEM*, White paper, Microsoft Philanthropies. Available at: https://bit.ly/2Q3Ba6q, accessed 10 May 2021.

Misa, T.J. (ed) (2010) *Gender Codes: Why Women Are Leaving Computing*, Hoboken, NJ: IEEE Computer Society and John Wiley & Sons.

NOU (2019) *Jenterom, gutterom og mulighetsrom: likestillingsutfordringer blant barn og unge*, Oslo: Kulturdepartementet.

OECD (2016) *Pisa 2015 Results (Volume I): Excellence and Equity in Education*, Paris: OECD Publishing.

Oldenziel, R., Mohun, A. and Lerman, N.E. (eds) (2003) *Gender & Technology: A Reader*, Baltimore: Johns Hopkins University Press.

Plant, S. (1997) *Zeros + Ones: Digital Women + the New Technoculture*, London: Fourth Estate.

Seibel, S. and Veilleux, N. (2019) 'Factors influencing women entering the software development field through coding bootcamps vs. computer science bachelor's degrees', *Journal of Computing Sciences in Colleges*, 34(6): 84–96.

Simonsen, M. and Corneliussen, H.G. (2020) 'What can statistics tell about the gender divide in ICT? Tracing men and women's participation in the ICT sector through numbers', in D. Kreps, T. Komukai, T.V. Gopal and K. Ishii (eds) *Human-Centric Computing in a Data Driven Society*, Cham, Switzerland: Springer, pp 379–97.

Strauss, A. and Corbin, J. (1998) *Basics of Qualitative Research: Techniques and Procedures for Developing Grounded Theory*, London: Sage.

Tænketanken DEA (2019) *Hvordan får vi STEM på lystavlen hos børn og unge? – Og hvilken rolle spiller køn for interesseskabelsen?* Available at: www.datocms-assets.com/22590/1589284030-pixi-stempaalystavlenhosboernogunge.pdf, accessed 10 May 2021.

Talks, I., Edvinsson, I. and Birchall, J. (2019) *Programmed Out: The Gender Gap in Technology in Scandinavia*, Oslo: Plan International Norway.

UNESCO (2017) *Cracking the Code: Girls' and Women's Education in Science, Technology, Engineering and Mathematics (STEM)*, Paris: UNESCO.

Vainionpää, F., Kinnula, M., Iivari, N. and Molin-Juustila, T. (2019) 'Gendering and segregation in girls' perceptions of IT as a career choice: a nexus analytic inquiry', in A. Siarheyeva, C. Barry, M. Lang, H. Linger and C. Schneider (eds) *Information Systems Development: Information Systems Beyond 2020 (Isd 2019 Proceedings)*, Toulon, France: ISEN Yncréa Méditerranée, pp 1–12.

Wajcman, J. (2004). *TechnoFeminism*, Cambridge: Polity Press.

Woodfield, R. (2000) *Women, Work and Computing*, Cambridge: Cambridge University Press.

5

Changes in Funding and the Intensification of Gender Inequalities in Research and Innovation

Marja Vehviläinen, Hanna-Mari Ikonen and Päivi Korvajärvi

Introduction

The availability of funding is one of the central institutional constituents of research and innovation (R&I) in current universities and other R&I institutions. Universities are increasingly neoliberal and entrepreneurial (Ylijoki, 2003; Pereira, 2017; Rodrigo and Clavero, 2020), and access to competitive funding and the publications produced in competitively funded projects are key indicators when the success and trajectories of R&I are evaluated. The award of competitive funding justifies the subjects worth researching, researchers and R&I institutions, and it shapes gender and its intersecting differences in R&I. There has been a systematic disadvantage in women's and other minorities' access to competitive R&I funding (SHE Figures, 2018: 174; Burns et al, 2019; Rodrigo and Clavero, 2020). Although some funding agencies, in Ireland (Doona, 2020) and Nordic countries in particular, have conducted gender equality planning (Husu and de Cheveigné, 2010), gender inequalities have nonetheless remained persistent also in Nordic R&I (Griffin and Vehviläinen, 2021). In spite of the importance of the topic, the implications of R&I funding practices for gender and gender (in)equalities are under-researched, as Husu and de Cheveigné (2010) and Steinþórsdóttir et al (2020) have also observed.

R&I institutions are key sites for R&I work. These institutions respond to neoliberal science policies, and reward research groups and units as well as researchers that bring in highly competitive funding while simultaneously employing researchers on fixed-term precarious work contracts (Ylijoki et al, 2011; Siekkinen et al, 2017). They also continue to perpetuate gendered practices and cultures, 'corridor talk' (Pereira, 2017), which shape the practices of R&I groups and units, including gender inequalities in recruitment and career promotion, and sexual harassment, implying disadvantage for women and minority groups (Husu, 2001; Acker and Armenti, 2004; van den Brink and Benschop, 2011; Nielsen, 2016; Murgia and Poggio, 2019). Researchers and researcher groups, women and minority groups in particular, grapple with the simultaneous presence of neoliberal and gendered practices in R&I, precarious work contracts and various gendered inequalities, and try to secure the continuity of their R&I work through gaining competitive funding, often in collaboration with international networks (Pereira, 2017).

The interplay between R&I funding and R&I work – and gender in R&I – is complex and has local variations across countries, funding agencies and R&I institutions. Governments allocate core funding to R&I institutions and resources to funding agencies which deliver these through an application process. Supranational actors such as the European Commission also grant competitive funding. Once secured, competitive funding gives credit in later applications. The sources of R&I funding fluctuate over time. The research intensities of countries, the share of Gross Domestic Product (GDP) spent on R&I, and resources delivered by funding agencies expand and decline (Eurostat, nd). Although the gendered access rates to competitive grants and the gendered practices of funding agencies are recognized in discussions about gender and R&I (that is, Van der Lee and Ellemers, 2015), there is little knowledge about the gendered complexity of R&I funding and its relations to actual R&I, and even less regarding specificities such as the gendered effects of the fluctuation in research intensities and changing resources provided by funding agencies.

This chapter addresses the changes in R&I funding sources since the mid-1990s, and in particular the expansion and subsequent decline in resources distributed by funding agencies in Finland. It examines the interplay between funding opportunities and gendered practices (Korvajärvi, 2011) in R&I that produce gender inequalities: intersecting social inequalities 'that are more often experienced by women than men' and that cause disadvantage for women (Evans, 2017: 9). Finnish R&I intensity was relatively high in relation to GDP by 2008 and then dropped dramatically from 2010 to 2015 (Eurostat, nd), with consequences for the resources of the funding agencies and the availability of competitive funding. It thus provides an interesting case study regarding this issue. Our data consist of biographical interviews, covering periods of expansion and decline in funding, with women who work in R&I, namely Health Technology (HT), a field that has been prioritized in Finnish R&I policies and is largely dependent on competitive funding and changes to the latter. We explore gender inequalities embedded in R& work and the R&I work trajectories of women produced in part by changes in competitive R&I funding. We argue that significant changes in R&I funding involve a risk of deepening gender inequalities and can have negative implications for women's R&I work. The chapter articulates how this risk manifested itself in the reported lived experiences of women in R&I and in the (often contradictory) gendered practices of R&I institutions.

In the following, we discuss the literature on gender and R&I funding, and then describe the R&I funding system in the Finnish context as well as the data and methods and, before our discussion and conclusions, move to three key accounts of our analysis of gender and gender inequalities in the context of changes to R&I funding.

Gender in competitive R&I funding

The gendered implications of competitive R&I funding have been discussed in an increasing manner during the last decades by focusing on R&I funding agencies and the austerity measures in academia (that is, Husu and de Cheveigné, 2010; Moscowitz et al, 2014). However, the complex interplay of funding, R&I institutions and the grassroots level experiences of women has rarely, if at all, been researched.

European and North American researchers have examined how R&I funding agencies make funding decisions in gendered ways. Generally, they found various forms of gender bias, for example that women get relatively fewer and smaller grants both in the US (Hechtman et al, 2018) and in Europe (Van der Lee and Ellemers, 2015. Rodrigo and Clavero, 2020; Steinþórsdóttir et al, 2020). Husu and de Cheveigné (2010: 58) further noted that the European countries vary significantly in gender equality planning by the R&I funding agencies. The Nordic agencies have paid the most attention to their gatekeeping roles in selecting the researchers and research to be supported. While women are in the minority in expert groups and decision-making bodies in many other countries, the Nordic research councils have introduced gender equality planning and gender balance in expert boards. For example, the Finnish National Research Council, the Academy of Finland, developed these practices from the 1980s (Husu 2001: 85–9). However, there is some variation among funding agencies within individual countries. In Finland, differently from the Academy, the Agency for Innovation has not incorporated gender equality planning in its activities, and in the US, Burns et al (2019) found differences in gender equality among the funding institutions. Gender equality planning is hence not self-evident, not even in Nordic R&I funding agencies.

The effects of austerity and cutbacks of research funding in the neoliberal academy have also been widely researched. These effects are often negative for R&I work, as austerity is used as a rationale for implementing neoliberal values in academia and marginalizing minorities and work for diversity and equality (Ahmed, 2012; Moscowitz et al, 2014). However, an ethnographic study by Maria do Mar Pereira (2017) has shown that success in obtaining external competitive funding in cutback situations may also provide opportunities for the development of critical research.

In this chapter, we contribute to research on the gendered effects of competitive funding in R&I. Distinctly from studies of gender in funding agencies we contribute with a rarely acknowledged perspective of the reported experiences of women who work in neoliberal R&I institutions. And differently from austerity studies, we raise another rarely remarked upon phenomenon, changes in research funding in terms of national research intensities and the actual changes in the resources of funding agencies across previous decades. In the following, we describe more closely these contexts and explain the R&I funding system in Finland.

Funding in research and innovation

R&I work is primarily carried out in universities, research institutes, private companies and non-profit organizations. It is funded through various public and private sources: business enterprises, governments, private non-profit and higher education institutions, as well as international sources (Frascati Manual, 2002). Finnish universities receive governmental core funding through annual negotiations and agreements with the Ministry of Culture and Education and, furthermore, they can receive additional, largely competitive funding from various public and private sources. University structures vary but they usually consist of units with financial responsibility (faculties, departments, centres) which employ researchers and research groups. All these, from universities to individual researchers, apply for competitive funding. Competitive sources of funding have overtaken governmental funding in several countries (that is, Ireland, Sweden); in Finland they exceeded governmental core funding for the first time in 2001 (Tieteen tila, 2003: 54–5).

The level of R&I intensity, the R&I expenditure relative to GDP, has risen in the European Union since the turn of the century (Eurostat, nd). In Finland, however, it peaked in 2009 (3.73 per cent), after having grown from the mid-1990s (OECD, 2017: 18), and declined strongly from 2010 until 2016 (2.72 per cent). R&I expenditure nevertheless stayed at a relatively high level, with the EU average hovering at around 2 per cent (OECD, 2017: 18–19; Eurostat, nd). The increase of R&I expenditure in Finland until 2009 was largely due to the strong performance of information and communication technology (ICT) and the Nokia company in particular. Nokia was a major actor in research and development for several decades and then shut down substantial parts of this activity from the 2010s (OECD, 2017: 18). Private funding dropped from over 70 per cent of total R&I

funding in 2008 to 53.5 per cent by 2014 (Eurostat, nd). Conversely public R&I expenditure remained at around 1 per cent of GDP for decades (OSF, nd). Although the share of international funding for R&I in Finland grew between 2008 and 2018, varying from 6 to 14 per cent (Eurostat, nd), it did not offset the decline in national private funding. One effect was that the total number of full-time researchers declined both in the private sector and in higher education and R&I institutions in Finland, while it kept growing in Sweden, for example (Eurostat, nd). These changes in funding in Finland had significant effects on R&I institutions and the structure, work contracts and working conditions of their personnel.

Competitive governmental project funding has been distributed in Finland mainly through the Academy of Finland and the Finnish Funding Agency for Innovation which became Business Finland in 2018. The Academy of Finland funds individual researchers (postdocs, senior researchers and professor levels), research projects, centres of excellence in universities and research institutions, and more recently also universities as they build new research profiles. Its resources have remained steady and grown slightly (Tieteen tila, 2018: 12). The Agency for Innovation used to finance innovations and research-industry collaboration, where the funded project groups consisted of university research units and their researchers, private companies and often also public sector actors. Agency for Innovation funding increased until 2010 and then started to decline rapidly after 2011, following the pattern of the prevailing national research intensity (Tieteen tila, 2014, 2018). As the Agency for Innovation changed into Business Finland, the Academy of Finland to some extent took over its strategic funding function.

Research fields vary significantly in their use of competitive funding (Ylijoki et al, 2011). ICT sciences in Finnish universities covered nearly all their R&I costs through competitive funding in 2012, while in biomedicine it was 80 per cent, in electronics 60 per cent, about half in medicine, biochemistry, cell and molecular biology, and less than half in all other fields (Tieteen tila, 2014: 20–1). HT, a multidisciplinary field consisting of life sciences, medicine and technology, addressed in this chapter, has been one of the gainers of competitive funding. It was also one of the fields which was hit hard by the decline in funding resources from 2009. We shall now describe how we collected and analyzed our data in HT before we move to our analysis.

Data and method

The data consist of interviews, conducted between 2018 and 2020, with women in R&I under the multidisciplinary umbrella of HT. Twenty-eight of 30 interviewed women had PhD degrees, most commonly in bio or health sciences, or engineering, but also in social sciences, humanities or business studies. All 30 interviewees were White, all but two born in Finland. Their ages ranged roughly from 30 to 60. Twenty-six had children (usually one to three). About half worked in universities and the others mainly in private companies and research institutes. Many of the interviewees had worked through the period when R&I funding expanded strongly in the first decade of the 2000s, and the period of declining funding (2009–16). Many had started research groups and had continuously acquired competitive research funding, even when national resources were scarce, while others had moved to research institutes outside academia or to the private sector.

The interviewees first talked about their R&I work histories. The interview themes consisted of their current work situations and future plans, the role of gender in R&I work and their work-life balance. The interviews lasted one to two hours and were transcribed verbatim. They were conducted and analyzed in Finnish, and extracts were translated into English for the purposes of this chapter. Our methodological approach is institutional ethnography which starts the analysis 'in the actualities of everyday world, with the concerns and perspectives of people located distinctively in the institutional process', and the 'work knowledge' produced in the interviews, and uncovers 'the social relations implicated in the local organization of the everyday' (Smith, 2005: 34–5). The analysis goes beyond the everyday world and explicates also translocal forms of coordination that organize the local activity, for example, the patterns of R&I funding, even if those were not always articulated in the interviews. We read the interviews several times and, firstly, used thematic analysis to identify experiences regarding gender that were reported in the interviews. All interviewees had observations to make about gender. Gender neutrality/irrelevance and individuals' equal opportunities were emphasized (Korvajärvi, 2021). However, many also talked about gender inequalities in mundane R&I work and a few about sexual harassment and gender discrimination in detail, some in the context of declining funding sources. We traced gendered practices (Korvajärvi, 2011) that produced gender inequality in R&I work. Secondly, based on a thematic analysis, we selected key interviewees among the ones who talked about research funding (about half of all) and more specifically among the six interviewees who described how their R&I work and career had been affected by the changes in R&I funding, even though they had not been asked about funding (financial cuts in R&I were broadly discussed in Finland during the years of the interviews). Two of the chosen interviewees talked about gender inequalities and further explained two different kinds of funding arrangements taking place widely in the Finnish R&I (Academy of Finland, Agency for Innovation). The third selected interviewee was the one who articulated most clearly the effects of both the growth and decline of funding for her career, and we analyzed how mundane gender inequalities intersected her career. We built accounts based on each interview by highlighting their 'work knowledge' regarding the effects that R&I funding had on their R&I work. We analyzed the interplay between gender inequality and the changes in funding in our data through the lens of these three accounts. In the following sections, we present our analysis through these accounts. The first one involves steady resources from the Academy of Finland and serious gender inequality as the funding declined in the research unit and at the university; the second turns to the Agency for Innovation funding and gender inequality as sources became scarce in the university unit. The third one did not articulate gender inequalities at all. However, the changes of funding again affected that person's R&I work and career path in R&I.

Gender inequality in recruitment within declining funding

The first account centres on Mirjam (about 50 years old) who had a background in engineering and had worked in multidisciplinary research since her Master's degree. Her unit provided excellent guidance and projects, implying a good funding period. She made extended visits to foreign universities through her supervisor's contacts, which is considered an important dimension of academic career development in Finland. She established a research area of her own at the 'frontlines' of international research. Additionally, she learnt to write successful grant applications. She wrote her PhD thesis as part of a funded research school (four years). After completing her PhD, she received, through her own applications, individual and research group funding from the Academy of Finland. She said that she was well respected in the unit that she worked in and was invited to join various funding consortia.

Mirjam's career path began along the four-stage career model promoted by the Ministry of Education and Culture (MEC, 2016: 17) and the European Science Foundation: doctoral student, postdoc, senior researcher and professor. She had moved to career stage three, senior researcher, with a research group of her own. In contrast to most other higher education positions, stage four professor posts, funded by university core funding, are mainly available through advertised vacancies, and their number is limited (Vipunen, nd). In Finland, as in several other countries (van den Brink and Benschop, 2011; Nielsen, 2016), there is no self-evident continuation from stage to stage of the four-stage career model. Mirjam did not get a professor position to run her research group. She explained that research funding had started to decline and described how male networks worked to give the professor position to one of their members: "And then this person, he quite quickly got a professorship here at the university, and I've still not ever gotten anything at all. … They're part of this circle of friends and it makes sense that this person is a professor there, there supporting those other friends who are men." When resources became scarce, male networks banded together. Although Mirjam, with her successful external funding and research group, had been welcomed and supported throughout her early and mid-career in the period of expanding funding, she now became excluded. Male networks were mentioned in many interviews. The interviewees were aware that they existed at the university and in the region. They are not a new phenomenon (Husu, 2001; van den Brink and Benschop, 2014), and are present in male-dominated fields in particular. They remained idle and relaxed as long as funding resources were plentiful. During that time, expanding projects needed a labour force, and women's participation was useful there. During periods of plentiful funding, all successful funding, including that of women, gave credit to the network members. However, as the resources declined, the network closed ranks.

At the time of the interview Mirjam continued to do R&I work in an R&I institution through international collaboration. Her university unit welcomed prestigious (international) resources, and she had also once more received national research funding. Nevertheless, her situation in the local academic hierarchy remained precarious.

Coping with innovation funding and gendered inequality

The second account features Katarina (also about 50 years old) who did her Master's degree during the period of expanding funding. She taught and worked in projects funded by the national Agency for Innovation and had a place in a funded doctoral school. Just a few weeks after completing her PhD she gave birth and spent the following year on parental leave, but continued to teach for a few hours weekly. Her PhD thesis established a new field and her unit received additional funding to develop it further. However, as she was on leave, she was not given any role in the new project that was based on her PhD:

> 'There were two kinds of disadvantages as a woman, I'd say, so one was that I've now sort of created a new field there, which would be worthwhile to research and they got the project and the money. And I couldn't be part of it because I was on maternity leave ... it's that when you have a project you hire the people when you get the money, you can't wait like, let's wait a year, for that person to come back.' (Katarina)

Katarina acknowledged that the Agency for Innovation funding involved industry partners and deadlines, and the R&I unit could not wait for particular researchers to come back from their leaves, even if they had been the initiators and innovators of the project. However, another interviewee explained that the head of her unit made sure that she had a place to come back to from parental leave into an Agency for Innovation-funded project. Katarina's unit did not do this but instead excluded her from the project. In her own mind, she had not faced gender discrimination, even though she thought that being a woman was a disadvantage. She said that there was nothing to be done. However, she did not receive all possible support from her superiors either. Furthermore, she did not get the academic credit that she would have deserved as her thesis was the starting point for the new project, and this points to gender inequality. There is also the obvious penalty that she paid for having gone on parental leave.

Katarina also had a Business Studies background and, after coming back from parental leave, she found a new job to commercialize university research: "So I've gone into this chief development officer position that was selling the university's research findings, specifically in this bio field, overseas." Science commercialization was emphasized and intermediaries and science parks were built within or near universities, following the national science policy. This was also the case in other western countries (Pelkonen, 2003). Katarina worked broadly internationally. In her own words, she worked successfully for a couple of years with a colleague and wrote a business plan for a new research centre. However, this was when the funding situation started to change; private R&I funding had already declined, and Agency for Innovation resources were also declining. She was not offered a job in the new centre, although she had been a main planner for it, and instead her male colleagues arranged the job to go to her male collaborator:

> 'Unfortunately that endeavour ended when the funding ended and [the new RI centre] didn't have funding yet. And at that point it felt a bit like, men were drawing together, how should I say it, that although I was such a big part of [the preparations], it felt like it was each to their own, and there was one person who got sort of temporary funding, for him but not for me. I feel like it was a grave injustice. And at that point I left for [private company] [laughs].' (Katarina)

This interview account is reminiscent of the interview with Mirjam and two other interviewees. These women were appreciated as competent colleagues as long as a good funding situation prevailed. When the funding declined, the male networks excluded them and treated them unequally (Berger et al, 2015). As the other cases were examples of professorship recruitments based on university core funding, Katarina's account shows that such exclusions could happen both at lower career stages in R&I organizations, and also in the context of innovation funding. Katarina acted differently from Mirjam who continued to carry out research at the university with competitive project funding. Katarina had worked in science commercialization and was invited to join an R&I company. By the time of the interview, she had worked in a leading position there for several years.

From hype to declining resources

The third account concerns Tuija (35–40 years old) who entered a female-dominated research group during the heyday of a newly emerging field. Although she was rather ambivalent about her aims and her 'match' with that field, she became drawn into a research group to do her Master's thesis, even though she was still completing her Bachelor degree, and into doctoral research while she was still working on her Master's. She got four-year funding for her doctorate:

> 'We had big Agency for Innovation funding, Academy funding and money did also come in then. It was like money came to money, that we got research funding pretty well in the beginning. And, of course at that point it's pretty nice to jump into the academic world, when it is in that kind of hype.' (Tuija)

Like Katarina, Tuija gave birth to her first child right after completing her PhD. After her parental leave, and a few months of unemployment, she started at another university in Finland. She was supposed to write research applications for herself and for a newly established group to help the group leader, and then she faced the decline of funding: "2015, … then at the same time as these cuts in education started coming from the government … research funding decreased all the time". Several interviewees described how application writing had become more demanding, requiring more and more persistent and continuous work as the competition became fiercer. During the same years, she had a second child and took further parental leave. She was supposed to write an individual application to gain funding for herself and her research right after she came back to work. Academy funding had not decreased at that stage, and she might have got some, but she failed to write an application and moved to a private company as a particular kind of expert.

Other interviewees shared these experiences. They had received secure funding for their doctoral research and at the point of declining resources became anxious since they were expected to acquire their own funding, common for fixed-term employees in academia in Finland (Siekkinen et al, 2017). They, like Tuija, left academia with ambivalent feelings and found relevant work in private companies.

Tuija's case demonstrates a particular risk in relation to major changes in R&I funding. When there was significant funding, large groups of researchers were recruited at the same time, differently from the gradual recruitment that occurs in periods of steady funding. Although these circumstances of multiple simultaneous appointments provide research opportunities, they also tend to have negative effects on researcher training and productivity in research (Poropudas, 2018). Here the interviewee did not need to learn to write applications independently, although she might have participated in applications led by others. As the funding opportunities diminished, the competition became harder, and she badly needed the skills necessary to write a successful funding application.

Tuija did not mention gender inequality at all. Rather, she stated that she had never experienced any discrimination. She had received funding for her PhD and collegial support in her groups. She was not dealing with any straightforward gender inequality that took place in the context of funding changes. Instead, there were subtle processes during the change from expansion to decline that made her vulnerable and unable to move on in academic research. Furthermore, the period of declining funding hit Tuija while she was on parental leave. She took one-year parental leaves twice, as is commonly done by highly educated women in Finland (Salmi and Närvi, 2017: 71). The first time she did not have a job waiting for her, and the second time she returned to a fixed-term position for her 'mission impossible', to write a highly competitive application. The changing financial situation and precarious work situation were a double-edged sword for her: it invited one to take parental leave, as this was an attractive personal solution in precarious work situations, and it also made it hard to come back and continue in highly competitive academic R&I. There were subtle gendered relations that came together and produced disadvantages for her and her trajectory in R&I.

Discussion

The expansion of R&I funding in Finland until 2009 provided opportunities for many interviewees to become qualified researchers and to visit foreign universities with world-class research groups, the latter being an important requirement in Finnish academe. Many interviewees were offered full-time job contracts to do their PhD, which was, if not the norm, a common practice in natural, medical and technical sciences, different from the social sciences and humanities where doctoral students often had to secure their grants themselves (Hakala, 2009). Many were able to establish research groups of their own with competitive funding (SHE Figures, 2018: 174).

In this chapter, we analyzed how the significant changes in Finnish R&I funding intersected with gender inequalities. Although not all gender inequalities in our data were rooted in funding changes alone, we suggest that the major decline in funding after 2009 provoked particularly prominent forms of gender inequality, as both Mirjam and Katarina experienced. As studies by Berger et al (2015) and van den Brink and Benschop (2014) also showed, male networks, in academia, and between academia and industry, worked to provide positions for male colleagues in male-dominated research communities when resources became scarce. This particular form of inequality had major effects on both Mirjam's and Katarina's opportunities and trajectories in R&I work. They could not get the promotions that would have enabled them to continue their career paths as they had intended. It also disrupted researchers' work in their groups as they needed to find new supervisors and new institutional settings.

The third account, Tuija's, hints at a more subtle relation between gender inequality and funding. The rapid expansion of funding provided great opportunities for (too) many, and research groups did not oversee and instruct young academics in all academic skills, as suggested also by Poropudas (2018). When the decline of resources hit, many were not prepared for this and it became difficult to act and continue R&I work in a purposeful way. Many researchers with fixed-term contracts were distressed by constant application work in situations of heightened competition (Siekkinen et al, 2017), and the major decline in funding intensified this further. This affected more women than men as fixed-term contracts in Finnish higher education, more than the EU average, involved almost twice as many women as men in 2016 (respectively 12.6 per cent and 6.9 per cent: SHE Figures, 2018: 99).

Furthermore, discussions of the reproductive body and having young children appeared in all of our three key interviews. The significance of the reproductive body is difficult to recognize and articulate, as has been shown in Pecis' (2016) study. Katarina's original contribution to a new project was not acknowledged because she was on parental leave in the early stages of the new project. Mirjam also told us that she started to lose support in her unit after she had had children. Tuija was on parental leave twice and then experienced difficulties returning to fixed-term work. She was no longer as well supported as she had been during her doctoral studies. The negative effects of a neoliberal science policy and the academy for women have been reported across the globe, for example, in Australia (Blackmore and Sawers, 2015; Toffoletti and Starr, 2017); Italy (Pecis, 2016); Norway (Thun, 2020) and Finland (Nikunen, 2014). Pregnancy and the period when children are young stand out as particularly vulnerable times for mothers in the neoliberal academy. Our study suggests that the reproductive body and young children intensify gender inequalities and diminish opportunities when significant changes in R&I funding take place. More research is needed on this phenomenon.

The practices of the funding agencies matter. Many interviewees received funding from the Academy of Finland – although it could take as long as three years of repeat applications to succeed – and this funding supported their R&I work and career. Agency for Innovation resources require university-industry collaboration, and projects are built on networks in both. In contrast to the Academy and the Swedish Innovation Funding Agency, the Finnish National Agency for Innovation had done little if any gender equality planning. Although some R&I units were able to see that researchers on parental leaves maintained ownership of their work, including in Agency for Innovation-funded projects, other applications and projects markedly made room for old boys' networks. The Agency for Innovation did not pay attention to the continuity of the R&I careers of those temporarily on parental leave – women more often than men. Innovation funding stands out as a resource where the expansion and decline of funding created a particular risk of gender inequality.

The practices of particular funding agencies intertwined with the overall changes in R&I intensity. (Professor) positions funded through university core funding became more valuable as R&I intensity declined, and not even excellent competitive funding brought into the unit could pave the way to those positions, if they were controlled by old boys' networks. Competitive funding provided only conditional, precarious R&I paths, as Pereira (2017) has also observed.

Conclusions

In this chapter we have explored how major changes in competitive R&I funding, one of the cornerstones of the neoliberal academy and R&I, produced risks for women and their opportunity to advance their R&I work and career paths. Our study supports findings from elsewhere that financial cutbacks cause gender inequalities in neoliberal universities (that is, Blackmore and Sawers, 2015; Pereira, 2017). Additionally, it suggests that major fluctuations in funding, expansion and decline following on from each other, create a significant risk of creating and/or reinforcing gender inequalities.

From the perspective of women in R&I work, it is the R&I institutions that play the significant role (also Griffin and Vehviläinen, 2021). Neoliberal R&I institutions, their units and research groups welcome competitive funding in growth periods and recruit personnel to conduct R&I. Some research groups train those recruited to cope with the expanded tasks of the neoliberal university and support women through their parental leaves, while others do not. And it is R&I institutions that allow old boys' networks to dominate as resources become scarce and women find themselves excluded in R&I. These gender inequalities played a role when women unintendedly leave academia for good or remained in marginal positions. Our study calls for gender equality work that takes into account changes in R&I funding that inevitably occur in R&I institutions, funding agencies and R&I policies.

Acknowledgements

The research was done in a Nordforsk funded Centre of Excellence Nordwit. We would like to thank Tiina Suopajärvi and Minna Leinonen who conducted the interviews and Oili-Helena Ylijoki for insightful comments.

References

Acker, S. and Armenti, C. (2004) 'Sleepless in academia', *Gender and Education*, 16(1): 3–24.

Ahmed, S. (2012) *On Being Included: Racism and Diversity in Institutional Life*, Durham: Duke University Press.

Berger, L., Benschop, Y. and van den Brink, M. (2015) 'Practising gender when networking: the case of university–industry innovation projects', *Gender, Work and Organization*, 22(6): 556–78.

Blackmore, J. and Sawers, N. (2015) 'Executive power and scaled-up gender subtexts in Australian entrepreneurial universities', *Gender and Education*, 27(3): 320–37.

Burns, K.E.A., Straus, S.E., Liu, K., Rizvi, L. and Guyatt, G. (2019) 'Gender differences in grant and personnel award funding rates at the Canadian Institutes of Health Research based on research content area: a retrospective analysis', *PLOS Medicine*. Available at: https://journals.plos.org/plosmedicine/article?id=10.1371/journal.pmed.1002935, accessed 8 April 2021.

Doona, A. (2020) 'Addressing gender inequality in academia: the role of Irish funding agencies', in E. Drew and S. Canavan (eds) *The Gender-Sensitive University: A Contradiction in Terms?*, London: Routledge, pp 154–65.

Eurostat (nd) Science, technology and innovation. Available at: https://ec.europa.eu/eurostat/web/science-technology-innovation/data/database, accessed 8 April 2021.

Evans, M. (2017) *The Persistence of Gender Inequality*, Cambridge: Polity Press.

Frascati Manual (2002) *Proposed Standard Practice for Surveys on Research and Experimental Development*. Available at: https://ec.europa.eu/eurostat/ramon/statmanuals/files/Frascati_Manual_2002_EN.pdf, accessed 8 April 2021.

Griffin, G. and Vehviläinen, M. (2021) 'The persistence of gender struggles in Nordic research and innovation', *Feminist Encounters*, 5(2): 28.

Hakala, J. (2009) 'Socialization of junior researchers in new academic research environments: two case studies from Finland', *Studies in Higher Education*, 34(5): 501–16.

Hechtman, L.A., Moore, N.P., Schulkey, C.E., Miklos, A.C., Calcagno A.M., Aragon, R. and Greenberg J.H. (2018) 'NIH funding longevity by gender', *PNAS*, 115(31): 7943–8.

Husu, L. (2001) *Sexism, Support and Survival in Academia: Academic Women and Hidden Discrimination in Finland*, Helsinki: Department of Social Psychology, University of Helsinki.

Husu, L. and de Cheveigné, S. (2010) 'Gender and gatekeeping of excellence in research funding: European perspectives', in B. Riegraf, B. Aulenbacher, E. Kirsch-Auwärter and U. Müller (eds) *GenderChange in Academia*, VS Verlag für Sozialwissenschaften, pp 43–59. DOI: 10.1007/978-3-531-92501-1_4.

Korvajärvi, P. (2011) 'Practicing gender neutrality in organizations', in E. Jeans, P. Yancey Martin and D. Knights (eds) *Handbook of Gender, Work and Organization*, London: Sage, pp 230–44.

Korvajärvi, P. (2021) 'Doing/undoing gender in research and innovation: practicing downplaying and doubt', *Feminist Encounters*, 5(2): art. 27.

MEC (2016) *Tutkijanuran tilannekuva* [*Situational Picture of Research Career*], *Tutkijanuratyöryhmän loppuraportti* [*Final Report of the Research Career Work Group*], February, Helsinki: Ministry of Education and Culture. Available at: https://julkaisut.valtioneuvosto.fi/handle/10024/64967, accessed 8 April 2021.

Moscowitz, D., Jett, T., Carney, T., Leech, L. and Savage, A. (2014) 'Diversity in times of austerity: documenting resistance in the academy', *Journal of Gender Studies*, 23(3): 233–46.

Murgia, A. and Poggio, B. (eds) (2019) *Gender and Precarious Research Careers: A Comparative Analysis*, London and New York: Routledge.

Nielsen, M.W. (2016) 'Limits to meritocracy? Gender in academic recruitment and promotion processes', *Science and Public Policy*, 43: 386–99.

Nikunen, M. (2014) 'The "entrepreneurial university", family and gender: changes and demands faced by fixed-term workers', *Gender and Education*, 26(2): 119–34.

OECD (2017) OECD *Reviews on Innovation Policy: Finland*. Available at: https://read.oecd-ilibrary.org/science-and-technology/oecd-reviews-of-innovation-policy-finland-2017_9789264276369-en#page20, accessed 8 April 2021.

OSF (nd) *Government R&D Funding in the State Budget*. Helsinki: Statistics Finland. Available at: www.stat.fi/til/tkker/tie_en.html, accessed 19 January 2021.

Pecis, L. (2016) 'Doing and undoing gender in innovation: femininities and masculinities in innovation processes', *Human Relations*, 69(11): 2117–40.

Pelkonen, A. (2003) 'Intermediary organizations and commercialization of academic research', *Vest*, 16(1): 47–77.

Pereira, M. do Mar (2017) *Power, Knowledge and Feminist Scholarship: An Ethnography of Academia*, London and New York: Routledge. Available at: www.taylorfrancis.com/books/9781315692623, accessed 8 April 2021.

Poropudas, O. (2018) 'Miksi suomalaisen tutkimuksen tuottavuus kasvoi, mutta laatu heikentyi?' ['Why did the productivity of Finnish research grow and the quality decrease?'], *Informaatiotutkimus*, 1(37): 5–16.

Rodrigo, R. and Clavero, S. (2020) 'The challenge of neoliberalism and precarity for gender sensitivity in academia,' in E. Drew and S. Canavan (eds) *The Gender-Sensitive University: A Contradiction in Terms?*, London: Routledge, pp 16–27.

Salmi, M. and Närvi, J. (2017) 'Pienten lasten vanhempien työmarkkina-asema, työn epävarmuus ja toimeentulo'['Labour market position, work insecurity and livelihood of parents of small children'], in M. Salmi and J. Närvi (eds) *Talouskriisi ja sukupuolten tasa-arvo*, Raportti 4/2017, Helsinki: Finnish Institute for Health and Welfare, pp 36–63.

SHE Figures (2018) Brussels: European Commission. Available at: https://op.europa.eu/en/publication-detail/-/publication/9540ffa1-4478-11e9-a8ed-01aa75ed71a1, accessed 19 January 2022.

Siekkinen, T., Kuoppala, K., Pekkola, E. and Välimaa, J. (2017) 'Reciprocal commitment in academic careers? Finnish implications and international trends', *European Journal of Higher Education*, 7(2): 120–35.

Smith, D.E. (2005) *Institutional Ethnography*, Langham: Altamira Press.

Steinþórsdóttir, F.S., Einarsdóttir, Þ., Pétursdóttir, G.M. and Himmelweit, S. (2020) 'Gendered inequalities in competitive grant funding: an overlooked dimension of gendered power relations in academia', *Higher Education Research and Development*, 39(2): 362–75.

Thun, C. (2020) 'Excellent and gender equal? Academic motherhood and "gender blindness" in Norwegian academia', *Gender Work and Organization*, 27: 166–80.

Tieteen tila (2003) [*State of Scientific Research 2003*], *Suomen tieteen tila ja taso* [*State and Level of Finnish Scientific Research*], Helsinki: Academy of Finland.

Tieteen tila (2014) [*State of Scientific Research 2014*], Helsinki: Academy of Finland.

Tieteen tila (2018) [*State of Scientific Research 2018*], Helsinki: Academy of Finland. Available at: www.aka.fi/globalassets/2-suomen-akatemian-toiminta/2-tietoaineistot/aka_tieteen_tila_2018_web.pdf, accessed 8 April 2021.

Toffoletti, K. and Starr, K. (2017) 'Women academics and work–life balance: gendered discourses of work and care', *Gender, Work and Organization*, 23(5): 489–504.

van den Brink, M. and Benschop, Y. (2011) 'Gender practices in the construction of academic excellence: sheep with five legs', *Organization*, 19: 507–24.

van den Brink, M. and Benschop, Y. (2014) 'Gender in academic networking: the role of gatekeepers in professorial recruitment', *Journal of Management Studies*, 51(3): 460–92.

Van der Lee, R. and Ellemers, N. (2015) 'Gender contributes to personal research funding success in the Netherlands', *PNAS Proceedings of the National Academy of Sciences*, 112(40): 12349–53.

Vipunen (nd) *Education Statistics Finland.* Available at: https://vipunen.fi/en-gb/, accessed 8 April 2021.

Ylijoki, O.-H. (2003) 'Entangled in academic capitalism? A case-study on changing ideals and practices of university research', *Higher Education*, 45: 307–35.

Ylijoki, O.-H., Lyytinen, A. and Marttila, L. (2011) 'Different research markets: a disciplinary perspective', *Higher Education*, 62: 721–40.

6

Promoting Gender Equality in STEM-oriented Universities: Institutional Policy Measures in Sweden, Finland and Norway

Charlotte Silander, Ida Drange, Maria Pietilä and Liza Reisel

Introduction

Equal access to research-intensive careers for talented academics of all genders and backgrounds is vital to secure social justice and to ensure efficient research and knowledge production. Still, gender inequalities endure in academia. Although Sweden, Norway and Finland have been identified as forerunners in promoting gender balance in research (Lipinsky, 2013), the share of women in top academic positions in science, technology, engineering, and mathematics (STEM) remains well below the threshold for a gender balance (European Commission, 2019).

Previous studies on women's under-representation in STEM have noted that female talent is lost at every critical career transition phase ('the leaky pipeline' metaphor; Berryman, 1983; Ong et al, 2011; Liu et al, 2019). This approach has, however, been criticized for its focus on the 'supply-side' (Metcalf, 2010), linearity and inability to account for varied career paths (Xie and Shauman, 2003; Etzkowitz and Ranga, 2011). Another stream of literature notes that maths and science continue to be perceived as male domains, and the perception of scientists in STEM is predominantly male (Makarova et al, 2019). This emphasizes that women are viewed as deviating from the norm of the ideal worker (Acker, 2012). Male domination makes the lack of access to networks (Fox and Colatrella, 2006; Terosky et al, 2014) and role models more evident. In addition, intensified international competition requires early career researchers to be mobile (Herschberg et al, 2018), influencing women's chances for recruitment and promotion (Jöns, 2011).

The under-representation of women in STEM has created the necessity for national and institutional measures to promote gender equality at universities. National measures are particularly relevant in the Nordic countries which have comprehensive gender equality legislation that also applies to higher education institutions. In addition, the state may provide different incentives for universities to promote equality. Nevertheless, the effectiveness of these policies depends on both the type of measures and their implementation at university level. Previous studies on measures for improving gender balance and diversity in organizations indicate that transparency in hiring and promotion, policies that establish clear responsibility for increasing diversity within the organization, and affirmative action plans in combination with responsibility structures have the largest effects (Naff and Kellough, 2003; Holzer and Neumark, 2006; Kalev et al, 2006; Timmers et al, 2010; Dobbin et al, 2015).

Only a few studies have investigated the types of equality measures used in Nordic higher education institutions (Bergman and Rustad, 2013; Nielsen, 2017; Moratti, 2020). Nielsen (2017) analyzed the use of such measures in six Nordic universities, two each in Norway, Sweden and Denmark. Nielsen concluded that measures aimed at creating equal opportunities and revising existing organizational cultures were the most efficient in countering organizational inequalities. Based on a longitudinal study from one Norwegian university, Moratti (2020) found no detrimental effect on (rarely used) low-transparency and low-openness procedures. However, more controversial proactive measures, such as affirmative action policies, showed clear positive effects, but they have become less available due to stricter European legislation over the past decades. These results indicate a need for further studies on organizational gender equality policy that focus on types of policy in more detail.

Against this background, in this chapter we seek to investigate how the changes in the proportion of women in grade A positions in STEM-oriented universities are related to the use of gender equality measures. Grade A positions are the highest academic positions, typically full professorships. Bacchi (2009) argues that policy always makes assumptions about the problem the policy is meant to solve. In line with this, building on prior research (for example, Kalev et al, 2006; Timmers et al, 2010; Dobbin et al, 2015), we categorize gender equality measures (GE measures) according to how they seek to reduce gender inequalities. We investigated what GE measures have been used by the universities that have achieved significant positive changes in the proportion of women in grade A positions. This was done by analyzing how the proportion of women in grade A positions has developed in each university between 2000 and 2018, and by investigating if the detected variation is related to the use of these measures. We discuss which potential implications the use of specific GE measures have for the academic career progression of women.

The skewed gender distribution in STEM fields, especially in the highest academic career positions, has attracted high-profile policy attention, calling for states, research organizations and universities to take action to improve gender equality in research (for example, Council of the European Union, 2015). Against this background, we expect STEM-oriented universities to face pressing issues related to gender equality, which may be reflected in their institutional gender equality work. To our knowledge, previous research has not investigated what measures STEM-oriented universities have taken to address gender inequalities in academic careers. Thus, this study provides new knowledge on how STEM-oriented universities in three Nordic countries – Sweden, Norway and Finland – have used policy measures to support and promote gender equality among academic staff.

We define STEM-oriented universities as universities that have a high proportion of academics working in STEM fields and that have a strong research and teaching environment in those fields, reflected in a high proportion of PhD graduates in STEM fields. The study uses institutional survey data which were collected as part of the Nordic Centre of Excellence NORDICORE. The data provide a unique opportunity to compare the universities' use of equality measures, and to relate this to the changes in female representation in STEM fields.

Categorization of gender equality measures

Policies that seek to combat gender inequality in organizations can be studied from several perspectives. One approach is to investigate how the policies relate to different assumptions about men and women (Rees, 2005; Squires, 2008). Another is to analyze GE measures based on what they seek to target. Timmers et al (2010), based on Fagenson (1990), distinguish between measures that target individuals, the culture and organizational structures. In another study on the efficacy of diversity measures, Kalev et al (2006) use three broad approaches for promoting diversity: initiatives to establish organizational responsibility for diversity, initiatives to reduce bias through training and initiatives to reduce the social isolation of women and minority workers. In another study, the same team (Dobbin et al, 2015) focus on how managers are motivated to influence change by activities that influence managerial motivation for promoting diversity, activities that constrain managers' discretion to discriminate and activities that increase transparency and monitoring within the organization.

Policymakers can use different policy measures to achieve their intended goals. Here we distinguish between policies that target individuals and policies that target structures. The approach by Dobbin et al (2015) focusses on changing the behaviour of actors, while Kalev et al (2006) focus on policies emphasizing both social structures and actors. In this chapter actor-oriented policies include measures that target members of the under-represented sex, and training measures to reduce bias and stereotyping. Structure-oriented policies include measures establishing organizational responsibility and measures of preferential treatment (see Table 6.2, under the section 'Findings', for an overview of the included measures in the study).

Targeted measures

Targeted measures are actor-oriented as they aim to target members of the under-represented sex (in STEM, women) and seek to remedy their 'deficiencies' so that they advance in the prevailing career structures. Gender differences are addressed by targeting women through measures that aim to change individual behaviour and the choices made by women (although these can be influenced by societal norms and values). These measures seek to 'fix' the women through intervention strategies that support them (Kalev et al, 2006). Such measures are often based on 'deficit' analyses that assume that women lack the required knowledge or networks, or behave in ways that make them less competitive (for example not taking enough risks, not applying for promotion). Thus, women are offered targeted training, coaching, networking, mentoring and leadership programmes to help them meet the norms of the ideal academic.

Questions in the survey referring to targeted measures were about i) special funding for women to qualify for promotion; ii) the possibility for women to earn research leave in a shorter time compared to men; iii) mentoring programmes for women; iv) career development workshops for female academic staff; v) networking gatherings for female academic leaders; and vi) leadership development programmes for women.

Training measures

Training measures seek to change the culture of the organization and prevent research and teaching staff, managers and gatekeepers from holding implicit bias and stereotypes which may reproduce existing patterns of inequality (Kalev et al, 2006). Although academia is often presented as gender neutral, previous research indicates that many practices in fact privilege men (Broadbridge and Hearn, 2008). Processes of assessment, selection and evaluation are at risk of being performed by managers and gatekeepers who hold stereotypes of men and women (Fagenson, 1990). Thus, training measures target the norms and values of staff in an organization, especially department heads and members of recruitment and promotion committees.

Questions in the survey encompassed i) diversity training for academic staff; ii) diversity training for department heads; iii) diversity training for hiring or promotion committees; iv) sexual harassment training for academic staff; v) written instructions for hiring or promotion committees about gender and diversity bias; and vi) promotion of equality as part of the qualification for department heads.

Organizational responsibility measures

This first category of measures among the structure-oriented policies includes measures to support organizational responsibility in gender equality work. These are warranted because even if a policy sets out the direction for change, this can be lost on the way if the policy is decoupled from the overall goals and objectives of the organization. Based on the ideas of Max Weber, Kalev et al (2006) argue that decoupling is likely to occur when there is a lack of structures of responsibility, such as a diversity office or expert to monitor progress. If diversity efforts become everyone's responsibility, they risk becoming no one's primary responsibility and policy might become decoupled from practice. If organizations fail to assign responsibility for diversity goals to a specific office or person, these goals risk being lost when line managers need to meet competing demands from scholars (Kalev et al, 2006). Weber's recommendation is to assign responsibility for setting goals, allocating means and evaluating progress, which Kalev et al (2006) interpret as actions plans, internal monitoring and the introduction of diversity committees.

Policies that seek to make structural changes in organizations aim to change the way rules, structures, decisions and processes are organized, for example by increasing representation or transparency within the organization. This may mean transparent procedures for workload allocations and promotion criteria (Probert, 2005) or official publishing of positions for recruitment (van den Brink, 2010). A number of policies representing organizational responsibility in promoting gender equality, such as the requirement to have a gender equality plan and salary reviews by sex, are part of the legislation in the Nordic countries.

The organizational responsibility measures included in the survey were i) office or full-time person devoted to equality/diversity; ii) a standing gender equality committee or equivalent; and iii) written procedures for discrimination or sexual harassment grievance for academics.

Preferential treatment measures

Our second category of structure-oriented policy focusses on organizational structures which can influence individuals' entry and promotion in academic careers (Ragins and Sundstrom, 1989; Fagenson, 1990). Existing organizational structures and institutions are not gender neutral but favour one gender (usually men) in a variety of subtle and often invisible ways. This calls for policies that seek to enhance equality among historically excluded groups with the help of preferential treatment. It should be noted that affirmative action in the manner in which it is understood and exercized in the US, for example, is not in use in the Nordic countries. Through deconstruction and redistribution, preferential treatment measures tackle deeply rooted organizational cultures and work to increase the participation of the under-represented group while trying to even out the imbalance (Rees, 2005). In international studies preferential measures have proven to have limited effect (Holzer and Neumark, 2006; Kalev et al, 2006), but a study in Norway proved them effective (Moratti, 2020). Such measures may entail recruitment and promotion procedures in favour of women, for example earmarking funding for the under-represented sex, or organizational incentives to recruit women academics.

In our survey, preferential treatment measures included i) promoting the use of proactive measures to increase the proportion of the under-represented sex among academic staff; ii) use of invitation procedures to professorships to increase the proportion of the under-represented sex; iii) earmarking of funding to support hiring members of the under-represented sex; iv) use of nationally granted money to develop GE measures; and v) special funds for start-up packages to support hiring women faculty.

Methodological underpinnings of the study: Case selection

We define STEM-oriented universities as institutions that fulfil two criteria.[1] First, they have a high density of academics working in STEM fields, which we measured based on the proportion of grade A positions located in STEM fields. Second, STEM-oriented universities have a strong research and teaching environment in STEM fields, which we measured based on the proportion of PhD graduates in the university that were in STEM fields. We calculated these proportions using data from the official databases for statistics on higher education in Norway, Sweden and Finland (DBH, Statistics Sweden, Vipunen Database).

To be part of the dataset, at least 45 per cent of grade A positions in the university had to be in STEM and at least 55 per cent of PhD graduates had to be from STEM fields. We calculated the grade A proportions using university-level data from 2018. As there is some yearly fluctuation in the number of completed PhD degrees, we calculated these proportions with university-level data from 2018, 2019 and 2020 for Norway and Finland, and for 2018 and 2019 for Sweden and used the average proportion from these years. It should be noted that as we used proportions of grade

A positions and PhD graduates for each university in defining STEM-oriented universities, the dataset mostly comprises technical universities and universities specializing in natural sciences. Thus, the analysis excludes comprehensive universities that have extensive natural science faculties, because STEM fields are not dominant in these university organizations.

Based on these criteria, nine universities in the three countries qualified as STEM-oriented universities in 2018. Of these, eight participated in the NORDICORE study and are included in this dataset. Three of these are located in Sweden, two in Norway and three in Finland.

Data and method

The study uses organizational survey data on Swedish, Norwegian and Finnish STEM-oriented universities' gender equality and diversity policies. For the collection of the survey data, we targeted all institutions in Sweden, Norway and Finland which in 2018 had a legal status as universities. For this study, we employ data from the eight STEM-oriented universities.

We collected the survey data between 2018 and 2020 in phone interviews (including Skype/Zoom) and face-to-face interviews. Most respondents to the survey were human resources (HR) personnel (for instance, HR directors or administrators) or equality coordinators. In many cases, especially in large institutions, we interviewed several people. The survey included questions on universities' formal central-level policies and measures to promote gender equality and diversity and the timing of policies (start and end year of each policy). Due to increased institutional autonomy and the strengthening of the central governance of universities, we expected policies on the institutional level to be important (cf. Enders et al, 2013; Hansen et al, 2019).

The survey was strongly inspired by the work of Alexandra Kalev and Frank Dobbin, who have studied diversity management in the US. The research group worked together to develop the survey and to collect and analyze data. This enabled us to verify consistency in the interpretation of questions across the countries and institutions. The individual survey questions represented binary variables, where the main response alternatives were 'yes' and 'no' (with the option to respond 'I don't know' and 'I don't want to answer'). When respondents were not able to answer questions, they were asked to consult colleagues or institutional records.

For the analysis, we chose the variables (20 in total) which, according to our estimation, represent the analytical categories presented earlier. The analysis was based on the frequency of the measures by university and graphic illustration of the results. We excluded measures derived directly from national legislation from the analysis. That is, the analysis only included measures that the universities had voluntarily chosen to use to promote equality.

Findings

Table 6.1 provides an overview of the proportion of women in grade A positions in the studied universities. It presents the situation in the universities at three time points (2000, 2010 and 2018) and visualizes the pace of development in the 2000s and 2010s.

Table 6.1: Proportion of women in grade A positions in the studied universities in 2000, 2010 and 2018

University	Total FTE/share of women	2000	2010	2018	Factor change of the proportion of women	Absolute change of the proportion of women (pp)
SE1	Total FTE	57	98	150		
Univ with significant changes	women %	2.6	14.9	25.2	9.6	22.6
NO1	Total FTE	485	597	782		
Univ with significant changes	women %	8.5	19.0	25.6	3.0	17.1
SE2	Total FTE	132	182	214		
Univ with significant changes	women %	6.7	8.0	16.6	2.5	9.9
SE3	Total FTE	194	288	308		
Univ with significant changes	women %	11.1	20.8	24.0	2.2	12.9
NO2	Total FTE	110	128	194		
Univ with significant changes	women %	12.9	17.3	25.6	2.0	12.7
FI1	Total FTE	264	338	243		
Univ with small changes	women %	10.2	0.2	15.0	1.5	4.8
FI2	Total FTE	52	80	74		
Univ with small changes	women %	11.5	18.0	15.0	1.3	3.5
FI3	Total FTE	106	146	94		
Univ with small changes	women %	4.7	7.6	5.6	1.2	0.9

Note: The dataset includes two universities which merged during the timeframe of the analysis. Figures for years prior to the mergers were calculated with data from the former pre-merger institutions.

In Table 6.1, the overall change in the proportion of women for each university is presented in factor and absolute terms. In the table, the order of the universities is set according to the factor change of the proportion of women. It should be noted that the starting point in 2000 differed in the eight universities: the universities had an average of 8 per cent women in grade A positions, however, with variation from 3 per cent to 13 per cent. In 2018, the universities had reached an average of 19 per cent of women in grade A positions, again with significant variation from 5 per cent to 26 per cent. It should also be noted that in the Swedish and Norwegian universities, the number of grade A positions increased, whereas in two of the Finnish universities, it decreased.

Based on the size of the change in grade A positions (in both factor and absolute terms), we composed two groups of universities. In the first group, the proportion of women increased significantly between 2000 and 2018. The group includes five universities (SE1, NO1, SE2, SE3 and NO2). In the second group, changes were smaller or ambiguous. The group includes three universities (FI1, FI2 and FI3). It is notable that the universities in the two groups are located in different countries: universities with high-level changes are located in Sweden and Norway, whereas all universities with low-level changes are located in Finland. The differences may partly reflect national regulation and activity in gender equality work, such as higher education legislation with different emphasis on gender equality issues (Borchorst et al, 2012).

This study focusses on how the variation in grade A positions is related to the differences between universities in gender equality activity. Based on previous literature, we expected some measures at the organizational level to be more effective than others in promoting equality.

Table 6.2 displays the use of GE measures per university by the analytical categories presented above. The order of the case universities is defined according to the overall activity in gender equality work for each university. The universities range from left to right from those with higher levels of activity in gender equality to those with lower levels of activity.

STEM-oriented universities in the three countries vary considerably in the use of organizational GE measures. Table 6.2 shows the pattern involving the use of measures and the scale of change in grade A positions. Active use of GE measures seems to be related to significant changes in the proportion of women in grade A positions between 2000 and 2018: the universities which witnessed the biggest growth of women had, on average, used a variety of measures to promote gender equality. By contrast, the universities with a low use of GE measures all belong to the group with small changes in the proportion of women in grade A positions.

When looking at the GE measures per category, the three measures that reflect organizational responsibility were used most widely. For example, all universities had gender equality and diversity committees. There is more

Table 6.2: The use of GE measures in STEM-oriented universities

	Universities							
	NO1	SE1	SE2	NO2	SE3	FI1	FI3	FI2
Targeted measures								
Funding for women to qualify for promotion								
Research leave for women in a shorter time compared to men								
Mentoring programme for women academic staff	(X)							
Promotion or tenure workshops for women academic staff								
Networking gatherings for women academic leaders								
Funding for women academics' participation in leadership development programs								
Amount	5	5	3	0	0	0	0	0
Training measures								
Diversity training programme for academic staff								
Diversity training for department heads								
Diversity training for hiring or promotion committees								
Sexual harassment training for academic staff								
Written instructions for hiring or promotion committees about gender and diversity bias								
Promotion of equality part of the qualification for department heads								
Amount	4	2	2	2	1	2	0	0

Table 6.2 cont.: The use of GE measures in STEM-oriented universities

	Universities							
Organizational responsibility measures								
Office or full-time person devoted to faculty equality/diversity								
Standing gender equality or diversity and equality committee								
Procedure for discrimination or sexual harassment grievance for academic staff					(X)			
Amount	3	2	3	2	3	2	2	2
Preferential treatment measures								
Proactive measures to increase the prop. Of the under-represented sex among academic staff	(X)							
Invitation procedures to professorship to increase the prop. Of the under-represented sex				(X)				
Earmarking, funds or faculty lines to support hiring members of the under-represented sex								
Granted money to develop gender equality measures								
Special funds for start-up packages to support hiring women academic staff								
Amount	5	3	2	4	1	0	1	0
All measures (count)	17	12	10	8	5	4	3	2
% of measures (20 in total)	85	60	50	40	25	20	15	10

Note: Dark grey indicates that the measure was in use in 2018. Light grey indicates that the measure was used, but then stopped. (X) indicates that the measure was used, but it is not known whether it was in use in 2018. Black indicates missing data.

variation in the use of targeted measures, training measures and preferential treatment measures. It is clear that while all the universities used organizational responsibility measures, the universities with significant changes in the proportion of women more often also used preferential treatment measures and targeted measures for women in promoting equality. The universities with only small changes, all located in Finland, used preferential treatment and targeted measures marginally or not at all.

Table 6.2 also displays which measures were in use in 2018 and which had been in use but were discontinued. Overall, there was a clear upward trend in GE activity. However, there was a distinction between the measures that were used only temporarily and measures which seemed to be longer-lasting. Once adopted, the training measures and the organizational responsibility measures represent enduring structures for universities' equality work: the majority of universities which had adopted these measures continued to use them in 2018. In contrast, the use of targeted measures and preferential treatment measures was more temporary in nature. For example, the use of the strongest version of preferential treatment, earmarking, was discontinued in many Swedish and Norwegian universities as it was considered discriminatory towards men after being ruled out by the European Court of Justice in 2002 and 2003 (Lerwall, 2001; Husu, 2015).

Conclusions and discussion

Our analysis shows that the STEM-oriented universities which saw the biggest growth of women in grade A positions between 2000 and 2018 used or had used, on average, a variety of measures to promote gender equality. In contrast, the universities with small changes used fewer measures. It is striking that the universities which had significant positive changes in the proportion of women in grade A positions had on average been more active in using preferential treatment measures and targeted measures. The connection between preferential treatment measures and targeted measures on the one hand and female representation on the other is interesting because these measures reflect politically controversial intervention strategies to promote equality.

All studied universities used measures that aim at strengthening organizational responsibility via institutional gender and diversity committees and internal procedures to report on discrimination or sexual harassment. Measures aimed at strengthening organizational responsibility seem to form the institutional base for STEM-oriented universities' equality work. However, when compared to preferential treatment and targeted measures, their influence (without simultaneous use of other measures) is questionable. Case university SE3 is an exception, with only minor use of preferential treatment and targeted measures and still significant growth in the proportion of women in grade A positions.

The use of equality measures by the STEM-oriented universities increased over time. However, we also saw differences in the type of measures used and their longevity. Training measures and measures that aim at strengthening organizational responsibility represent universities' enduring gender equality structures, whereas activities in preferential treatment and measures for women were, in many cases, used only short-term. Overall, the use of targeted measures for women and preferential treatment was uneven across the universities. This calls for discussions on the operationalization and implementation of gender mainstreaming and future strategies for GE measures in Nordic STEM-oriented universities to change still-persistent gender inequalities.

We cannot make any causal conclusions about the relationship between the use of GE measures and the differences in the outcomes in grade A in this study because the adoption of measures is endogenous (that is, the adoption of measures may be related to university-specific characteristics that affect the gender balance). Also, we did not include any data on other variables that might affect the gender balance, such as the gender distribution among PhD graduates or academic staff other than professors in the case universities. Still, the findings point to interesting hypotheses for further research that seek to study what works when pursuing tangible changes in the highest academic career positions in STEM-oriented universities.

Note

1 STEM refers to science, technology, engineering, and mathematics. The exact definitions of STEM fields or disciplines vary by national context and organization (see, for example, Koonce et al, 2011). In this chapter, we incorporate the fields listed under 'natural sciences' and 'engineering and technology' in the OECD Classification of Sciences as STEM fields.

References

Acker, J. (2012) 'Gendered organizations and intersectionality: problems and possibilities', *Equality, Diversity, and Inclusion: An International Journal*, 31(3): 214–24.

Bacchi, C.L. (2009) *Analysing Policy*, French Forest: Pearson Higher Education AU.

Bergman, S. and Rustad, L.M. (2013) *The Nordic Region: A Step Closer to Gender Balance in Research? Joint Nordic Strategies and Measures to Promote Gender Balance among Researchers in Academia*, TemaNord 2013: 544. Copenhagen: Nordic Council of Ministers.

Berryman, S. (1983) *Who Will Do Science? Minority and Female Attainment of Science and Mathematics Degrees: Trends and Causes*, New York: Rockefeller Foundation.

Borchorst, A., Freidenvall, L., Kantola, J., Reisel, L. and Teigen, M. (2012) 'Institutionalizing intersectionality in the Nordic countries: anti-discrimination and equality in Denmark, Finland, Norway, and Sweden', in A. Krizsan, H. Skjeie and J. Squires (eds) *Institutionalizing Intersectionality: The Changing Nature of European Equality Regimes*, London: Palgrave Macmillan, pp 59–88.

Broadbridge, A. and Hearn, J. (2008) 'Gender and management: new directions in research and continuing patterns in practice', *British Journal of Management*, 19(1): S38–49.

Council of the European Union (2015) *Advancing Gender Equality in the European Research Area*, Brussels: Council Conclusions. Available at: http://data.consilium.europa.eu/doc/document/ST-14846-2015-INIT/en/pdf, accessed 9 April 2020.

Database for Statistics on Higher Education (DBH) (2017) Available at: https://dbh.nsd.uib.no, accessed 30 March 2021.

Dobbin, F., Schrage, D. and Kalev, A. (2015) 'Rage against the iron cage: the varied effects of bureaucratic personnel reforms on diversity', *American Sociological Review*, 80(5): 1014–44.

Enders, J., de Boer, H. and Weyer, E. (2013) 'Regulatory autonomy and performance: the reform of higher education re-visited', *Higher Education*, 65(1): 5–23.

Etzkowitz, H., and Ranga, M. (2011) 'Gender dynamics in science and technology: from the "leaky pipeline" to the "vanish box"', *Brussels Economic Review*, 54(2–3): 131–47.

European Commission (2019) *SHE Figures 2018*, Directorate-General for Research and Innovation, Luxembourg: Publications Office of the European Union.

Fagenson, E.A. (1990) 'At the heart of women in management research: theoretical and methodological approaches and their biases', *Journal of Business Ethics*, 9: 267–74.

Fox, M.F. and Colatrella, C. (2006) 'Participation, performance, and advancement of women in academic science and engineering: what is at issue and why', *The Journal of Technology Transfer*, 31(3): 377–86.

Hansen, H.F., Geschwind, L., Kivistö, J., Pekkola, E., Pinheiro, R. and Pulkkinen, K. (2019) 'Balancing accountability and trust: university reforms in the Nordic countries', *Higher Education*, 78: 557–73.

Herschberg, C., Benschop, Y. and van den Brink, M. (2018) 'Selecting early-career researchers: the influence of discourses of internationalisation and excellence on formal and applied selection criteria in academia', *Higher Education*, 76(5): 807–25.

Holzer, H.J. and Neumark, D. (2006) 'Affirmative action: what do we know?', *Journal of Policy Analysis and Management*, 25(2): 463–90.

Husu, L. (2015) 'A comprehensive national approach to promote gender equality in science: the case of Norway', in W. Pearson, Jr., L.M. Frehill and C.L. McNeely (eds) *Advancing Women in Science: An International Perspective*, London: Springer, pp 327–9.

Jöns, H. (2011) 'Transnational academic mobility and gender', *Globalisation, Societies and Education*, 9(2): 83–209.

Kalev, A., Dobbin, F. and Kelly, E. (2006) 'Best practices or best guesses? Assessing the efficacy of corporate affirmative action and diversity policies', *American Sociological Review*, 71: 589–617.

Koonce, D.A., Zhou, J., Anderson, C.D., Hening, D.A. and Conley, V.M. (2011) 'What is STEM?', in *2011 ASEE Annual Conference & Exposition*, pp 22–1684.

Lerwall, L. (2001) *Könsdiskriminering: en analys av nationell och internationell rätt.* [*Gender Discrimination: An Analysis of National and Internatonal Law*] Dissertation. Uppsala, Juridiska institutionen, Uppsala universitet: Justus förlag.

Lipinsky, A. (2013) *Gender Equality Policies in Public Research: Based on a Survey Among Members of the Helsinki Group on Gender in Research and Innovation*, Brussels: European Commission.

Liu, S.-N.C., Brown, S.E.V. and Sabat, I.E. (2019) 'Patching the "leaky pipeline": interventions for women of color faculty in STEM academia', *Archives of Scientific Psychology*, 7(1): 32–9.

Makarova, E., Aeschlimann, B. and Herzog, W. (2019) 'The gender gap in STEM fields: the impact of the gender stereotype of math and science on secondary students' career aspirations', *Frontiers in Education*, 4: 60.

Metcalf, H. (2010) 'Stuck in the pipeline: a critical review of STEM workforce literature', InterActions *UCLA Journal of Education and Information Studies*, 6(2): 1–20.

Moratti, S. (2020) 'Do low-openness, low-transparency procedures in academic hiring disadvantage women?', *Social Sciences*, 9(6): 1–13.

Naff, K.C. and Kellough, J.E. (2003) 'Ensuring employment equity: are federal programs making a difference?', *International Journal of Public Administration*, 26(12): 1307–36.

Nielsen, M.W. (2017) 'Scandinavian approaches to gender equality in academia: a comparative study', *Scandinavian Journal of Educational Research*, 61(3): 295–318.

Ong, M., Wright, W., Espinosa, L. and Orfield, G. (2011) 'Inside the double bind: a synthesis of empirical research on undergraduate and graduate women of color in science, technology, engineering, and mathematics', *Harvard Educational Review*, 81(2): 172–208.

Probert, B. (2005) '"I just couldn't fit it in": gender and unequal outcomes in academic careers', *Gender, Work and Organization*, 12(1): 50–72.

Ragins, B.R. and Sundstrom, E. (1989) 'Gender and power in organizations: a longitudinal perspective', *Psychological Bulletin*, 105(1): 51–88.

Rees, T. (2005) 'Reflections on the uneven development of gender mainstreaming in Europe', *International Journal of Feminist Politics*, 7(4): 555–74.

Squires, J. (2008) *Gender in Political Theory*, Cambridge: Polity Press.

Statistics Sweden (2021) Available at: www.scb.se, accessed 30 March 2021.

Terosky, A.L., O'Meara, K. and Campbell, C.M. (2014) 'Enabling possibility: women associate professors' sense of agency in career advancement', *Journal of Diversity in Higher Education*, 7(1), 58–76.

Timmers, T.M., Willemsen, T.M. and Tijdens, K.G. (2010) 'Gender diversity policies in universities: a multi-perspective framework of policy measures', *Higher Education*, 59(6): 719–35.

van den Brink, M. (2010) *Behind the Scenes of Science: Gender Practices in the Recruitment and Selection of Professors in the Netherlands*, Amsterdam: University Press.

Vipunen Database (2018) *Education Statistics Finland*. Available at: https://vipunen.fi/en-gb/, accessed 30 March 2021.

Xie, Y. and Shauman, K. (2003) *Women in Science: Career Processes and Outcomes*, Cambridge: Harvard University Press.

7

Uniformity Dressed as Diversity? Reorienting Female Associate Professors

May-Linda Magnussen, Rebecca W.B. Lund and Trond Stalsberg Mydland

Introduction

> 'I have not been very strategic in the past, and I realize that, when I talk to others, primarily men, who have been focussed on becoming professors as soon as possible. They have been more systematic when it comes to what they have said yes and no to, and given thought to what benefits them when it comes to that specific goal. But I have not been like that myself. I have been like "Oh, that's interesting and that's something I'm really committed to", and I say yes and I want to be kind and then suddenly, when I'm sitting there and am supposed to assemble what I've done in a CV and application, I think "Why did I prioritize that instead of that?" So, I wish someone had knocked on my door a long time ago and made me more aware of this.'

This quote is from an interview with a female associate professor at the University of Agder (UiA), Norway. At the time of the interview, she was taking part in a gender equality action programme for increasing the number of female professors at the university. This programme was enveloped in a rhetoric suggesting that female associate professors should be more strategic and self-assertive – 'lean in'.[1] The programme taught her that her tendency to 'say yes' was an obstacle to her becoming a professor, and that she had to develop an ability to 'say no' (see Lund, 2020b). Many other female associate professors at UiA talked of similar experiences.

In this chapter we investigate whether, how and with what consequences preliminary evaluations speed up female associate professors' processes of becoming full professors. To make sense of the effects of the evaluations, we use Dorothy Smith's (2005) concept of 'ruling relations' together with Sara Ahmed's emotional politics (2014) and queer phenomenology (2006). We explore textually mediated understandings of the 'ideal academic' (Lund, 2015) in the preliminary evaluation action, and how emotions 'stick' to these textually mediated discourses. Thus, we attend to the discursive as well as the emotional (re)orientations the evaluations can produce. We furthermore reflect on the particular understanding of gender equality embedded in this action programme, and its consequences for diversity in the sense of widening notions of what a good academic might be.

The *Balance project* at the University of Agder

In response to continued vertical and horizontal gender segregation in Norwegian academia (Ulvestad, 2017; KIF-info, 2021), the Norwegian Research Council (NRC) established the Balance Programme in 2013. The programme aims at increasing the share of female professors and research leaders through co-funding local research-based knowledge and action measures. To ensure local commitment, the university leadership has to be involved and willing to allocate funding. When UiA applied for funding from the Balance Programme in 2014, only 22 per cent of professors/readers (*dosents*) at UiA were women.[2] The university received funding and implemented its so-called *Balance project* between 2015 and 2018.

The aim of the project was to contribute to 'structural and cultural change' towards gender equality. The university asked for co-funding[3] for three gender equality actions. One was the *integration of gender and gender equality perspectives in leader gatherings and courses*, aimed at providing leaders with knowledge about the gendering of academia and tools to change it. Another was *search-and-find-committees*, aiming at increasing the share of female applicants for professorships at the university. The third was the *preliminary evaluations*, which we focus on in this chapter. The latter measure was directed at female associate professors already working at the university. In Norway, associate professors employed in a 50–100 per cent position can apply for personal promotion to full professor and are therefore not dependent on getting a professorship based on open-call applications. Those who received preliminary evaluations as part of the *Balance project* sent a preliminary application for professorship promotion to an evaluation committee with one internal and one external member. The committee provided, in return, a written evaluation of the associate professors' academic work. The associate professors could also contact committee members for strategic advice concerning promotion. Administrative staff at the university facilitated the process, while department heads often identified candidates for the evaluations and facilitated the actions for improvement recommended by the committee. In practice, this frequently meant facilitating more (coherent) research time.

In addition, all female associate professors at UiA were invited to participate in 'professorship promotion seminars' and 'shut-up-and-write-seminars'. Promotion seminars provided information about what it would take to achieve promotion, and gave participants access to the career experiences and advice of recently appointed female professors or female associate professors close to promotion. In the 'shut-up-and-write-seminars', female associate professors would sit in the same room and write academic texts for a whole day, following a fixed schedule of writing periods and breaks. While these two seminars were not part of the action measures funded by the NRC, they aligned with the overall strategic ideas being transmitted through the evaluations, as we will show later.

In addition to getting funding for the three original gender equality actions, UiA received funding from the NRC for carrying out research on local gender relations and inequality at the university. One pillar of the research focussed on exploring female associate professors' everyday lives and research careers, seeking to theorize the social organization of academic working lives, without paying direct attention to the action measures (Magnussen et al, 2018; Lund, 2020b). Another pillar focussed on the effects of the gender equality action measures. This chapter is an outcome of the second pillar and zooms in on the effects of the preliminary evaluations, which turned out to be the most successfully implemented of the three action measures.

Beyond body counts: understanding the production of uniformity

Substantial amounts of research demonstrate that gender equality actions are often reduced to body counts and incorporated in managerial quality or excellence strategies with economic purposes (Eisenstein, 2009; Rottenberg, 2018; Lund, 2020b). Gender quality strategies in academic institutions also tend to be based on the assumption that women are a uniform group, thus downplaying differences between women while simultaneously reproducing inequalities along lines of sexuality, class and ethnicity/race (for example Tzanakou and Pearce, 2019). We argue that the merger of competitive agendas and gender equality agendas produce and (re)produce particular discursive and emotional practices that result in increased uniformity rather than diversity. The equality agenda, rather than nurturing space for a diversity of people and practices within academia, becomes a measure for ensuring that the people in the organization are equally oriented towards narrow, institutionally defined goals of quality.

Identifying ruling relations

Dorothy Smith developed institutional ethnography as a 'method of inquiry' for exploring and challenging institutional processes and power from the standpoint of people's everyday lives and embodied experiences (Smith, 2005). The choice of standpoint, in our case that of the female associate professors, is empirically and contextually justified as pointing towards new perspectives, and challenging ways of knowing and doing which are considered unquestionable, neutral and objective (Smith, 2004a; Smith, 2004b).

In producing data, the researcher first aims to assist her research participants in articulating as much as possible of the physical, mental and emotional 'work' that a certain kind of practice – such as trying to become a professor – consists of, as well as the *social relations* this is being done in. If the production of data is successful, these descriptions will contain clues regarding the institutionalized and objectified knowledge that shapes work and activities across diverging local sites (Lund, 2015). Smith labels this knowledge *ruling relations*, and defines these as:

> text-mediated and text-based systems of 'communication', 'knowledge', 'information', 'regulation', 'control' and the like. The functions of 'knowledge, judgment, and will' that Marx saw as wrested from the original 'producer' and transferred to capital become built into a specialized complex of *objectified* forms of organization and relationship. ... Knowledge, judgment, and will are less and less properties of the individual subject and more and more of objectified organization. They are constituted as actual forms of concerting and concerted activities and can be investigated as such. ... The concept of the ruling relations identifies a historical development of forms of social consciousness that can no longer be adequately conceived as arising in the life conditions of actual individuals. (Smith, 2004a: 77–8)

Ruling relations are mediated through material and replicable texts. Their coordinating and generalizing capacity lies in the fact that they can be read, heard and seen in many places, by different people, at the same time. Having identified material texts, such as the preliminary evaluations and the intertextual hierarchy these are part of,[4] the researcher returns to the chosen standpoint, explicating how the identified texts shape the experience she started out exploring. She aims to show *how* power works in the informants' everyday lives and the *consequences* it has. She also aims to explore whether and how the ruling relations are reproduced, challenged or even dismantled, and whose interests this supports.

Emotional reorientation

In addition to identifying the ruling relations shaping the experiences of female associate professors engaged in preliminary evaluations, we used Ahmed's (2006, 2014) emotional politics and queer phenomenology to make sense of how emotions such as fear, shame, disappointment, discomfort, hope and pride become attached to discourses mediated through the ruling relations, thus hooking into broader textual-affective higher education regimes of ranking and competition (for example Shahjahan et al, 2020).[5] This involves representations of the objects and subjects that people direct their emotions towards and ultimately how people categorize and label objects and subjects. According to Ahmed, with time, certain emotions tend to 'stick' to some people and objects, but not to others. This is relevant because the gender equality action programme we explore in this chapter involves 'orienting' people towards particular objects and relations and away from others. This institutionally driven process of 'reorienting' encourages positive emotions towards objects and relations that provide exchange-value, and benefits the women's own careers. It also encourages neutrality or negative emotions directed at use-value and care for others (for example Ahmed, 2006). Furthermore, deep engagement with and concentration on particular objects and relations that benefit the self involves cultivating blindness towards the work that other people must engage in to make this possible for you (Ahmed, 2014). People are differently (dis)posed in terms of feeling 'at home' and 'comfortable' with orienting towards objects and relations in the ways that are institutionally and textually encouraged (for example Threadgold, 2021).

The case of UiA and our research data

UiA is one of many Norwegian university colleges that achieved university status in the 2000s. Although the university's activity and funding are closely tied to professional study programmes (such as teaching, nursing and engineering), the focus on research is increasing. The 2016 strategy stated that the university aimed at delivering 'world-leading research' and at increasing its participation in international research projects and programmes (University of Agder, 2021). Statistically, the Agder region has the most gender-segregated work life in Norway, and research substantiates that the associations between femininity and care work and masculinity and paid work are particularly strong here (Magnussen, 2015). Faculty and other staff at UiA are not unmarked by these regional particularities. Many have grown up in the region or have lived there for a long period of time, have family there and engage in social relations transcending the university.

The main data for this chapter are 57 personal, semi-structured qualitative interviews with staff at the university, conducted between October 2015 and

November 2018.[6] Thirty-two of these were with female associate professors, and out of these, 13 had had preliminary evaluations. Some of the associate professors we interviewed also sent us experience notes on specific issues. We conducted two workshops about career challenges for female associate professors. In these, many women who were not interviewed contributed with their experiences. In addition, we attended meetings and events at the university – such as promotion seminars, meetings in the university's gender equality and inclusion committee, as well as leadership gatherings – throughout the time period of the *Balance project*. The *Balance project* financed one administrative staff member or faculty member in the four university faculties with the lowest shares of female professors to spend 20 per cent of their working hours facilitating preliminary evaluations and search-and-find-committees. These people became important informants in the project and provided us with valuable insights into their experiences of these measures.

The remaining 25 interviews were carried out with male associate professors and professors, as well as with male and female management and other administrative staff. In the interviews with faculty, the goal was to make our informants articulate as much of their everyday academic activity, and as specific and detailed, as possible. In all interviews, we aimed at making our informants put the relations and institutional texts shaping their activities and experiences into words. The interviews with the managers and other administrative staff, moreover, focussed on explicating their understandings of the research careers of female associate professors at the university, as well as their own experiences with and reflections concerning the *Balance project* measures.

In the next section, we begin with female associate professors' experiences regarding the preliminary evaluations. We draw on our other data from UiA to explore the ruling relations mediated in and through the evaluations, and the ways emotions 'stick' to these.

The practical, mental and emotional 'work' of preliminary evaluations

When the *Balance project* ended in 2018, 24 female associate professors at UiA had participated in preliminary evaluations. Most of these were handpicked by their department heads.[7] Our interviews with 13 of these women substantiated that the evaluations often did speed up their processes of becoming professors. Many told us how the evaluations made them more certain that aiming for promotion to professor was worthwhile, while also providing direction to and speeding up the process. Some mentioned the usefulness of assembling their work, writing up an application and tailoring a CV that they could improve – based on the evaluation – and use in their real application for promotion to professor. In addition, several women used the evaluation and the connected career advice to negotiate more research time with their department heads. One woman said that for her, getting more research time – "time to think and to breathe" – was her main take-away from, and her main reason for, having a preliminary evaluation. The advice she had received from the evaluation committee did not add anything to what she had already learnt from participating in promotion seminars.

Many of the women we interviewed also voiced important emotional aspects of being invited to a preliminary evaluation. Some expressed becoming motivated by being identified as "professor material", which made them feel "seen". One woman said: "Preliminary evaluations are about being seen and feeling that somebody thinks that it's important to acknowledge you." Other informants said that the evaluations' external validation made them feel more confident about their research interests. Even in cases where the evaluations were in line with the associate professors' self-evaluation, they expressed how it felt reassuring to "have it on paper". Feeling acknowledged and seen is particularly valuable in an affective economy where you can easily become either invisible or hyper-visible if you are not perceived as being oriented towards the 'right' goals. Being one of the few selected for preliminary evaluation may have made the female associate professors feel special and worthy of consideration. Such processes can be seductive, hooking people into what has been termed 'neuroliberalism', capturing the combination of principles of neoliberalism combined with the insights of behaviourism (Morley and Lund, 2020). The more you align, and direct yourself towards the 'right' things, the more acknowledgement you receive and the less resistance you experience. In other words, everyday life, in some respects, becomes easier (Ahmed, 2006: 14–21).

Our data substantiates that 'being seen' may have a stronger reorienting effect on the academic work of women than that of men. Among the emotional work in our data, we found many traces of highly gendered emotional work, particularly dealing with feelings of insecurity and the so-called imposter syndrome (Chandra et al, 2019). We understand such feelings as themselves produced by and shaped in gendered social relations in academia (Lund, 2020a). For instance, some of the interviewed women said that they were preoccupied with ensuring that they would get promoted when they did send in the real application for promotion. Being overqualified was seen as better than overestimating themselves, and the preliminary evaluation helped them to navigate this terrain. In our material, this was only one of many signs indicating that the female associate professors we interviewed manoeuvred contradictory gendered ideals on their way towards a professorship. While the gender equality rhetoric dominating the *Balance* activities told them to be more strategic on their own behalf, and thus counter feminine stereotypes, they were often simultaneously expected to conform to such stereotypes by being emotionally invested in the well-being of students and colleagues (see also Magnussen et al, 2018) and avoiding 'boastful' behaviour (Lund, 2020a). Thus, the self-promotion encouraged by gender equality action measures can be risky for the women we interviewed.

Another emotional aspect of the preliminary evaluations in our data was that some of the interviewed women said that setting a professorship as a clear goal motivated them and lent speed to the process of becoming a professor. Some said that the signalling effect of the preliminary evaluation also provided such extra impetus. Certain expectations, capacities and potentials were attached to them by their surroundings, thus generating a sense of urgency and focus. One woman talked about how the evaluation generated high expectations and a sense of pressure from her leader and colleagues: "I notice that I have speeded up. I have felt that pressure a little bit, because you get many questions about when you're going to send the application for promotion. Some think that there is a lot of support. But it's not actually like that." This associate professor met expectations to perform more and faster, without having much extra support and time, and later on in the interview she said that this resulted in recurring health problems. Speeding up had a cost.

Not all of our informants were that interested in becoming professors, however. Being a professor "is a title and I'm not that into titles", one woman said, suggesting that the meaning of the status attached to a professorship was not self-evident. Another interviewee would have liked some discussion about the reasons for wanting to become a professor and about institutional expectations regarding professors. A third woman said that she was not motivated by the prestige of a professorship, but by specific research and teaching agendas and how becoming a professor opened certain doors. When asked about what motivated her, she said that:

> 'I think what I do is important. It helps people. … I don't need any other motivation than that. So, I think it's important. And teaching, that's perhaps the part I enjoy most of all. Really. … But the evaluation gave me a small push to at least think about [professorship promotion]. Because the days pass so quickly, so I seldom sit down and think about promotion. For my part, it doesn't mean that much. In a busy everyday life that's not important, but I can see that in applying for research projects and in international collaboration the title actually has something to say. So, I think that's a reason to become a professor.'

However, the majority of the women we interviewed told us how the preliminary evaluations *had* changed the way they thought and felt about academic work. The criteria used to evaluate their research careers, combined with the gathering of emotions, bodies and resources around the aims of reformulating their goals and redirecting their attention, made several think that they should have made better – that is, more 'strategic' – choices throughout their careers. They began to attach value to the standardized quality measures used to evaluate their work and to the seductive notion of 'making it'. It made them think that their work should have been less shaped by, for instance, teaching and commitment to solving societal challenges, and more by choices that would have speeded up their own processes of becoming professors. Saying 'no' was, however, not only invoked as a way of speeding up the strategic path to a professorship, but also as self-care. In the face of pressure to perform in particular standardized ways, responsibility for well-being at work was experienced as individualized, adding another layer to the redirection and emotional orientations of the female academics we interviewed. They were responsibilized and had to carefully manage their 'investments' of time and resources, both for the sake of becoming professors and for keeping healthy.

Gendered academic ideals

By February 2021, 12 of the 24 women involved in preliminary evaluations during the *Balance project* period were full professors, and the share of female professors at UiA had increased to 30 per cent, from 22 per cent in 2014. The preliminary evaluations probably contributed to this increase. However, they also had problematic side effects. In the following sections, we investigate these by unpacking the ruling relations (Smith, 2005) of the preliminary evaluations. More specifically, we explore understandings of the good academic that are promoted through them and, in turn, what kind of academia these contribute to.

Our total data material from UiA shows that the understanding of academic ideals as neutral and as equally desirable and attainable for all is widespread (Magnussen et al, 2018). One woman we interviewed about these preliminary evaluations, however, connected the ideals promoted through the action measures – individualism and careerism – with masculinity and male-coded practices:

> 'I know some [women] who have stated very clearly that they want to become professors, but what is obvious to me is that if you're kind of a competitive lonely rider, if you're only running your own race, if you're not a team player, you will not to the same degree be invited to join projects. … But is it the women who use their elbows and who say no to everything and sit by themselves, are they the ones who succeed the most and become professors quicker? That would be interesting for me to know. Because even if it is so, I might not choose that strategy, because it doesn't match what I stand for. But of course, it's still interesting to see if that's the way it is, if the women who are a bit more like men, if you know what I mean, are those who are most successful.'

This associate professor probably did not change her orientations as a consequence of the understandings promoted in the *Balance* action measures, even if they might be the quickest way to a full professorship. She also pointed to the risks of doing academic work in this way, as mentioned earlier.

While women doing academic work "more like [some] men" probably contribute to numerical gender equality, merely increasing the presence of female bodies in professorship positions does not automatically translate into a more equality- and diversity-favouring culture (Ahmed, 2017; Lund, 2020b). Instead, this as a one-sided approach will probably strengthen already dominant academic ideals that favour particular ways of being an academic, historically associated with certain men (Bailyn, 2003; van den Brink and Benschop, 2012). At UiA, as well as in academia more broadly, publication points, citations and certain kinds of international collaboration, the main currency of a global competitive 'excellence industry', increasingly shape academics' everyday lives (Lund, 2015; Magnussen et al, 2018). Individual self-promotion, in the form of publication output and external funding, seems to become more important, while tasks such as pastoral work around students, mentoring, reviewing for journals and so on tend to become invisible. This is work that the female associate professors we interviewed (still) did a lot of and often regarded as important, but are encouraged to reduce in order to get promoted to professor. The 'competitive ethos underpinning the university produces a binary of winners and losers' (Morley and Crossouard, 2016: 4) that is in turn associated with particular emotions.

The preliminary evaluations and other actions measures responsibilized (Lemke, 2001; Wright, 2014) the interviewed associate professors: they provided tools with which the women could work on their thoughts, emotions and actions. Academic work they had hitherto not been particularly aware of or had negative emotions towards, gradually became attached to other and more positive emotions such as pride, joy and a sense of being seen. Such affective and emotional shifts are central to complying with and internalizing neoliberal value systems (Morley and Crossouard, 2016; Morley and Lund, 2020) and, ultimately, for the exclusion of those positioned as losers. Through the reponsibilization of individuals, differences in opportunity structures are concealed (Lund, 2020b).

Repurposing feminism

The preliminary evaluations and other action measures at UiA also promoted specific understandings of gender equality. In line with much feminist research on organizations, the NRC (2021) states that actions funded by the Balance Programme should not 'fix women', as many 'traditional' actions for gender equality have done (for example De Vries and van den Brink, 2016). The UiA's application for funding included the feminist intention of 'changing gendered cultures and structures' at the university. Even so, the project to a large degree ended up helping women 'fix themselves' to fit standardized, seemingly neutral quality standards (Magnussen et al, 2018).[8] This conclusion is supported by the fact that one of the other action measures, *integration of gender and gender equality perspectives in leader meetings and courses*, encountered a lot of resistance at UiA and was not successfully implemented. In addition, initiatives such as 'shut-up-and-write' sessions and promotion seminars all focused on shifting how individual women prioritized their time and efforts. These offered generalized advice of 'saying no' to (assumed) non-meritorious work in order to, as one top manager said, 'make it' (Lund, 2020b). Presenting academic ideals as neutral and unproblematic reduced gender equality to a question of numbers, glossing over more subtle and informal gendering in the university. The *Balance project* at UiA helped women play the gendered academic game more effectively, rather than critically engage with the structural and cultural forces at play (Colley and White, 2018). That female associate professors were asked to be more individualistic and careerist, *and to code this as feminist*, concerns us.

The gendered global knowledge economy

Considering the reflections in the previous sections of this chapter, the reorienting of the female associate professor behind the opening quote of this chapter becomes problematic. Even if she aims at gender equality, she can be understood as first and foremost contributing towards strengthening the competitiveness of UiA and Norwegian academia in the so-called global knowledge economy (Wright, 2014; Hazelkorn, 2015). This process probably contributes to a less diverse academia, effectively hidden within the language and discourses of research excellence and feminism. Even if the NRC (2021) states that having more female professors is important for bringing new perspectives into Norwegian academe, it is also framed as a means towards increasing the sector's competitiveness. The European Union, for instance, has made gender equality in grant-awarding a clear ambition although no clear penalties or rewards ensure this in practice. As a result, numerical gender equality has become a currency in the excellence industry (Lund, 2020b). Moreover, it is based on the assumption that gender is the main (or only!) category of difference, while other signifiers such as class, sexuality, race or age, are made invisible, creating a problematic institutional assumption of universality and sameness among women, in turn justifying a one-size-fits-all 'reorienting'. This may very well have consequences concerning epistemic diversity (Aarseth, Bråten and Lund, forthcoming).

Concluding remarks

In this chapter we have explored how women engaged in preliminary evaluation action measures became re-oriented through the ruling relations mediated in textualized quality criteria. We have shown how gender equality measures ended up fostering uniformity rather than diversity through an action measure that ultimately aimed at 'fixing the woman' rather than 'fixing the system and culture'. Actions directed at individual women can be a smart entry to working with gender equality in academia, seeing that actions focussed on furthering women's individual careers align with dominant understandings of gender equality and feminism, as also De Vries and van den Brink (2016) have pointed out. And indeed, as we showed, numerically, such individualized action measures turned out to be a success. However, such measures should not stand alone. Instead, they should be supplemented with developing knowledge and collegial practices that challenge the subtle ways gendered and intersecting differences become (re)produced in everyday practices, as well as in gender equality action measures. In carrying out research as part of the *Balance project* we encountered many women who had never reflected on their academic work from a gender perspective. Coming together, articulating experience and finding commonalities and common concerns – the consciousness-raising tools of the early women's liberation movement – do not seem to have lost their relevance and may serve as an important driver for taking the agenda for equality and diversity further. While consciousness raising does not provide a quick-fix solution to subtle, inadvertent and unintentional forms of gendered bias in academic structures and cultures, it does provide faculty members with a sensibility for noticing, and a language for expressing, the complexities of inequality (see for instance Carnes et al, 2015; Remich et al, 2017 for such consciousness-raising initiatives and interventions in US context). This is ultimately a first step towards cultural and structural transformation over time.

Acknowledgements

This research was funded by the Norwegian Research Council and the University of Agder. Norwegian Research Council project number: 245466.

Notes

1 Here, we refer to Sheryl Sandberg's *Lean In* (2013).

2 10 per cent less than the national average (KIF-info, 2021).

3 The Norwegian Research Council demanded 50 per cent co-funding from the institutions receiving funding for gender equality action from the Balance Programme.

4 The researcher often identifies local texts that shape the experience she aims to understand. These are texts with which the informants in their research interact directly, for instance criteria for promotion to a professorship. The researcher then moves on to explore how these texts are part of a trans-local intertextual hierarchy. This means that the texts that the people she started her research with, engage with and which shape their actions, are themselves shaped by texts of a higher order, such as white papers about higher education and research.

5 *Being* 'affected' differs from *having* ownership of certain 'emotions' (Probyn, 2005). Ahmed (2006) theorizes emotions as operating within an 'affective economy'. Emotions are understood as intentional in the sense of being 'directed' towards something or someone in particular ways – either attracting us or repelling us. The capacity to affect, and be affected, is, however, shaped by *what* we come into contact with. According to Ahmed (2006: 2), 'emotions involve affective (re)orientations'. This means that in order for something or someone to make a particular emotional mark on us, we must be affectively oriented towards it in a particular way, and this orientation is, in turn, shaped by 'our accumulated history' (Threadgold, 2021: 58). As such, Ahmed's theory of an affective economy points towards how people become (re)oriented emotionally towards particular objects and subjects, and explains why some people feel comfortable while others feel uncomfortable with this (re)orientation.

6 We recorded and transcribed most of the interviews. When recording was not possible, we wrote interview or field notes. Rachel Fishberg, former Master's student at the University of Aarhus, contributed to developing our interview data.

7 However, some also contacted the administrative staff connected to the *Balance project* directly or were encouraged by them to have preliminary evaluations. Furthermore, towards the end of the project, female associate professors who were further from being qualified were invited to have these evaluations done.

8 Some of the female associate professors we interviewed understood academia and the lack of gender equality there this way, but we found these understandings much more often among male faculty, leaders and administrative staff at the university.

References

Aarseth, H., Bråten, B. and Lund, R.W.B (forthcoming) 'Kjønnslikestilling eller Perspektivmangfold?' ['Gender Equality or Epistemic Diversity?'], in H. Aarseth and I. Owesen (eds) *Kjønnsbalansei*, Bergen: Fagbokforlaget.

Ahmed, S. (2006) *Queer Phenomenology*, Durham, NC: Duke University Press.

Ahmed, S. (2014) *The Cultural Politics of Emotion* (2nd edn), Edinburgh: Edinburgh University Press.

Ahmed, S. (2017) *Living a Feminist Life*, Durham, NC: Duke University Press.

Bailyn, L. (2003) 'Academic careers and gender equity: lessons learned from MIT', *Gender, Work & Organization*, 10(2): 137–53.

Carnes, M., Devine, P.G., Manwell, L.B., Byars-Winston, A., Ford, C.E., Forscher, P., Isaac, C., Kaatz, A., Magua, W., Palta, M. and Sheridan, J. (2015) 'Effect of an intervention to break the gender bias habit for faculty at one institution: a cluster randomized, controlled trial', *Academic Medicine*, 90(2): 221–30.

Chandra, S., Huebert, C.A., Crowley, E. and Das, A. (2019) 'Imposter syndrome: could it be holding you or your mentees back?', *CHEST: Commentary: Teaching, Education and Career Hub*, 156(1): 26–32.

Colley, L. and White, C. (2018) 'Neoliberal feminism: the neoliberal rhetoric on feminism by Australian political actors', *Gender, Work & Feminism*. DOI: 10.1111/gwao.12303.

De Vries, J.A. and van den Brink, M. (2016) 'Transformative gender interventions', *Equality, Diversity & Inclusion*, 35(7–8): 429–48.

Eisenstein, H. (2009) *Feminism Seduced*, London: Routledge.

Hazelkorn, E. (2015) *Rankings and the Reshaping of Higher Education*, Basingstoke: Palgrave Macmillan.

KIF-info (2021) 'Statistikk om kjønnsbalanse og mangfold' ['Statistics on gender equality and diversity']. Available at: http://kifinfo.no/nb/content/statistikk-0, accessed 30 March 2021.

Lemke, T. (2001) '"The birth of bio-politics": Michel Foucault's lecture at the Collège de France on neo-liberal governmentality', *Economy and Society*, 30(2): 190–207.

Lund, R.W.B. (2015) *Doing the Ideal Academic: Gender, Excellence and Changing Academia*, Doctoral dissertation, Helsinki: Aalto University.

Lund, R.W.B. (2020a) 'The social organization of boasting in the neo-liberal university', *Gender & Education*, 32(4): 466–85.

Lund, R.W.B. (2020b) 'Becoming a professor requires saying *no*: merging equality and quality agenda in a Norwegian gender balance project', in H. Lawton, C. Henry, H. Etzkowitz and A. Poulovassilis (eds) *Gender, Science and Innovation: New Perspectives*, Cheltenham: Edward Elgar Publishing, pp 35–58.

Magnussen, M.-L. (2015) *Familieforsørgelse i menns hverdag* [*Breadwinning in men's everyday lives*], Doctoral dissertation, Department of Sociology and Human Geography, University of Oslo.

Magnussen, M-L., Lund, R.W.B. and Wallevik, H. (2018) 'Et kjønnet rom for akademisk skriving: Den akademiske skrivingens sosiale organisering, sett fra ståstedet til kvinnelige førsteamanuenser ved Universitetet i Agder' ['A gendered space for academic writing: the social organization of academic writing, seen from the standpoint of female associate professors at the University of Agder, Norway'], *Tidsskrift for Kjønnsforskning* [*Norwegian Journal for Gender Research*], 42(1–2): 85–103.

Morley, L. and Crossouard, B. (2016) 'Gender in the neoliberalised global academy: the affective economy of women and leadership in South Asia', *British Journal of Sociology of Education*, 37(1): 149–68.

Morley, L. and Lund, R.W.B. (2020) 'The affective economy of feminist leadership in Finnish universities: class-based knowledge for navigating neoliberalism and neuroliberalism', *Discourse: Studies in the Cultural Politics of Education*, 42(1): 114–40.

Norwegian Research Council (NRC) (2021) 'Program Plan 2017–2022. Program, Kjønnsbalanse i toppstillinger og forskningsledelse – BALANSE' ['Programme Plan 2017–2022. Programme, gender balance in top positions and research leadership']. Available at: www.forskningsradet.no/siteassets/sok-om-finansiering/programplaner/balanse-work-programme.pdf, accessed 19 January 2022.

Pereira, M.M. (2017) *Power, Knowledge and Feminist Scholarship: An Ethnography of Academia*, London: Routledge.

Probyn, E. (2005) *Blush: Faces of Shame*, Minneapolis: University of Minnesota Press.

Remich, R., Jones, R., Wood, C.V., Campbell, P.B. and McGee, R. (2017) 'How women in biomedical PhD programs manage gender consciousness as they persist toward academic research careers', *Academic Medicine*, 91(8): 1119–27.

Rottenberg, C. (2018) *The Rise of Neoliberal Feminism*. Oxford: Oxford University Press.

Sandberg, S. (2013) *Lean In: Women, Work and the Will to Lead*, New York: Alfred A. Knopf Publishing.

Shahjahan, R., Sonneveldt, E.L., Estera, A.L. and Bae, S. (2020) 'Emoscapes and commercial university rankers: the role of affect in global higher education policy', *Critical Studies in Education*. DOI: 10.1080/17508487.2020.1748078.

Smith, D.E. (2004a) 'Ideology, science and social relations: a reinterpretation of Marx's epistemology', *European Journal of Social Theory*, 7(4): 445–62.

Smith, D.E. (2004b) *Writing the Social: Critique, Theory, and Investigations*, Toronto: University of Toronto Press.

Smith, D.E. (2005) *Institutional Ethnography: A Sociology for People*, Lanham, MD: AltaMira Press.

Threadgold, S. (2021) *Bourdieu and Affect: Towards a Theory of Affective Affinities*, Bristol: Bristol University Press.

Tzanakou, C. and Pearce, R. (2019) 'Moderate feminism within or against the neoliberal university? The example of Athena SWAN', *Gender, Work & Organization*, 26(8): 1191–211.

Ulvestad, J.M. (2017) 'Fremad i alle retninger: Implementering af Kjønnsbalanse i Akademia' ['Forward in all directions: implementing gender balance in academia'], *Tidsskrift for Kjønnsforskning* [*Norwegian Journal of Gender Research*], 41(1): 5–21.

University of Agder (2021) *Strategy 2016–2020*. Available at: www.uia.no/en/about-uia/organisation/strategy-2016-2020, accessed 31 March 2021.

van den Brink, M. and Benschop, Y. (2012) 'Gender practices in the construction of academic excellence: sheep with five legs', *Organization*, 19(4): 507–24.

Wright, S. (2014) 'Knowledge that counts: points systems and the governance of Danish universities', in D.E. Smith and A. Griffith (eds) *Under New Public Management: Institutional Ethnographies of Changing Front-Line Work*, Toronto: University of Toronto Press, pp 294–338.

8

"Should I Stay or Should I Go?" How Early Career Researchers Imagine the (Im)Possible Future in Academia

Siri Øyslebø Sørensen and Guro Korsnes Kristensen

Introduction

Interviewer:	What do you think about the possibilities to pursue what you described as your plan A, an academic career?
Post doc:	To stay in academia? … It's not like that. It doesn't feel like that is something one can just choose to do.

This short exchange captures the ambiguous situation early career researchers find themselves in: regardless of any genuine desires to pursue an academic career, the fact that it is not up to the young scholar alone to make the desired future happen was a strongly present awareness among several of the 29 postdocs that participated in the study presented in this chapter. There are multiple ways of dealing with and making sense of this situation. The purpose of this chapter is to explore how early career researchers reflect upon their potential future within academia, and the ways in which these reflections draw on their experiences of entering an academic career.

A better understanding of how early career researchers perceive their potential futures in academia is crucial for informing future work on gender balance (Murgia and Poggio, 2019). This is particularly relevant to the current Nordic context, where one policy goal is to enhance the gender balance among professors (Brandser and Sümer, 2017). Despite longstanding efforts to promote women in academia, 74 per cent of all professors in Norway are men (Wendt, 2019). Even in fields where women outnumber men in the student population, and the numbers of female and male PhD candidates have been equal for more than a decade, an imbalance persists in top positions (Næss et al, 2018). The postdoc period of an academic career trajectory is in other words crucial in terms of gender balance.

Postdoc researchers are potential future professors. However, their position within academic institutions is ambiguous: on the one hand, they have already made their way into a narrow and highly competitive working life which suggests that they are both ambitious and privileged. On the other hand, as their position within this system is still by definition temporary, they are in an ambiguous and precarious situation, commonly referred to as a 'career stage'. By studying careers and perceptions of career choices, one gets to understand how societal context, organization and individual agency relates (Inkson et al, 2012). Thus, we argue that exploring their experiences and reflections provides valuable insights into the ongoing efforts to promote a gender balance and inclusion in research and innovation. To guide the empirical investigation and analysis, we asked the following questions: how do early career researchers make sense of their academic endeavours? How are past and current experiences within academia linked to perceptions of possible futures in academia? And whether and how is gender made part of these reflections?

In the following, we describe the contextual background of the chapter, before introducing the empirical data, methods and analytical strategies. The analysis is organized into three sections, exploring i) how the postdocs make sense of finding opportunities and starting an academic career; ii) how they view challenges in pursuing a career; and finally iii) what makes them want to continue. The chapter ends with a concluding reflection on how crucial elements in assembling research careers for early career scholars provide the basis for future change towards a better gender balance.

Gendered career trajectories: patterns and perceptions

Nordic higher education institutions (HEIs) have seen rapidly growing numbers of postdoc scholars in recent years and in Norway, where our study was conducted, there has been a particularly sharp increase in that number over the last decade (Kwiek and Antonowicz, 2015; Kyvik, 2015). Postdoc positions provide opportunities for PhD graduates to qualify for a permanent academic position. However, the substantial increase in use of postdoctoral positions and temporary research contracts across Europe has coincided with changes in funding structures and an increased demand on universities to engage directly with partners outside of academic institutions, suggesting that postdoc positions potentially also enable alternative career trajectories outside of academic institutions (Chantwell and Taylor, 2015; Yudkevich et al, 2015).

Academic career trajectories are not identical across national contexts. Thus, local situations influence how early career researchers make sense of their opportunities (Le Feuvre et al, 2018). For example, tenure track positions do not exist in Norwegian HEIs, but once one is employed as an associate professor, a full professorship can be achieved based on personal merits, that is, through personal promotion (Kyvik, 2015). Since the early 1990s there has been a tendency in Norway to announce positions at associate professor level as a means in particular to keep women in the academy (Olsen et al, 2005).

This structural change has contributed to an increasing number of women staying on the academic career path in science, technology, engineering, and mathematics (STEM) and technology (Suboticki et al, 2021). It has been combined with targeted recruitment and efforts to redefine the gendered symbolism of STEM and technology studies, both discursively and in representations (Lagesen, 2007; Lagesen et al, 2021), as well as funding schemes to support women academics, alongside with women's networks and mentoring programmes.

However, there are gender differences across academic careers, after achieving permanent positions. Women outnumber men in teaching positions, while men to a larger extent occupy research positions (Frølich et al, 2018). Model calculations based on Norwegian data still show that if you compare female and male associate professors of equal age within the same academic discipline, employed at the same type of institution, the probability of becoming a full professor is four percentage points lower for women compared to men (Frølich et al, 2018). Thus, it is important to explore whether and how early career scholars navigate this gendered landscape. Does it influence their experiences and perceptions of future possibilities? Are they aware of gender in how they make sense of their career experiences, choices and prospects?

The extant literature shows that scientists' sense of professional self is shaped by understandings of research as purposes and 'passion', and also strongly influenced by gendered perceptions of the self (Søndergaard, 2005; Armano and Murgia, 2013; Bozzon et al, 2019). Some have emphasized how discourses of ambition and practices of boasting are inherently gendered, resulting in patterns of gender inequality (Benschop et al, 2013; Lund, 2020). Furthermore, gender stereotypes are shown to influence perceptions of competence and merit in the peer review processes (Tregenza, 2002; Reuben et al, 2014). We also know that precariousness in relation to family situation influences the likelihood of pursuing an academic career (Manzi and Ojeda, 2014; Bataille et al, 2017; Sutherland, 2018). Ideals of work-life balance are known to be discursively gendered (Sørensen, 2016, 2017), and empirical studies have shown how women academics take on the responsibility for managing that balance (Toffoletti and Starr, 2016).

When we planned our study, we expected early career researchers to be more or less conscious about the various obstacles and drivers identified in previous research in how they navigate the landscape of academia. And, as we will show, ideas about work-life balance, required merits, international mobility, self-esteem and social background did play significant roles in the narratives, but not always in coherent or consistent ways – and not always according to our anticipation.

Empirical data, methods and analytical strategies

The empirical data analyzed in this chapter are based on group interviews with early career scholars, conducted by the authors and research colleagues in a project entitled 'Gender balance from below: Towards a gender-balanced NTNU 2025'. This project aimed to enhance the gender balance at departmental level at Norway's largest university, the Norwegian University of Science and Technology (NTNU). As part of an initial mapping of the situation we conducted individual interviews with professors and heads of departments, as well as group interviews with PhDs and postdocs from across the university.

For this chapter, we draw on the eight group interviews we conducted during 2017 and 2018 with 29 postdocs in total: 12 women and 17 men. Approximately half of the participating postdocs had done their entire education in Norwegian institutions, while the other half had an international background, with either a Master's or a doctoral degree from institutions outside of Norway. Their ages varied from late 20s to early 40s. This is indicative of the fact that the average age of Norwegian PhDs and postdocs is relatively high (Kyvik, 2015).

The research participants were recruited from departments at NTNU with different levels of gender balance and gender balance change patterns, representing a broad range of academic disciplines, including both human and social sciences and the STEM disciplines (Sørensen et al, 2019). The interviews were conducted by two, sometimes three, researchers taking part. One researcher led the conversation, while the other(s) observed, took notes and joined the conversation with additional questions. The interview guide was structured around career experiences, career expectations, perceptions and opinions about gender balance and inclusion in academia.

All the interviews were recorded and later transcribed verbatim. The study was approved by the Norwegian Center for Research Data, and the participants signed consent forms to enable us to use their data in publications from this research. The interviewees were given pseudonyms and those who participated in the same conversation were given names starting with the same letter. This allows for some sensitivity towards the interactional context of the individual voices. The transcribed conversations were coded thematically, using the software Atlas.ti.

We used thematic analysis to categorize the different narratives of how the postdocs entered their academic career trajectory in the first place (Braun and Clarke, 2013). The stories were then further processed by drawing on the tools of dialogical narrative analysis (Riessman, 2008; Frank, 2012). According to Bakhtin (1981: 426) the dialogical constitutes an epistemological mode. Instead of being occupied primarily with identifying the narrative structure or any coherent pattern that can be labelled a narrative, dialogical narrative analysis allows one to pay attention to and capture the complexity of how stories come to make sense. Language use is always saturated with meaning, both in descriptive and ideological ways. By paying attention to what utterances respond to, both in terms of capturing pasts and imagining futures, we were able to identify not only the material obstacles facing early career researchers, but also the subtle and less tangible barriers and possibilities that are experienced by prospective academics.

Our main interest lay in exploring how these stories relate to images of a future career. We looked at how ideas about a future career were perceived in the context of a broader notion of a future life situation. The main themes addressed by the early career scholars were work-life balance, geographic mobility and scholarly identity or 'sense of self'. In order to keep the complexity of individual voices accessible and visible we have chosen to focus on a limited number of research participants in the empirical analysis. All the interviewees in this chapter are white and born in a Nordic country. The selected voices represent diverse backgrounds in terms of family situations. The voices we will meet in the analysis, belong to the following interviewees:

Agnes was 37 years old at the time of the interview, lived with a partner and had two children. She was in her fifth year of postdoc research within life sciences. Berit was also a 37-year-old woman, without children. She lived with her partner, a dog and a cat. She worked in social science and was one year into her postdoc period. Henriette was 35 years old and had completed her PhD three years previously. She combined academic work with paid work as a consultant. She had two children, both born during her PhD period. Hilde was 38 years old and had four children. She had had various temporary lecturer and teaching contracts since finishing her PhD five years previously, and recently started her postdoc. Both Henriette and Hilde worked within the humanities.

Are was a 29-year-old man, one year into his postdoc. He was single, with no kids. Børre was another 29-year-old man, two years into his postdoc, also single with no kids. Are worked in engineering, whereas Børre worked in social science. Harald was the third man in our sample. He was in his mid-30s, married and the father of two young kids. He worked in the humanities, and just a month before the interview took place he had landed a permanent position after several years on temporary postdoc and research contracts.

In the following, we explore some of the complex dynamics and ambiguities that came to the fore when the interviewees were encouraged to share their reflections upon their life in academia, voicing career-choice considerations.

"Skills, help and luck, basically"

When asked about why and how they took the first step into an academic career, the postdocs shared a variety of experiences. Most of them, regardless of family situation and other circumstances, talked about their motivations for being in academia, closely linked to a sense of purpose. The majority talked about their research as a desirable activity in its own right. A good example of this was Are:

> 'I started on my PhD studies because I wanted to become a researcher, not necessarily to become a professor. I just want to learn new things all the time, thus becoming a researcher would be optimal. But, I guess one has to become a professor at some point, and then you need to apply for funding, take on responsibility for other people and things like that, tasks that are less tempting to me.' (Are)

At the core of Are's expressed motivation was an urge to "learn new things", and the idea of a researcher embodies this motivation in his story. Still, he responded to the idea of an expected future in which becoming a professor was implicitly understood to be the goal of an academic career. There is a dissonance between the expressed genuine, personal motivation and the institutionalized expectations – embodied by the professor. Thus, becoming a professor did not emerge as a goal in itself, but rather as a means to being able to continue to do research, at least part-time.

This ambiguity regarding a professorship was also articulated in other career-choice narratives, for example in Børre's who told quite a different story from Are. Børre did not base his story on a sense of purpose or a genuine research interest. Instead, he talked about almost randomly starting his academic career path, currently "making something good out of it":

> 'I never had an ambition to become a professor, or to do anything within academia so I was kind of also just a bit thrown into it because I was offered a PhD position, and didn't have any other job offer at the time, and then we received funding for further research so I could continue into a postdoc. And now that I am in academia, I want to do the best that I can do and use my energy to make something good out of it.' (Børre)

Børre's story illustrates a 'seizing the opportunity' narrative. He describes how he was offered a position and had no better alternative for an income at the time. The next step was described as seemingly random as well through the use of the passive "we received funding". There were no visible traces of hard work or luck in this narrative of career moves. Børre articulated his agency by stating that since he happened to be in academia he would "make something good out of it". Interestingly, this type of story too responded to an implied expectation of becoming a professor as an end-goal, by distancing itself from the idea of pursuing an academic career as such and instead emphasizing the "making something good".

Another way of framing one's career start, different from Are's and Børre's narratives, was presented by Berit. Berit, like Are, expressed genuine interest in her research subject and for that reason wanted to pursue an academic career. In her story, the opportunities she had had were not represented as arbitrary, nor invisible. Instead, she stated quite clearly:

> 'I have definitely been helped. I am not a bad scholar, because I guess there would be no point in helping me if I was. But I guess someone needs to get involved, to personally make an effort. And I was very lucky to have that. First for my PhD, and then also for my postdoc. But, then it was also a matter of luck. I was the right person at the right place at the right time. And someone saw that. So, skills, help and luck, basically.' (Berit)

The striking contrast between this story and the two previous excerpts of the men's narrative is the distribution of agency in creating a career. Whilst Are and Børre both narrate their career starting from issues of their individual agency – purposeful or lucky – centre stage, Berit highlights the relational aspect, and the crucial helpers she has had. In her story Berit responds to a potential sense that being helped implies one is somehow incapable. But she regarded the fact that "someone" had decided to make an effort on her behalf as a confirmation of being a good scholar. The way Berit narrated her story resembles an element central to several narratives, namely 'being seen and supported' by someone in power.

This was also the case for Agnes. In her story, the supervisor was an important figure: "In my experience, my supervisor really wanted me to continue, even though they did not have the money to fund further research. I have the impression that if they really want to keep you, there are ways." These quotes reference a combination of hard work and dependence on people in power for 'finding ways' to support one's career. In our material, both women and men told stories about being supported as part of how they had succeeded in academe. However, there was a gendered difference in these narratives about support, in the sense that the women more explicitly articulated and highlighted this as a significant factor, whereas more of the men tended to downplay any direct dependence on others – as we saw in

Børre's story, who narrated the same kind of circumstances in an altogether more passive way when explaining how he was "offered a PhD position, and didn't have any other job offer at the time, and then we received funding for further research so I could continue into a postdoc". Both instances, however, echo the statement by Henriette, the postdoc quoted at the beginning of this text: "It doesn't feel like that is something one can just choose to do."

A striking feature across the stories about opting for a career in academe was that the general idea of what a professor is, portrayed across the narratives, was construed as less desirable, and not compatible with pursuing one's research interests as the main motivation. This might seem surprising, given a general notion of the supposed desirability of achieving higher ranks. However, for these early career researchers, pursuing a professorship seemed to be a consequence of wanting a permanent position, rather than a goal in its own right.

"If you want to live a balanced life, it is difficult to become a professor"

When we asked explicitly about career aspirations and expectations it quickly became evident that the most important threshold was having a permanent position. Becoming a professor was expressed as a rather reluctant ambition. This is illustrated in the exchange between Berit and Børre:

> 'I want to see a future in academia, that, I mean you have to kind of decide to pursue a permanent position because living on these temporarily contracts never knowing when you will get work again, that is not really a good way of living. So I have to say that my ambitions in the end have to be to become a professor. Even though I don't want to say that I want to become a professor, but that seems like the option. Because you can't say that my main goal in life is to become an associate professor. That's not valid in a way to, to say that, to stop there.' (Berit)

The idea of a predictable future seemed to be the rationale behind pursuing a professorship in Berit's narrative. Børre responded: "If you want to be a professor you have to sacrifice a lot of things. I think if you want to live a balanced life, it is difficult to become a professor." Berit quickly followed up on Børre's claim about this required sacrifice:

> 'I agree. I don't have a family, I have my job and my partner and a dog and a cat, and it is hard enough to balance them with the type of academic work that we do. You become your career in a way. If I am to become a professor, that is not just my job, that's my identity.

> And to separate those things I can easily see myself not managing that very well.' (Berit)

'Sacrificing things' did not merely seem to be about time or effort; rather, the idea of pursuing an academic career was linked to identity. The quotes show how it seemed impossible to keep work and life separate if one was to be a professor, and this merging of work and life was portrayed as so comprehensive that there was no room for anything but work – work becomes everything, so to speak, in the expectations expressed by these early career researchers. Bringing it down to personal desires and expectations, it seemed more difficult to envision a work-life balance as something that could be reconciled with becoming a professor.

Several of the postdocs who were not sure if they wanted to pursue an academic career talked about conflicts regarding the investments necessary to succeed. They talked about time as a scarce resource, that it was too time-consuming to do high-quality – or in many cases – high-quantity ('enough papers') research to succeed in academia, if one wanted more in life, either a family or to pursue other, non-academic activities. They also talked about time in the sense of life course, particularly in relation to starting a family and having children. Hilde expressed it like this:

> 'There is something about having children in parallel with building your career, both in terms of time-management, but also – at least I think it influences my self-confidence. There is something about that feeling of being stuck at home with the laundry, while others travel to conferences and write up their articles. It is just as if it creates a self-fulfilling prophecy in a system where you are supposed to brand yourself as the person who is willing to go "all in"'. (Hilde)

Hilde's comments made it clear that if one could not see oneself mainly as an academic, the risk of losing self-confidence was very present and explicitly linked to a feeling of not living up to a perceived expectation of going "all in". Housework – the laundry – represents the counterpart to academic work and career advancement in this story.

"Being stuck at home"

Being "stuck at home" was also a concern with regard to the issue of international mobility in several interviews. Typically, mobility was on the one hand presented as an opportunity that would potentially open up new possibilities in academia, and on the other hand as a problem when the early career researchers or their family members (partner, children) did not want to relocate. Agnes explained:

> 'My contract now is for one more year. I really want to continue in academia as long as possible. But I have a daughter that is in school, and a husband with a permanent position here. The focus on mobility is really strong, so I guess it would be possible for me to get a position somewhere, but when your family is here and they don't want to go elsewhere, it is hard.' (Agnes)

The conflict between family commitments and mobility as a requirement for pursuing an academic career was not only expressed by the women taking part in our study. Harald expressed a similar frustration related to short-term mobility and travel requirements:

> 'It is difficult to balance it all, when conferences are taking place at weekends, and you have to work late nights, and then taking care of your kids. I was actually supposed to be at a conference right now, I really should have, but I can't since my wife is on a job trip abroad at the moment, all the traveling makes it difficult.' (Harald)

Several of the men in our study expressed similar concerns for balancing family responsibilities with their work as a researcher. Common to all of them, however, was that they talked about a partner equally committed to their career, and how they adapted to that – implicitly presenting themselves as gender-equal spouses. Women in our study, on the contrary, tended to narrate their own agency in planning family and career, implicitly taking the responsibility for 'being equal'. Henriette explained how she deliberately planned ahead and made sure to have a longer research stay abroad before she had children:

> 'I had my stay abroad before I had children. I made that choice consciously, because I knew you have to go abroad, and I knew I wanted to have children. Of course, the stay was beneficial in many ways, but I have to admit that I did it mainly to "tick the box"'. (Henriette)

The timing of having children became a topic in most of the interviews, here illustrated by an exchange between Agnes and Are:

> 'You really cannot wait until you have reached professor level to have kids, because by then you might be 45 or 50. It will be too late to have kids, at least for women.' (Agnes)

> 'That is true, but then it is a bit like as if I, as a man, could be expected to be 40 and successful and then find a much younger partner to start a family. I don't find that right either.' (Are)

In this dialogue, we can see how gendered perceptions of age and prioritizing family and children are challenged by expectations regarding academic careers. Prioritizing family is first portrayed, implicitly, as optional for men who can pursue their career first, and thereafter family. Implicit in this dialogue are heteronormative stereotypes of age difference and status difference between heterosexual partners. Are challenges this idea by arguing that the same problematic is also relevant for men. The orientation towards gender-equal relations expressed both by Harald and Are is significant as it paves the way for an allegiance between women and men in creating liveable lives in academia. Equally important to note is the fact that the women in our study talked about how they adapted to and assessed themselves according to assumed work standards and gendered constraints that are embedded in understandings of personal choice (Gascoigne et al, 2015; Sørensen, 2017).

"When you've already invested a lot, it is hard to let go"

Despite the fact that becoming a professor was associated with great sacrifice, and many of the early career researchers explicitly stated that they were not pursuing an academic career in order to become a professor, they also explained that they had already invested so much time and effort in their academic career that it was difficult to imagine leaving academia. This dynamic has been labelled a 'trap of passion' and 'promise dispositif' (Bozzon et al, 2019). The following conversation took place between Hilde, Henriette and Harald:

> 'I have been willing to live on temporary contracts because I have already invested so much, both time and energy in this work, and I don't want to let go of that.' (Harald)

> 'I agree, it is such a huge choice to make to give up, to let go of the idea that one day I will be sitting there, looking out.' (Hilde)

Here a sense of purpose as the motivation for staying in academia becomes self-fulfilling through the way in which Harald explains why he has put up with years on temporary research contracts. Letting go, giving up, suggests being defeated, while the idea of "sitting there, looking out [from the ivory tower]" indicates victory and satisfaction.

It was not only the individual defeat or victory that mattered in the postdocs' narratives. Henriette commented: "Sometimes I think that it is such a waste if the knowledge I have accumulated just disappears from the university." The underlying sense of purpose here relates to the efforts of the university as a collective, rather than the individual career. Hilde added: "A frustrating thing about not getting hold of a permanent position is also the fact that you have to keep giving, without getting anything in return. At the end of the day, your voice doesn't count." Implicit in this statement is the longing for a position with the authority to be listened to. Interestingly, having a permanent position was constructed as the relevant threshold for achieving this status, not 'becoming a professor'. Thus, the sense of purpose and genuine interest in the research in itself was entangled with a desire for getting a reward for one's efforts, and the end of precariousness seemed to be the most desirable reward.

Assembling academic career choices: discussion and concluding remarks

In this chapter our main interest has been to explore how early career researchers perceive their agency and possibilities for pursuing an academic career. By analyzing qualitative interviews with postdocs employed at the largest university in Norway, we explored how early career researchers reflect upon their potential future within academia and how their experiences and expectations were potentially gendered.

Focusing first on the postdocs' reflections about their own experiences when entering academia and being early career researchers, we found what we labelled a narrative about having the right skills and motivation, being supported *and* fortunate (lucky). This finding reinforces the notion that careers in academia are difficult to plan (Riordan, 2011). This narrative was articulated across the gender divide, but the notion of being supported turned out to be more strongly expressed by the women interviewees. In the stories presented by the men the efforts of others were more implicit, and rarely explicitly highlighted. Our interpretation of this is that even though both men and women to a great extent depend on active support to succeed in making an academic career, the narrative of 'being helped' is subtly gendered.

The main narrative about having the right skills and motivation as well as being supported and fortunate included elements of a sense of finding a purpose in research. Others too have found that academics tend to express great personal passion for their job, and that they tend to appreciate autonomy, independence and opportunities for individual self-expression (Lindholm, 2004; Loveday, 2018; Murgia and Poggio, 2019). On the other hand career-coaching models emphasizing community building and collective support has been developed as a supplement to traditional research mentoring to support minority academics. Evaluations of such schemes suggest that collective career mentoring, informed by social theory, can promote persistence in pursuing academic careers (Thakore et al, 2014; Williams et al, 2016).

Our study indicates that career mentoring should, however, include not only theoretical insights about gender and diversity, and peer solidarity, but should also aim to open up knowledge about varieties of experiences of becoming and being a professor (see also Ylijoki, 2013). We argue this as the ideas about what a professor is, and what it entails to be a professor, played a crucial role in how the postdocs made sense of their own choices. A strong perception of being a professor as an all-consuming endeavour left the early career scholars with a sense of being incapable, and 'stuck' in life outside of the university. This was true for both women and men. However, while women to a greater extent talked about taking active agency and planning strategically to fulfil the requirements of international mobility, the men's stories revolved around negotiating family concerns with an equally committed spouse. Again, the gendered perceptions of the obstacles were subtly gendered.

Becoming a professor was explicitly discussed as something unattractive, and involved a narrative of sacrifice, overwork and multiple responsibilities, a situation that the early career scholars found undesirable. Nevertheless, becoming a professor was also and simultaneously portrayed as an obligatory career goal, due to the fact that academics who have the possibility of becoming a professor are likely to have invested much time and energy into the process leading up to it. This means that a trap between passion and overwork, as discussed by Bozzon et al (2019), was also implied in the narratives of these Norwegian early career researchers. Embedded in the narrative of becoming a professor was a strong perception of a permanent position as the threshold that could potentially resolve stress and ambiguity.

In contrast to the ideas circulating among early career researchers, professors at the same university regard academia as flexible and adjustable to family needs. Our understanding of this discrepancy is that the shift from precariousness to predictability that comes with a professorship is of crucial importance to how both work within, and life outside of, academia is made sense of. This discrepancy needs to be acknowledged in future work to promote a gender balance. Furthermore, the inherent and often subtle ways in which gender works in how early career researchers make sense of their career need to be discussed more openly in order to support early career scholars and promote a better gender balance.

References

Armano, E. and Murgia, A. (2013) 'The precariousnesses of young knowledge workers: a subject-oriented approach', *Global Discourse*, 3(3–4): 486–501.

Bakhtin, M. (1981) *The Dialogic Imagination: Four Essays*. Trans. M. Holquist and C. Emerson. M. Holdquist (ed), Austin: University of Texas Press.

Bataille P., Le Feuvre, N. and Kradolfer Morales, S. (2017) 'Should I stay or should I go? The effects of precariousness on the gendered career aspirations of postdocs in Switzerland', *European Educational Research Journal*, 16(2–3): 313–31. DOI:10.1177/1474904116673372.

Benschop Y., van den Brink M., Doorewaard, H. and Leenders, J. (2013) 'Discourses of ambition, gender and part-time work', *Human Relations*, 66(5): 699–723. DOI:10.1177/0018726712466574.

Bozzon, R., Murgia, A. and Poggio, B. (2019) 'Gender and precarious careers in academia and research: macro, memo and micro perspectives', in A. Murgia and B. Poggio (eds) *Gender and Precarious Research Careers: A Comparative Analysis*, London: Routledge, pp 15–49.

Brandser, G. and Sümer, S. (2017) 'Kjønnsbalanse i akademiske toppstillinger: med blikk for brytninger og nye muligheter' ['Gender balance in academic top positions: focus on change and new opportunities'], *Tidsskrift for kjønnsforskning*, 1(41): 22–38. DOI: 10.18261/issn.1891-1781-2017-01-03.

Braun, V. and Clarke, V. (2013) *Successful Qualitative Research: A Practical Guide for Beginners*, London: Sage.

Frank, A. (2012) 'Practicing dialogical narrative analysis', in J.A. Holstein and J.F. Gubrium (eds) *Varieties of Narrative Analysis*, Thousand Oaks, CA: Sage, pp 33–52. DOI: 10.4135/9781506335117.n3.

Frølich, N., Wendt, K., Reymert, I., Tellmann, S.M., Elken, M., Kyvik, S., Vabø, A. and Larsen, A. (2018) *Academic Career Structures in Europe: Perspectives from Norway, Denmark, Sweden, Finland, the Netherlands, Austria and the UK*. Report 2018: 4, Oslo: Nordic Institute for Studies in Innovation, Research and Education (NIFU).

Gascoigne, C., Parry, E. and Buchanan, D. (2015) 'Extreme work, gendered work? How extreme jobs and the discourse of "personal choice" perpetuate gender inequality', *Organization*, 22(4): 457–75.

Inkson, K., Gunz, H., Ganesh, S. and Roper, J. (2012) 'Boundaryless careers: bringing back boundaries', *Organization Studies*, 33(3): 323–40. DOI: 10.1177/0170840611435600.

Kwiek, M. and Antonowicz, D. (2015) 'The changing paths in academic careers in European universities: minor steps and majore milestones', in T. Fumasoli, G. Goastellec and B. Kehm (eds) *Academic Work and Careers in Europe: Trends, Challenges, Perspectives*, Dordrecht: Springer, pp 41–68.

Kyvik, S. (2015) 'The academic career system in Norway', in M. Yudkevich, P.G. Altbach and L.E. Rumbley (eds) *Young Faculty in the 21st Century: International Perspectives*, New York: Suny Press, pp 173–200.

Lagesen, V.A. (2007) 'The strength of numbers: strategies to include women into computer science', *Social Studies of Science*, 37(1): 67–92. DOI:10.1177/0306312706063788.

Lagesen, V.A., Pettersen, I. and Berg, L. (2021) 'Inclusion of women to ICT engineering: lessons learned', *European Journal of Engineering Education*. DOI: 10.1080/03043797.2021.1983774.

Le Feuvre, N., Bataille, P., Kradolfer, S., Carral, M.R and Sautier, M. (2018) 'The gendered diversification of academic career paths in comparative perspective', in A. Murgia and B. Poggio (eds) *Gender and Precarious Research Careers: A Comparative Analysis*, London: Routledge, pp 50–80.

Lindholm, J.A. (2004) 'Pathways to the professoriate: the role of self, others, and environment in shaping academic career aspirations', *The Journal of Higher Education*, 75(6): 603–35.

Loveday, V. (2018) 'Luck, chance, and happenstance? Perceptions of success and failure amongst fixed-term academic staff in UK higher education', *The British Journal of Sociology*, 69(3): 758–72.

Lund, R.W.B. (2020) 'The social organisation of boasting in the neoliberal university', *Gender and Education*, 32(4): 466–85. DOI: 10.1080/09540253.2018.1482412.

Murgia, A. and Poggio, B. (eds) (2019) *Gender and Precarious Research Careers: A Comparative Analysis*, London: Routledge.

Næss, T., Gunnes, H. and Wendt, K. (2018) 'Likestilling blant professorene' ['Equity among professors'], *NIFU Arbeidsnotat*, 2018: 1. Oslo: NIFU. Available at: www.nifu.no/publications/1560591/, accessed 30 March 2021.

Olsen, T.B., Kyvik, S. and Hovdhaugen, E. (2005) 'The promotion to full professor: through competition or by individual competence?', *Tertiary Education and Management*, 11: 299–316. DOI: 10.1007/s11233-005-0981-6.

Reuben, E., Sapienza, P. and Zingales, L. (2014) 'How stereotypes impair women's careers in science', *Proceedings of the National Academy of Sciences*, 111(12): 4403–08. DOI: 10.1073/pnas.1314788111.

Riessman, C.K. (2008) *Narrative Methods for the Human Sciences*, Thousand Oaks, CA: Sage.

Riordan, S. (2011) 'Paths to success in senior management', in B. Bagilhole and K. White (eds) *Gender, Power and Management*, London: Palgrave Macmillan, pp 110–130. DOI: 10.1057/9780230305953_6.

Søndergaard, D.M. (2005) 'Making sense of gender, age, power and disciplinary position: intersecting discourses in the academy', *Feminism & Psychology*, 15(2): 189–208. DOI:10.1177/0959353505051728.

Sørensen, S.Ø. (2016) 'Karrierekvinne og mor: Et kulturanalytisk blikk på kombinasjonslivets balansekrav' ['Career woman and mother: a cultural analytical perspective on the expected ability to combine two ideals'], in M.N. Ravn, G.K. Kristensen and S.Ø. Sørensen (eds) *Reproduksjon, kjønn og likestilling i dagens Norge*, Oslo: Fagbokforlaget, pp 39–52.

Sørensen, S.Ø. (2017) 'The performativity of choice: postfeminist perspectives on work–life balance', *Gender, Work & Organization*, 24: 297–313. DOI: 10.1111/gwao.12163.

Sørensen, S.Ø., Lagesen, V.A., Sørensen, K.H. and Kristensen, G.K. (2019) 'Kjønnsbalanse gjennom aksjonsforskning og lokal kunnskaping' ['Gender balance through action research and local knowledge production'], *Tidsskrift for kjønnsforskning*, 43(2): 108–27. DOI: 10.18261/issn.1891-1781-2019-02-04.

Suboticki, I., Lagesen, V.A. and Unander, T.E. (2021) *En kartlegging og evaluering av tre kjønnsbalansetiltak ved NTNU: Startpakker, kvalifiseringsstipend og mentorprogram* [*A Mapping and Evaluation of Three Gender Balance Measures at NTNU: Starting Grants, Qualification Grants and Mentor Programs*], Trondheim: NTNU Report. Available at: https://docplayer.me/215207665-En-kartlegging-og-evaluering-av-tre-kjonnsbalansetiltak-ved-ntnu.html, accessed 25 January 2022.

Sutherland, K. (2018) *Early Career Academics in New Zealand: Challenges and Prospects in Comparative Perspective*, Wellington, New Zealand: Springer International Publishing.

Thakore, B.K., Naffziger-Hirsch, M.E., Richardson, J.L., Williams, S.N. and McGee, R. Jr. (2014) 'The academy for future science faculty: randomized controlled trial of theory-driven coaching to shape development and diversity of early-career scientists', *BMC Medical Education*, 14: 160.

Thun, C. (2020) 'Excellent and gender equal? Academic motherhood and "gender blindness" in Norwegian academia', *Gender, Work & Organization*, 27(2): 166–80. DOI: 10.1111/gwao.12368.

Toffoletti, K. and Starr, K. (2016) 'Women academics and work–life balance: gendered discourses of work and care', *Gender, Work & Organization*, 23: 489–504. DOI: 10.1111/gwao.12133.

Tregenza, T. (2002) 'Gender bias in the refereeing process?', *Trends in Ecology & Evolution*, 17(8): 349–50. DOI: 10.1016/S0169-5347(02)02545-4.

Wendt, K. (2019) *She Figures 2018 – hun teller: Presentasjon av hovedfunn* [*She Figures 2018 – She Counts: Presentation of Main Findings*]. Available at: http://kifinfo.no/nb/kjonnsbalanse-i-forskning-hun-teller, accessed 30 March 2021.

Williams, S.N., Thakore, B.K. and McGee, R. (2016) 'Coaching to augment mentoring to achieve faculty diversity: a randomized controlled trial', *Academic Medicine: Journal of the Association of American Medical Colleges*, 91(8): 1128–35. DOI: 10.1097/ACM.0000000000001026.

Ylijoki, O.-H. (2013) 'Boundary-work between work and life in the high-speed university', *Studies in Higher Education*, 38(2): 242–55. DOI: 10.1080/03075079.2011.577524.

Yudkevich, M., Altbach, P.G. and Rumbley, L.E. (eds) (2015) *Young Faculty in the 21st Century: International Perspectives*, New York: SUNY Press.

9

"If It Had Been Only Me, It Would Not Have Worked Out": Women Negotiating Conflicting Challenges of ICT Work and Family in Norway

Gilda Seddighi and Hilde G. Corneliussen

Introduction

This chapter centres on women working in information and communication technology (ICT), a male-dominated profession that continues to imagine the ideal worker according to the male norm of having little or no childcare responsibility. There is a well-established assumption that Norway is a 'world champion in gender equality' (Selbervik and Østebø, 2013: 205). However, despite family-friendly policies in the country, women struggle to reconcile work and care responsibilities (Kitterød and Halrynjo, 2019). How do women who work in ICT in Norway's gender egalitarian culture find the resources to negotiate the contradictory demands of work and family? In Norway, as elsewhere across the western world, most fields of ICT work are still male-dominated. Women make up only 25 per cent of those studying and working in ICT in Norway (Samordna opptak, 2018; Statistics Norway, 2018; Simonsen and Corneliussen, 2020). Despite the fact that digitalization is changing the landscape of ICT work and increasing the need for ICT expertise in general, women's under-representation in ICT has remained persistent (EIGE, 2020).

Family-oriented national policies in Norway such as flexible and long parental leave and a generous childcare system aim to increase women's participation in the workforce and to support their career development (Seierstad and Kirton, 2015). Although women make up 47 per cent of the workforce (Statistics Norway, 2018), traditional gender norms locating women as the primary family caregiver are still common (Seierstad and Kirton, 2015). Family-friendly policies have contributed to the increase in women's participation in the workforce and helped them return to work earlier following parental leave, but have also been criticized for not being beneficial to women's career development (Kitterød and Halrynjo, 2019). Unequal gendered divisions of labour in care and household responsibilities remain barriers to career development in the greedy work culture of ICT (Quesenberry et al, 2006; Bailey and Riley, 2018; EIGE, 2020). This is a matter not only of finding ways to make time for work and family, but also of navigating gendered work cultures and norms such as around parenthood (Ellingsæter, 2006; Hakim, 2006; Bø et al, 2008).

A recent European study found that women in ICT experience more flexible working conditions and a smaller pay gap than in other fields, but they also work longer hours, and a lower proportion have childcare responsibilities compared to women in other occupations (EIGE, 2018). In addition, fewer women in ICT work part-time as compared to other occupations (Simonsen and Corneliussen, 2020). These features indicate a double pressure on women, as they try to care as well as fit into a male-dominated field and style of work that favours men as ideal workers (Acker, 1990; Watts, 2009; Singstad, 2011). The specific context of ICT work in Norway, recognized for its progressive welfare regime and a high degree of gender equality, highlights the need to investigate how women working in ICT find the resources to reconcile family and work responsibilities while pursuing their career.

This chapter is based on interviews with 22 women working full-time in ICT research, development and innovation in Norway. Our findings suggest that the boundary-less work culture of ICT makes family-oriented national policies less relevant, while private resources are central to women's negotiation of the contradictory demands of work and care. We also found that the gendered patterns of work and family are being re-gendered, but without challenging work cultures that discriminate against women more than men (Padavic et al, 2019). Most importantly, our analysis reveals the need to take a critical view of the work-life balance discourse, as responsibility for creating this 'balance' tends to be given to the individual (Gregory and Milner, 2009). Taking such a critical view is important for policymakers' understanding of the economic and social structures that enable or restrict women's opportunities for careers in male-dominated fields such as ICT.

We begin with a literature review before presenting this study's theoretical and methodological framework. Following on from that, the chapter turns to the analysis of the women's accounts of the resources they use in reconciling work and family responsibilities. This will be discussed in terms of the shortcomings of public childcare and how family is able or unable to step in to cover these shortcomings.

Sources of negotiating the work-life balance for women working in ICT

The term 'work-life balance' has been defined as 'the relationship between the institutional and cultural times and spaces of work and non-work in societies where income is predominantly generated and distributed through labour markets' (Felstead et al, 2002: 56). It is a dominant discourse in policies seeking to increase women's workforce participation and improve conditions for them to pursue careers (OECD, 2007). As scholars have argued, achieving a work-life balance needs different levels of support, namely national policies, workplace policies and private support (Abendroth and den Dulk, 2011).

Norway, along with other Nordic countries, is often seen as a frontrunner with regards to gender equality, especially in terms of family-friendly policies aimed at supporting the reconciliation between work and family life (Öun, 2012). Family-friendly policies have a long tradition in the Nordic countries. They are 'part of the general social-democratic model of welfare emphasising economic growth, redistribution of wealth, social rights and social security' (Björnberg, 2016: 508). Norway often scores high in the international indexes (Chzhen et al, 2019), especially for its flexible parental leave (Rudlende and Bryghaug, 2017), paternal quota leave (Gram, 2019) and the extension of kindergarten access to one-to-two-year-old children. These policies have been established to increase women's participation in the workforce as well as to strengthen fathers' roles and engagement in care responsibilities (Brandth and Kvande, 2005; Kitterød and Halrynjo, 2019).

Despite these policies, the number of women who work part-time has remained high and is currently 37 per cent of employed women compared to 13 per cent of employed men (Statistics Norway, 2018). The statistics indicate a similar pattern observed across member states in the EU where on average one third of employed women work part-time (Eurostat, 2020). Although women's high participation in the workforce in Norway at 68 per cent (Statistics Norway, 2018) indicates the success of these national policies, the national policies for childcare have had little impact on mothers' career development (Halrynjo and Lyng, 2010; Johnsen and Løken, 2016). Studies suggest that fathers' career preferences are prioritized over those of the mother while mothers take the main care responsibilities (Halrynjo and Lyng, 2010).

Work-life balance policies in workplaces often refer to flexible working conditions and the management of time and place of work (Fleetwood, 2007; Lewis et al, 2007), implying that this balance relies on individual choice (Gregory and Milner, 2009). Controversially, Hakim suggests that women and men tend to choose different career paths, with women being drawn towards jobs that 'can be fitted around family life' (2006: 285). Focussing on a vocabulary of choice in her discussion of women's reconciliation of work and family life in Norwegian media, Sørensen (2017) identifies three subject positions for women: 'the part-time working, good mother' opting out of work; 'the exceptional career mother' who aims to have it all, both children and a career; and 'the failing mother', who also aims to have it all, but faces accusations of failing at motherhood. Sørensen (2017: 310) argues that invoking the vocabulary of choice here not only covers up power structures (McRobbie, 2009), it also produces differences and inequalities.

Pedersen and Egeland (2020) show that parents with flexible working hours who have to solve work-care conflicts during work hours catch up with their work in the late evenings or over weekends. Critical studies on work-life balance policies show that they make work-life balance issues appear to rely on individual choice while in actuality these issues are constrained by gender norms (Gregory and Milner, 2009) and thus do not challenge well-established structures such as gendered work cultures (Chung and Van der Lippe, 2018). In another study on women in high-commitment careers, Seierstad and Kirton (2015) found that flexible work conditions did not mean less work for the participants of their study; rather, it was a matter of adapting work to the family situation and vice versa. For mothers with flexible working hours, adapting their work to their family situation put more pressure on care responsibilities as these women are often the primary caregiver.

Research on working life in Norway has also shown that employees in some sectors such as ICT experience a greedy or boundary-less work culture where standard, full-time work is not enough (Brandth and Kvande, 2005; Nilsen and Skarsbø, 2009). In the male-dominated fields of ICT (Watts, 2009), where the need to continuously upskill is a precondition for a successful career (EIGE, 2018: 3), work cultures imagine the 'ideal worker' (Acker, 1990) as one who prioritizes work over care responsibilities (Williams, 2000), something men embody more than women (Singstad, 2011). As several studies have suggested, women in ICT work more than women in many other occupations (Watts, 2009; EIGE, 2018). Watts' (2009) study of women in engineering within the UK construction industry shows that women working full-time adopt work styles that include long hours, as they perceive this as necessary for acceptance in the workplace. Flexible working conditions in boundary-less work cultures mean that the boundaries between work time and private time, workplace and private space become blurred and intensify the challenges of negotiating between work and family time, for women more so than for men (Zerwas, 2019).

Interestingly enough, the women in Seierstad and Kirton's (2015: 401) study did not want more formal work–life balance policies, but rather a change of 'workplace culture to one where both women's and men's domestic responsibilities were more fully acknowledged'. In a Finnish context, Heikkinen et al (2014: 32–6) investigated how women managers experience the support given by their male partners and identified four ways in which spousal support of women's careers was constructed: harmoniously flourishing, irrelevant, deficient and inconsistent. It was only when the spousal support was consistent and included practical and psychological support, that this positively influenced the women's careers.

The flexible work arrangement in ICT might appear as an advantage for women as the focus of work-life balance policies has been on employees' autonomy and flexible working time and place. But women's work arrangement also hides the potential double pressure as women have main care responsibilities as well as trying to fit into a style of work that favours men as ideal workers. The double pressure remains invisible as the responsibility of achieving a work-life balance is left to the individual, while the gendered work culture is left untouched.

Theoretical framework

Some scholars critique the concept of work-life balance because it implies that work and life are two separate spheres (Warhurst et al, 2008). Others have argued that 'balance' in work and life has become a neoliberal postfeminist discourse that has produced a new feminist subject of autonomous and freely choosing individuals, searching for a balance to deal with the conflicting demands of work and family (Rottenberg, 2018). Women's investment in their sense of self has increasingly included mothering and the private space of life (Hays, 1996) as well as work (Rottenberg, 2018). Feminist technology studies have shown that across the western world cultures and stereotypes tend to associate men with ICT work more than women (Wajcman, 2004; Corneliussen, 2014). Watts' (2009) study suggests that gender stereotypes in ICT work culture are largely accepted. In this context, the concept of negotiation refers to women's attempts to overcome the competing demands and practices of work and family life while imagining a 'balanced' work-family life, that is, 'having it all'.

In Norway this negotiation includes an established idea of the dual-earner household (Melby and Carlsson Wetterberg, 2009; Singstad, 2011), though men as the main earner are still the norm (Elingsæter, 2006). Work practices create expectations favouring men (Acker, 1990) as the 'ideal worker' who prioritizes work over care responsibilities (Williams, 2000). Despite policies aimed at increasing men's participation in care responsibilities (Kitterød and Rønsen, 2012), the combination of the dual-earner household and this 'ideal worker' has created a pattern of a 'two-track parenthood': one track for mothers often taking long parental leave and part-time work, and another for men regardless of whether or not they have children (Ellingsæter, 2006; Bø et al, 2008). Focussing on how full-time working women with care responsibilities reconcile work and family, we look closer at how the negotiation of work and care responsibility in relation to a two-track parenthood model results in a 're-doing' of gender norms (West and

Zimmerman, 1987) associated with this two-track model, not by changing the model itself but by changing women and men's positions in the model. Compared to 'undoing' gender norms, which results in these norms losing their importance in social interactions (cf. Hirschauer, 2001), the concept of re-doing refers to social practices enacted in new ways but still with reference to the prevailing gender norms and values (Kelan, 2010).

Methodology

Interviews with women working in ICT

The data presented here are part of a larger dataset of 28 interviews we conducted in 2017–18. We recruited women working in ICT in the western region of Norway through organizations working with regional innovation, ICT development, research and funding agencies, as well as public and private companies. The 22 interviews analyzed were all with women who had childcare responsibilities. Fourteen of these women were born in Norway and eight women had immigrated to Norway due to work or higher education. The women were aged between 37 and 59. They had between one and four children. Some women also have children from several relationships. Thus, our participants represented a variety of heterosexual family constellations.

The selection criteria for the participants included: having at least a Bachelor degree, and diversity in terms of women working in the fields of ICT in different sectors and industries, as we recognize that digitalization is changing the landscape of ICT work. One interviewee had a Bachelor degree, seven had PhDs, and the rest had Master's degrees. Nine had degrees in ICT. These women worked in different fields of ICT, in management, design, programming, research, and implementation of new technology. Thirteen interviewees acquired ICT competence by combining an ICT education within a non-technical education, or training and upskilling combined with a non-technical profession. The latter women worked with ICT in a non-tech profession in positions including management, design, programming and implementation of new technology.

Our interviews lasted around one hour and followed an interview guide with a professional-life history structure, with questions about family, education, occupational history, career drivers, barriers and work-family arrangements.

The fieldwork gained ethical approval from the Norwegian Centre for Research Data and we followed their rules for data security. The informants were invited to participate voluntarily. In order to make the research process transparent for the informants, we told them about the project's aim before the interviews. The informants gave informed written consent to use the interview data in subsequent publications. The interview data were transcribed verbatim and anonymized.

Analytical framework

Our initial analytical encounter with the empirical material was through a grounded theory-inspired process, reading and coding the interviews while writing analytic texts, or 'memos' to further our analysis. Since this is part of a larger project, this was a rather open-ended process in which the coding resulted in the building of relevant categories. These categories were explored and developed around labels we identified in the analysis such as work, leisure and family. Key labels for this chapter were family, enablers, barriers, opting out and work-life balance.

Analysis

> 'Establishing a family, managing that, you could call it a barrier, but it was also a choice. It was completely voluntary'. (Gunn, late 30s)

The women in our study mentioned family both as a great support and as a barrier to their career though they described it as a conscious choice, as Gunn, one of the women in study, did in the aforementioned quote. Dual-earner parents experience time constraints in negotiating family and work duties. This is a result of specific working life structures and family policy schemes, and norms and values related to childcare and operating in the workplace (Hayes, 1996; Pedersen and Egeland, 2020). This is even more strongly experienced by women working in greedy work cultures (Hakim, 2006; Padavic et al, 2019) and male-dominated fields (Singstad, 2011). The relation between work and family entered the interviews most notably when we asked about barriers and drivers for career development. In this section we discuss how the women found resources to negotiate the conundrum of work and life when public childcare was not enough. This will be discussed in terms of how family was able or unable to step in and cover for these shortcomings.

The shortcomings of public childcare

The national work-life balance policies in Norway such as flexible parental leave, paternal quota leave and day nurseries for all children over one year old, are intended to regulate the conflicting demands of care and work experienced by women. Women in our study often took family-friendly policies for granted, and rarely talked about childcare services. When childcare services were mentioned, it was in relation to how the women arranged their working hours to leave and pick up children. As one of the participants put it: "Because I'm commuting, it is my husband who picks up and delivers in school and kindergarten every day" (Stine, 30s).

These women experienced a conflict between their working hours and the opening hours of the childcare service. This is in line with earlier research on daily family life in Norway (Pedersen and Egeland, 2020). Though picking up and leaving the children in childcare services needs planning, it was working odd hours that created the conflict between care and work responsibilities. Many participants described working odd hours such as in the evening and at weekends, in addition to being away due to work-related commuting and travelling. As Mari, one of the women, explained: "I worked very hard at the start of my career. I had small children but worked after they slept."

Many women in our study had taken part in training, Master's courses and upskilling, a crucial requirement in the fields of ICT as well as for one's career development. Ruth, one of the women in our study, described this as follows:

> 'I could not have attended a Master's degree or other courses I have taken, if it had not been for the support of my family and my husband. When I started the Master's degree in another city which was quite far away, the children were living at home at that time. If you have children, you need to have support and to know that it is okay that you are leaving and staying away from them for a week.' (Ruth, late 40s)

Since childcare services do not cover the needs of these women, the women had to find other solutions to deal with their childcare issues. Some described the work-life balance as a situation in which they took on *less* care responsibilities for family and children. This narrative challenged the two-track parenthood model where the mother is supposed to take the main responsibility. Like Sørensen's (2017) 'failing (career) mothers', these women probably risked being perceived as prioritizing their career and failing at motherhood. However, in their (non-judgemental) narratives (different from the judgemental tendency in the media discourses Sørensen analyzed), women described how they were dependent on other support. As one of our participants said: "If it had been only me, it would not have worked out" (Laila, 40s).

Unlike Sørensen's 'exceptional mothers' who bought support in the form of cleaners and au pairs, only one of the women in our study mentioned domestic help. Instead, their male partners took on the childcare responsibilities:

> 'Fortunately I had a man that used to do at least as much I used to do at home.' (Mari, 40s)

> 'My husband was very good at staying home. He has helped out there, and he is still the one making dinner at home. He has taken that over

> more and more, and now I don't even know what we're having for dinner.' (Ellen, 50s)

Among our interviewees, there were also examples of dual-career couples who both had greedy careers. In these cases, support from other close relatives was needed to help supplement the care for family and children, such as the women's parents: "My husband also has a demanding job. He is travelling and away a lot as well, and then we have my mother and father. … My father, he is still working, but he is working from home. He is looking after them [the children] a lot" (Laila, 40s).

The aforementioned examples involve two generations of dual-career couples and a grandfather solving work-life challenges, thanks to work arrangements that make him available for the children. However, this example is different from Pedersen and Egeland's study (2020) showing how grandparents contribute by helping to unburden families' everyday lives in relation to care, as here the grandparents contributed by making an intensive work culture possible.

Among our interviewees, aside from one case of a male partner who became a stay-at-home dad to support his wife's career, it was not the women's *flexible* working practices that helped, but something different: their partners had stable work positions with flexible and predictable hours and little or no work-related travel. Ellen, one participant, described her partner's work pattern as follows: "My husband has not changed his job much. He has not had jobs where he had to travel. If he also had a job where he had to travel a lot, things would have been much more difficult. He was always at home" (Ellen, 50s).

For our participants, it was not only the partners with flexible working hours who dropped off and picked up children from school that solved work and care conflicts, it was also the husbands who did not travel much and were available out of office hours, and the fathers who took extra leave. The women interviewed here identified their partners' flexible working hours as a support, so long as the work remained within and did not exceed either standard work times or a standard number of hours. Here men take on conventionally feminine roles of child- and other domestic care, thereby re-gendering care work and their role in the household. This happened only when the male partners had flexible and predictable working hours and used this to take on more care responsibilities at home.

Not having support in the private sphere

As many as two thirds of the women in our study mentioned family as a barrier to their career though they described this as a conscious choice. This narrative fits well with the dominant two-track model. Family could become a reason for their feeling that they were opting out from their career. Gunn, one of the participants, put it this way: "It's more when you have a family that things get difficult, but before that, I think that many women are encouraged to come forward" (Gunn, late 30s).

Although this narrative is reminiscent of the 'good mother' or home-centred woman narratives (Hakim, 2006; Sørensen, 2017) where the woman is often portrayed as a part-time worker and traceable in national statistics, these women were holding full-time positions in ICT but nonetheless spoke of prioritizing family over work and feeling that they were opting out: "I turn down travelling because I am away so much already. So, I avoided most of the travelling I could have done" (Karen, 40s).

Interviewees not only forewent work activities such as travelling, but also postponed career-developing training. For instance, five of our interviewees had left behind their desires to obtain a PhD. They were aware that they had lost certain opportunities when deciding to have children:

> 'The fact that I have chosen to have four children means that I cannot just take any job. That has to do with priorities. It was wanted and conscious. I could have chosen or prioritized differently.' (Bente, 40s)

> 'Every time you have a child ... I've never been promoted or gotten a pay raise when I've been on [maternity] leave. ... So, you stagnate a bit. (Lise, 30s)

Our participants justified their feeling of opting out by pointing to family and children as a choice. This explanation reproduces gender norms associating women with childcare responsibilities within a neoliberal individualizing ideology of 'choice'. As they presupposed a balance between work and life in their career development (Rottenberg, 2018), our interviewees calculated what their career might have been if they had 'chosen' differently: "I could have prioritized having fewer children and aimed for a higher position. I think I could have had that if I wanted, but I made a different choice" (Bente, 40s). Another interviewee explained:

> 'If you ask what barriers there are for me to be working more, then that [family] is it. If I had made other priorities, I could have been a professor. If you want to climb, you have to work more than one hundred per cent. I refrain from many things because I have a family and want to be with them, and that prevents me from climbing in the system.' (Karen, 40s)

These women's version of work-life 'balance' disguises the cost of prioritizing family over career-driving activities, costs that have notable and long-term consequences for their careers, such as *not* getting a PhD and *not* becoming a professor. In the long run these costs become visible in the gender gap in pay and pension. The rhetoric of 'choice' of our interviewees reflected the gender practices of the two-track parenthood model, where women generally take on more care responsibilities. It contributed to covering up the feeling of opting out. Thus, our findings support Sørensen's suggestion that the rhetoric of choice might reproduce traditional gender roles by defining motherhood according to a maternal presence in the family (Sørensen, 2017).

Discussion

While work-life balance policies take for granted that flexibility at work implies working *less* during office hours in order to spend time with family, the women in our study that spoke about this mostly described working *more*, with longer days, working odd hours and more travelling. Flexibility in greedy work cultures is not just a simple adjustment of work time and place. Rather, flexibility institutes working more than full-time as the norm. This conflicts with family responsibilities even if women do not 'prioritize' family. In contrast to literature suggesting that the discourse of work-life balance contributes to women's self-investment in both career and mothering (Rottenberg, 2018), the women in our study described a work pattern that indicates work invading private space and where ensuring a work-life balance was an individual responsibility (Gregory and Milner, 2009), relying on resources from the private sphere.

The co-production of work and family – evident in our interviewees' claims of prioritizing family while engaged in full-time work – indicates that working 'only' full-time was seen as limiting one's career development. This resonates with research showing that women in ICT feel the need to adopt a work style and long working hours that are said to be associated with men (Watts, 2009). It also indicates a greedy work culture with intense achievement targets and expectations of constant availability (Brandth and Kvande, 2005).

The work-life balance discourse's focus on time management and choice seems too narrow to precisely capture women's negotiation between work and family. As Biese and Choroszewicz (2019) point out, the issue of opting out has often been associated with women who leave the work force altogether. However, our participants' feeling of having to 'opt out' indicates that success in their work environments requires more than full-time commitment.

Hakim suggests that part-time working mothers are in danger of losing the competition with full-time workers due to the momentum of knowledge and experience full-time workers obtain (2006). However, Hakim's dividing line between part-time and full-time work is too optimistic for women working in fields of ICT. Instead, our findings support Watts' (2009) study, which highlights that women feel long working hours are required to develop a successful career in male-dominated fields.

Despite two-track parenthood being the main gender norm that is meant to help create a work-life balance in Norway (Ellingsæter, 2006), with equally shared parenting as the ideal (Pedersen and Egeland, 2020), in reality only private support enables the continuation of a two-track parenthood model. Here gender norms of care are re-done when men take more responsibility for children and family along the lines of the traditional female role. Not only the stay-at-home dad, but also partners with more flexible and predictable work hours were key to solving the work-life time squeeze and giving priority to women's careers. This might indicate changes in how couples negotiate and find arrangements for work and family, allowing women to develop a career. However, the re-gendering of two-track parenthood does not challenge the greedy work style that Padavic et al (2019) identify as the main obstacle to gender equality in working life, especially in ICT work.

Conclusion

Norway is often seen as having one of the world's most family-friendly policies (Seierstad and Kirton, 2015). Our study illustrates that even in Norway, the available public childcare and work-life balance solutions are not sufficient to support women in greedy work cultures such as ICT. From a work-life balance policy perspective, using flexible working conditions as a way to keep women in paid work has been a success. Our findings support a growing acceptance of women developing their careers (Metz-Goeckel, 2018). However, most women experience that they are required to work analogous to men's career development to achieve a career. Our study suggests an urgent need to reorient work-life discussions more towards career-life policies and solutions that acknowledge the challenges of greedy work styles.

As flexible working conditions are more often used by women working in ICT than in other occupations (EIGE, 2018), we need to look beyond the discourse of flexible working hours to truly understand what women's claims of prioritizing family in a greedy work culture really entail. Our informants' voices were united in describing how their career development required private support. Indeed, a male partner's predictable and less greedy work pattern, not work-life balance policies targeting women, was the main factor enabling women to combine work and family responsibilities in ICT research, development and innovation. The future of flexible working conditions that can function in favour of women's careers in the fields of ICT depend on changes in attitudes towards traditional gender patterns of work-family arrangements. This study's participants suggest that this is in part happening. However, the negotiation necessary to achieve this is left to individuals, and thus remains an issue of the private sphere.

References

Abendroth, A.-K. and den Dulk, L. (2011) 'Support for the work–life balance in Europe: the impact of state, workplace and family support on work–life balance satisfaction', *Work, Employment and Society*, 25(2): 234–56. DOI: 10.1177/0950017011398892.

Acker, J. (1990) 'Hierarchies, jobs, bodies: a theory of gendered organizations', *Gender and Society*, 4: 139–58.

Bailey, M. and Riley, S. (2018) '2018 Women in tech: unconscious bias, parity, and the path forward', *Woman in Technology International.* Available at: https://witi.com/IDC-2018-Women-in-Tech.pdf, accessed 10 April 2021.

Biese, I. and Choroszewicz, M. (2019) 'Opting out: professional women develop reflexive agency', *Equality, Diversity and Inclusion: An International Journal*, 38(6): 619–33.

Björnberg, U. (2016) 'Nordic family policies in a European context', *Sociology and Anthropology*, 4(6): 508–16. DOI: 10.13189/sa.2016.040610.

Bø, T.P., Kitterød, R.H., Køber, T., Nerland, S.M. and Skoglund, T. (2008) *Arbeidstiden-mønstre og utviklingstrekk* [*Working Time Patterns and Development*], Statistisk sentralbyrå (Statistics Norway), Oslo-Kongsvinger: Rapport 2008/12.

Brandth, B. and Kvande, E. (2005) 'Fedres valgfrihet og arbeidslivets tidskulturer' ['Fathers' freedom of choice and time culture of working life'], *Tidsskrift for samfunnsforskning*, 1: 35–54.

Chung, H. and van der Lippe, T. (2018) 'Flexible working, work–life balance, and gender equality: introduction', *Social Indicators Research*, 151: 365–81.

Chzhen, Y., Gromada, A. and Rees, G. (2019) 'Are the world's richest countries family friendly?', Policy in the OECD and EU, 22', Florence: UNICEF. Available at: https://vancouver.citynews.ca/wp-content/blogs.dir/sites/9/2019/06/13/Family-Friendly-Policies-Research_UNICEF_-2019.pdf, accessed 7 November 2021.

Corneliussen, H.G. (2014) 'Making the invisible become visible: recognizing women's relationship with technology', *International Journal of Gender, Science and Technology*, 6(2): 209–22.

EIGE (2018) *Women and Men in ICT: A Chance for Better Work–Life Balance: Research Note*, Luxembourg: EIGE: European Institute for Gender Equality, Publications Office of the European Union. Available at: https://eige.europa.eu/publications/women-and-men-ict-chance-better-work-life-balance-research-note, accessed 7 May 2021.

EIGE (2020) *Gender Equality Index 2020: Digitalisation and the Future of Work*, Luxembourg: EIGE: European Institute for Gender Equality, Publications Office of the European Union. Available at: https://eige.europa.eu/publications/gender-equality-index-2020-digitalisation-and-future-work, accessed 13 April 2021.

Ellingsæter, A.L. (2006) 'Nordiske permisjoner for foreldre: et columbi egg?' ['Nordic parental leave: Columbus' egg?'], *Tidsskrift for velferdsforskning*, 9(2): 73–87.

Eurostat (2020) *Women's Employment in the EU*. Available at: https://ec.europa.eu/eurostat/web/products-eurostat-news/-/EDN-20200306-1, accessed 7 November 2021.

Felstead, A., Jewson, N., Phizacklea, A. and Walters, S. (2002) 'Opportunities to work at home in the context of work-life balance', *Human Resource Management Journal*, 12(1): 54–76.

Fleetwood, S. (2007) 'Why work–life balance now?', *The International Journal of Human Resource Management*, 18(3): 387–400.

Gram, K.H. (2019) *The Paternity Leave is still Popular*, SSB. Available at: www.ssb.no/en/befolkning/artikler-og-publikasjoner/the-paternity-leave-is-still-popular, accessed 14 May 2021.

Gregory, A. and Milner, S. (2009) 'Work–life balance: a matter of choice?', *Gender, Work and Organization*, 16(1): 1–13.

Hakim, C. (2006) 'Women, careers, and work-life preferences', *British Journal of Guidance and Counselling*, 34(3): 279–94.

Halrynjo, S. and Lyng, S.T. (2010) 'Fars forkjørsrett: mors vikeplikt? Karriere, kjønn og omsorgsansvar i eliteprofesjoner' ['Father's right of way: mother's duty to yield? Career, gender and care responsibilities in elite professions'], *Tidsskrift for samfunnsforskning*, 51(2): 249–80.

Hays, S. (1996) *The Cultural Contradictions of Motherhood*, New Haven: Yale University Press.

Heikkinen, S., Lämsä, A.M., and Hiillos, M. (2014) 'Narratives by women managers about spousal support for their careers', *Scandinavian Journal of Management*, 30(1): 27–39. DOI: 10.1016/j.scaman.2013.04.004.

Hirschauer, S. (2001) 'Das Vergessen des Geschlechts: Zur Praxeologie einer Kategorie sozialer Ordnung', in B. Heintz (ed), *Geschlechtersoziologie*, 41: 208–35, Wiesbaden: Kölner Zeitschrift für Soziologie und Sozialpsychologie, Sonderheft.

Johnsen, J.V. and Løken, K.V. (2016) *Likestilling og framtidens familiepolitikk* [*Gender Equality and the Family Policy of Future*]. Available at: www.uib.no/sites/w3.uib.no/files/attachments/familiepolitikk-og-arbeidsliv-_feb_11_2016-v2.pdf, accessed 7 May 2021.

Kelan, E.K. (2010) 'Gender logic and (un)doing gender at work', *Gender, Work and Organization*, 17(2): 174–94. DOI:10.1111/j.1468-0432.2009.00459.x.

Kitterød, R.H. and Halrynjo, S. (2019) 'Mer likestilling med fedrekvote? Naturlige eksperimenter i norsk kontekst' ['More equality with father quota? Natural experiments in the Norwegian context'], *Tidsskrift for kjønnsforskning*, 43(2): 71–89. DOI: 10.18261/issn.1891-1781-2019-02-02.

Kitterød, R.H. and Rønsen, M. (2012) 'Non-traditional dual earners in Norway: when does she work at least as much as he?', *Work, Employment and Society*, 26(4): 657–75. DOI: 10.1177/0950017012445090.

Lewis, S., Gambles, R. and Rapoport, R. (2007) 'The constraints of a "work–life balance" approach: an international perspective', *The International Journal of Human Resource Management*, 18(3): 360–73.

McRobbie, A. (2009) *The Aftermath of Feminism: Gender, Culture and Social Change*, London: Sage.

Melby, K. and Carlsson Wetterberg, C. (2009) *Gender Equality and Welfare Politics in Scandinavia: The Limits of Political Ambition?*, Bristol: Policy Press.

Metz-Goeckel, S.H. (2018) 'The perfect course of life (CV) and double-career couples in science', *International Journal of Gender, Science and Technology*, 10(1): 7–23.

Nilsen, A. and Skarsbø, A.M. (2009) 'Familie, jobb og karriere: noen dilemmaer for likestilling' ['Family, work and career: some dilemmas for gender equality'], in I.K. Christensen and L.J. Syltevik (eds) *Kvinners arbeid* [*Women's Work*], Oslo: Unipub, pp 9–28.

OECD (2007) *Babies and Bosses: Reconciling Work and Family Life*, OECD: Paris.

Öun, I. (2012) 'Work-family conflict in the Nordic countries: a comparative analysis', *Journal of Comparative Family Studies*, 43(2): 165–84.

Padavic, I., Ely, R.J. and Reid, E.M. (2019) 'Explaining the persistence of gender inequality: the work–family narrative as a social defense against the 24/7 work culture', *Administrative Science Quarterly*, 65(1): 61–111. DOI: 10.1177/0001839219832310.

Pedersen, E. and Egeland, C. (2020) *Hverdagsliv og familieliv i Norge i 2020* [*Everyday Life and Family Life in Norway in 2020*], Oslo: Work Research Institute (AFI), Oslo Metropolitan University.

Quesenberry, J.L., Trauth, E.M. and Morgan, A.J. (2006) 'Understanding the "mommy tracks": a framework for analyzing work-family balance in the IT workforce', *Information Resources Management Journal*, 19(2): 37–53.

Rottenberg, G. (2018) 'Neoliberal feminism and the future of human capital', *Journal of Women in Culture and Society*, 42(2): 329–48.

Rudlende, L. and Bryghaug, R. (2017) *Familiens bruk av foreldrepenger etter fødsel* [*The family's use of parental benefits after birth*], Oslo: NAV. Available at: www.nav.no/no/nav-og-samfunn/statistikk/familie-statistikk/foreldrepenger, accessed 23 January 2021.

Samordna opptak (2018) *The Norwegian Universities and Colleges Admission Service (Samordna opptak)*. Available at: www.samordnaopptak.no/info/om/sokertall/, accessed 14 May 2021.

Seierstad, C. and Kirton, G. (2015) 'Having it all? Women in high commitment careers and work–life balance in Norway', *Gender, Work and Organization*, 22(4): 390–404.

Selbervik, M. and Østebø, M.T. (2013) 'Gender equality in international aid: what has Norwegian gender politics got to do with it?', *Gender, Technology and Development*, 17(2): 205–28. DOI: 10.1177/0971852413488716.

Simonsen, M. and Corneliussen, H.G. (2020) 'What can statistics tell about the gender divide in ICT? Tracing men and women's participation in the ICT sector through numbers', in D. Kreps, T. Komukai, T.V. Gopal and K. Ishii (eds) *Human-Centric Computing in a Data Driven Society*, Cham, Switzerland: Springer, pp 379–97. DOI: 10.1007/978-3-030-62803-1_30.

Singstad, B.N. (2011) *Det 'overbestemte' livet? Balansering av arbeid og familieliv i IT-bransjen i Norge, Malaysia og California* [The 'Over-determined' Life? Balancing Work and Family Life in the IT Industry in Norway, Malaysia and California], Trondheim: Norges teknisk-naturvitenskapelige universitet, Det humanistiske fakultet.

Sørensen, S.Ø. (2017) 'The performativity of choice: postfeminist perspectives on work–life balance', *Gender, Work and Organization*, 24(3): 297–313.

Statistics Norway (2018) *Dette er kvinner og menn i Norge* [*This is Women and Men in Norway*], Statistisk sentralbyrå. Available at: www.ssb.no/befolkning/artikler-og-publikasjoner/_attachment/341883?_ts=1632b8b8550, accessed 21 January 2022.

Wajcman, J. (2004) *TechnoFeminism*, Cambridge: Polity Press.

Warhurst, C., Eikhof, D.R. and Haunschild, A. (2008) *Work Less, Live More? Critical Analysis of the Work-Life Boundary*, Houndsmills: Palgrave Macmillan.

Watts, J.H. (2009) '"Allowed into a man's world": meanings of work–life balance: perspectives of women civil engineers as "minority" workers in construction', *Gender, Work and Organization*, 16(1): 37–57.

West, C. and Zimmerman, D.H. (1987) 'Doing gender', *Gender and Society*, 1(2): 125–51.

Williams, J.C. (2000) *Unbending Gender*, Oxford: Oxford University Press.

Zerwas, C.S. (2019) *Work-Life Balance and Women's Entrepreneurship: An Exploration of Influencing Factors*, Cham: Springer Nature.

10

Co-creative Platforms for Societal Impact of Research on Gender Issues: A Comparative Study of The Gender Academy and Gender Contact Point

Malin Lindberg, Ulf Mellström and Paula Wennberg

Introduction

Co-creative platforms for developing new knowledge and measures are increasingly common in Sweden and internationally, as part of a global trend to improve the societal impact and the societal relevance of science and innovation (Mauser et al, 2013; Owen et al, 2013; Reypens et al, 2016). Co-creation here means that experts and stakeholders jointly identify, explore and address societal and organizational challenges. The platforms may take the form of networks, partnerships, projects, events or labs, which involve actors from multiple societal sectors, organizations and communities. Research on social innovation suggests that co-creative platforms may reinforce the societal impact of science and innovation by enhancing structural transformation in organizations and society (Haxeltine et al, 2017; Westley et al, 2017).

Public policy in the European Union promotes co-creative platforms in science and innovation as part of policy agendas for smart, sustainable and inclusive growth (European Union, 2016; The Knowledge Coalition, 2016). The European Regional Development Fund (ERDF) provides funding for such platforms in the member states. The fund has, for example, financed the initiation of two platforms in Sweden called The Gender Academy and Gender Contact Point. The purpose of these platforms is to improve the societal impact and the societal relevance of research on gender and gender equality, through knowledge-based gender equality measures, primarily in industrial companies. The platforms enable joint development of new knowledge and measures by researchers, managers, employees and other stakeholders.

In this chapter, the experiences from Gender Contact Point and The Gender Academy are harnessed with the purpose of advancing knowledge on how the societal impact and the societal relevance of research on gender issues may be reinforced by co-creative platforms for academia-society cooperation. In exploring Swedish cases, this study adds to the research stream on gender in regional innovation systems that was established by Scandinavian scholars (cf. Andersson et al, 2012; Alsos et al, 2016). The research questions addressed in the study are: i) how are these co-creative platforms organized and managed?; ii) what co-creative forms and forums are applied in the platforms?; and iii) what challenges and potentials are perceivable in the platforms' efforts to reinforce the societal impact and the societal relevance of research on gender issues? Previous research on social innovation helps address these questions, by pinpointing mechanisms for societal and organizational transformation in co-creative platforms (cf. Westley et al, 2017; Howaldt et al, 2018).

Previous research

Co-creation

The concept of co-creation stems from the design field, where it refers to the joint development of new insights and solutions by experts, users and other stakeholders (Sanders and Stappers, 2008). It shifts the focus of design studies and practices from products and technology to human experiences and social needs. The interest in co-creation rose among scholars in the 1970s, in regard to customer-involvement in the product development of American companies, as well as employee-involvement in the renewal of industrial workplaces in Scandinavian countries. Co-creation has thereafter increasingly been understood and applied as a strategy for organizational and societal development by researchers and practitioners in various fields and sectors. It has recently become part of a global trend of improving the societal impact and the societal relevance of science and innovation, manifested in the establishment of co-creative platforms for joint development of new knowledge and measures (cf. Dutilleul et al, 2010; Beunen et al, 2012; Mauser et al, 2013; Nevens et al, 2013; Owen et al, 2013; Baraldi et al, 2016; Reypens et al, 2016).

Co-creative platforms take the form of networks, partnerships, projects, events, labs, among others (Dutilleul et al, 2010; Beunen et al, 2012; Mauser et al, 2013; Nevens et al, 2013; Owen et al, 2013; Baraldi et al, 2016; Reypens et al, 2016). The platforms can either be permanent in specific locations, ambulate between different locations or be omnipresent by means of digital technology. The physical configuration of the platforms often enhances creativity and interaction in the form of open areas, flexible furnishing and art materials. The social configuration of the platforms draws on participatory and emancipatory traditions, where stakeholders are empowered to impact on society and their own lives. Co-creative forms, such as workshops, dialogues and design thinking, are applied in the platforms in order to enable experts and stakeholders to jointly identify, explore and address societal and organizational challenges. Multi-actor and multi-level mobilization from various societal sectors, organizations and communities is a key component of co-creative platforms (Mauser et al, 2013; Owen et al, 2013; Reypens et al, 2016).

Social innovation

Studies in the field of social innovation have engaged quite extensively with the role of co-creative platforms for societal and organizational renewal (cf. Haxeltine et al, 2017; Howaldt et al, 2018). Social innovation refers, on a general level, to the development of new solutions to societal challenges, that intend to improve people's lives in regard to health, education, employment, housing, environment or other issues (Moulaert et al, 2013; Nicholls et al, 2015). It can, for example, take the form of a new method for matching unemployed youth or immigrants with potential employers, a new service for health care provision in rural areas, or a new alliance of citizens and professionals for building affordable housing. Social innovation aspires specifically to life improvement among those who are disadvantaged in regard to these issues due to age, origin, disability, gender, place or other factors. Empowerment and social inclusion are thus recurrent ambitions in social innovation.

In order to match the complexity of the addressed challenges, social innovation often engage stakeholders from various societal sectors, organizations and communities (Howaldt et al, 2018). It commonly involves those citizens who are negatively affected by the addressed challenge and whose lives may be improved by new solutions. Organizations from the civil society are also frequently involved, based on their established roles as voice-bearers for disadvantaged groups of people and advocacy actors for citizen interests. Municipalities, governmental agencies and other public authorities are also recurrently involved, based on their formal responsibilities for providing policies and services related to the addressed issues. Commercial businesses may be involved to some extent, based on their provision of products, services and employment in relation to the issues in question. Researchers, students and other academic professionals are least involved, since citizens or other stakeholders tend to replace traditional experts in social innovation.

In social innovation, these stakeholders are engaged in joint identification, exploration and solution of societal and organizational challenges (Moulaert et al, 2013; Nicholls et al, 2015). This broad engagement intends to achieve a better understanding of the underlying causations of the challenge in question, and to develop holistic and apt solutions for this challenge. This helps, in turn, to achieve structural transformation, in the sense that existing understandings, solutions and institutions are challenged, changed or replaced, on the individual, organizational and societal levels. Studies show that such transformation is achieved through a complex interaction between the societal institutions that set the rules of the game – such as politics, regulations, resources, organizational models, roles and norms – and the societal actors trying to change these institutions (Haxeltine et al, 2017; Westley et al, 2017). This generally takes a much longer time than allowed for in time-limited projects, making long-term commitment and alliances among stakeholders crucial for achieving societal transformation through social innovation (Edvik and Björk, 2016). Such alliances also require successful mediation of conflicting interests among the involved actors (Howaldt et al, 2018).

Gendered social innovation

The cited research on co-creative platforms for social innovation serves in this chapter as a springboard for advancing our knowledge on how the societal impact and the societal relevance of research on gender issues may be reinforced by such platforms. This chapter thereby contributes to the research stream of gender in regional innovation systems that investigates gender-related patterns and dynamics in platforms for industrial innovation in Scandinavian countries. Research in this area shows that a delimited range of actors, industries and innovations are usually involved in these forums, with a distinct gendered pattern of segregation and hierarchy between women and men (Andersson et al, 2012). The segregation is perceivable in the male dominance of the networks, companies, industries and professions that are most often involved in the studied innovation systems. A gendered hierarchy is perceivable in the higher value and relevance ascribed to male-dominated settings and competences, as well as to technological innovation, in the platforms.

As a consequence, women are under-represented in these innovation systems, in the sense that the industries and sectors that employ most women – such as services industries and the public sector – as well as the types of innovations most common in these industries – such as service innovations and social innovations – are marginalized (Andersson et al, 2012). This means that power and resources are often unevenly distributed between women and men in these platforms. Studies suggest that the gendered patterns in innovation systems may be challenged and changed by acknowledging and involving a broader spectrum of actors, industries and innovations in these forums (Alsos et al, 2016). It is argued that such a challenge would improve the ability of these platforms to address complex societal and organizational concerns, which require both technological and social innovativeness.

Based on the combined insights from studies on gender in innovation and social innovation, the concept of 'gendered social innovation' has been elaborated in order to enhance the knowledge development regarding gendered transformation in innovation systems (Lindberg et al, 2015; Lindberg and Berglund, 2016). It refers to the identification of gender inequality as a societal and organizational challenge in regard to specific areas such as employment, education or entrepreneurship, as a basis for developing innovative solutions that counteract segregating and hierarchical patterns of gender in these areas. It thus helps pinpoint and analyze initiatives and mechanisms for the innovative transformation of gendered structures in organizations and society.

Research design

The research design consists of a comparative case study of two co-creative platforms for academia-society cooperation in Sweden: The Gender Academy and Gender Contact Point. These are rewarding to study since they provide valuable insights into the role of co-creative platforms for enforcing the societal impact and the societal relevance of research on gender issues. The primary criterion for the selection of these cases is thus relevance, rather than randomness, in line with recommendations for comparative case studies (cf. Yin, 2009; Wiebe et al, 2010). The relevance of these Swedish cases is based on their potential to add to the existing research on gender in regional innovation systems (cf. Andersson et al, 2012; Alsos et al, 2016). The comparative case study design makes it possible to gain in-depth insights into each case, while also distinguishing multi-faceted patterns of similarities and differences between them. This has helped identify similarities and differences regarding the platforms' aims, organization, strategies and challenges described in the subsequent parts of this chapter.

The in-depth and multi-faceted data from the case studies were enhanced by a participatory research approach, where researchers and stakeholders jointly investigated the topic in question (cf. Aagaard Nielsen and Svensson, 2006). This approach is inherent in the platforms, due to their purpose of enabling joint development of new knowledge and measures through academia-society cooperation. Continuous interaction between researchers and stakeholders, described further later, has, consequently, taken place throughout the entire process from the initial identification of relevant topics to study, to the planning and execution of activities, the processing of the data and the presentation of the results. Literature on participatory research conveys that this approach helps achieve new knowledge and measures that are both scientifically and practically relevant and valid, through continuous reconciliation of expert and stakeholder views (Gunnarsson et al, 2015). In order to enhance this further, the project managers of Gender Contact Point and The Gender Academy were involved as co-authors of this chapter. The processing of the data was reconciled both with the project managers' own experiences and expertise, as well as with their insights into the stakeholders' views from their interactions with them.

The data collection for the study discussed here was carried out during a three-year period, 2018–20, through a combination of participatory observations of platform activities, individual and group interviews with the researchers, facilitators and stakeholders involved in the platforms, as well as document analyses of project plans, external communication, internal meeting minutes and the digital tools developed in the platforms. In The Gender Academy, participatory observations were carried out at ten regular meetings of the university's project team, documented in field notes. Eighteen semi-structured qualitative interviews with individual researchers, facilitators and companies were conducted, documented in field notes. In addition, two workshops were carried out with the university's project team, where the planning and progress of the platform were discussed for the sake of this study, documented in field notes. In Gender Contact Point, participatory observations were carried out at 17 regular meetings of the university's project team, documented in field notes. Participatory observations were thereto carried out at three of the platform's workshops with researchers and stakeholders, and documented in field notes. In addition, one joint workshop was carried out with the project teams from both platforms, where their organization, management, stakeholder engagement, challenges and results were discussed and compared for the purposes of this study. These were documented in a transcribed recording. The collected data were analyzed by means of a thematic analysis approach, where the character and variations of the studied cases were distinguished regarding their aims, organization, strategies and challenges (cf. Guest et al, 2012).

No ethics approval was required for this study, since it did not concern any of the application areas regulated in the Swedish Law of Ethical Review (2003: 460). It did, however, require some ethical considerations, as individuals were continuously involved in the research process, through meetings, interviews and participatory observations. In this, the study was guided by the ethical guidelines provided by The Swedish Research Council (Vetenskapsrådet, 2017) as well as the extensive discussion on research ethics in the literature on the applied participatory research approach (cf. Aagaard Nielsen and Svensson, 2006). Informed consent was, for example, applied in that the participants were verbally informed about the aim, methods and voluntary participation in the study. They were also informed that their participation would be anonymized in the results dissemination. The participatory approach thereto implied that the participants were given regular opportunities to take part in and discuss the preliminary results of the study.

The Gender Academy

Aim and organization

The Gender Academy[1] was initiated in 2016 by Karlstad University – situated in the region of Värmland in central Sweden – in order to create a permanent platform for university-society cooperation on knowledge-based gender equality practices. The platform is part of the Centre for Gender Studies at Karlstad University and their research profile Action for Organisational Change. It is also part of a regional declaration of intent for university-society cooperation on smart specialization, signed by the university and the regional county council. The establishment of the platform was preceded by several individual projects on similar topics, involving university researchers, industrial companies and public authorities. During 2017–20, it was managed by the university as part of an ERDF-funded project that aimed to improve the competitive advantage, innovation capacity and gender equality among small and medium-sized companies (SMEs) through knowledge-based gender equality practices. The project plan stated that this would be achieved through joint learning by university researchers and company representatives, where they jointly manage gender equality measures in the companies, workshops with all companies for mutual learning, as well as the development of a digital tool for guiding gender equality measures in SMEs.

The Gender Academy involved managers and employees from eight companies, as well as representatives from the county council and business promoters in the region. The participating companies are mainly small and medium-sized, producing products and services primarily in male-dominated industries such as ICT, transports, steels and foods, except for one company that operates in the female-dominated wellness industry. The main incentive for the companies to engage with The Gender Academy was, according to the project plan and interviews with four of them, to gain access to useful knowledge and practical measures for improving their competitiveness and attractiveness through a more diverse workforce, a better work environment and by better meeting market demands. As SMEs, they have limited internal resources – in the form of expertise, staff and funding – to manage gender equality measures on their own and are thus in need of external support and practical tools for guidance.

The Gender Academy was managed by a project team from the university, with researchers and facilitators with expertise in gender and gender equality practices. One of the researchers was also the project manager. Their main incentive to engage in The Gender Academy was, according to interviews with them and participatory observations of their meetings, to develop new knowledge on the preconditions and potentials among industrial SMEs in regard to gendered patterns and gendered transformation. The university's team met regularly in order to plan and evaluate the project activities. For each of the involved companies, one researcher and one facilitator partnered up to support their process. The university's team conducted surveys, interviews and participatory observations at the companies to map their initial and evolving situation in regard to gendered patterns. They also arranged workshops with each company, in order to present and discuss the ongoing results with managers and employees, as well as workshops where all companies partake to exchange experiences and be inspired by invited expert speakers. The university's team also managed the development of the digital tool for guiding gender equality measures in SMEs.

Strategies and challenges

The limited internal resources among SMEs make it difficult for them to prioritize time-consuming development processes. This has complicated the recruitment and participation of companies in The Gender Academy, according to the interviews with the project team and the companies. Extensive dialogues between the university's team and company managements have often been required to seal the deal. Since the companies differ in size, industry and operations, which implies varying needs and preconditions, it has been fruitful to identify each company's specific needs and to tailor the process accordingly. The applied measures in The Gender Academy such as surveys, interviews, observations and workshops, have consequently been customized to each company. The use of surveys has proven difficult in the smallest companies, since the anonymity among the few employees is likely to be compromised. For this reason alternative measures have been used there, such as 'norm tours' where employees and the university's team jointly identified gendered norms in various parts of their workplaces.

The companies' differences have also restricted their benefits of exchanging experiences at the joint workshops and complicated the compilation and communication of results from The Gender Academy, according to the interviews with the project team and participatory observations of their meetings. The results have nevertheless formed the basis for developing a digital tool – named iGen[2] – that guides gender equality measures in various types of SMEs and other organizations. The tool presents knowledge, measures and examples in an inspiring and interactive manner. It was developed in cooperation with a professional communication agency, specialized in digital formats. It was also informed by professionals with personal experiences of developing similar tools. In relation to other digital tools for guiding gender equality measures, the project's own tool was perceived to offer added value by combining a solid knowledge-base in research on gender issues and a tailored design to meet the needs and prerequisites of SMEs with limited internal resources.

A continuous challenge has been to advance the joint process because of recurrent changes in the stakeholders' ability and willingness to prioritize participation due to personnel turnover, re-organization, ownership transfer and market fluctuation, according to interviews with the project team and the companies. The joint process has been further hampered by persistent resistance towards advancements among some stakeholder participants, expressed either as outright discredit of the applied measures and anticipated results or implicit refusal to scrutinize their operations or implement planned measures. Some managers have, for example, reacted with disbelief when receiving the results from surveys conducted among their employees. Others have restricted the university team's access to certain parts of their everyday operations. Some initially expressed a positive and progressive approach to gender equality in their companies, while preserving the status quo in practice by prioritizing their everyday business. These challenges have been addressed by further tailoring the activities and interactions to the stakeholders' needs and preconditions, with varying degree of success.

Gender Contact Point

Aim and organization

Gender Contact Point[3] was initiated in 2014 by Luleå University of Technology – situated in the region of Norrbotten in northern Sweden – in order to create a permanent platform for university-society cooperation on knowledge-based gender equality practices. The platform is part of an alliance of several departments at Luleå University of Technology. The establishment of the platform was preceded by several individual projects on similar topics, involving university researchers, industrial companies, public authorities and other stakeholders. During 2018–20, it was managed by the university as part of an ERDF-funded project called Gender Smart Arena[4] that aimed at smart, sustainable and inclusive growth through gender-equal business models in SMEs and other organizations. This was to be achieved through joint learning by researchers, companies and municipalities in the form of workshops where a framework for gender-equal business models is jointly developed. The framework formed the basis for the development of a digital tool for guiding gender equality measures in industrial SMEs and other organizations.

The Gender Smart Arena project involved managers and employees from six companies and three municipalities in the regions of Norrbotten and Västerbotten. The companies were mainly small and medium-sized, producing products and services in the male-dominated ICT industry. The main incentive for the companies and municipalities to engage in the project was, according to the project plan and participatory observations of the workshops, to access useful knowledge and practical measures for improving their competitiveness and attractiveness through being a gender-equal organization with gender-equal operations. Most of the companies had pre-established relations with the university in ICT innovation development but not with the university's researchers in gender studies. As SMEs, they also had limited internal resources for managing gender equality measures on their own. The municipalities lacked, in their turn, structures for continuous cooperation with the university on the topic of gender equality.

Gender Smart Arena was managed by a project team from the university, with a project manager and researchers with expertise in gender and gender equality practices in relation to relevant fields, such as business models, design, ethics, entrepreneurship, innovation and ICT. Their main incentive to engage in the project was, according to the project plan and participatory observations of their meetings, to develop new knowledge on gendered patterns and gendered transformation among SMEs and other organizations. The university's team met regularly in order to plan and evaluate the project activities. They arranged workshops with participants from the ICT companies and municipalities involved, as well as open seminars with a broader range of stakeholders, which involved inspirational talks by invited speakers as well as presentations and discussions of preliminary project results. The university's team also managed the development of the digital tool for guiding gender equality measures.

Strategies and challenges

Gender Smart Arena was preceded by another ERDF-funded project, where ICT companies and researchers jointly translated research results into practical tools for guiding gender equality measures. This resulted in a tool for gender-equal recruitment and a perceived potential to develop a practically useful framework for gender-equal business models, and motivated the initiation of the Gender Smart Arena project. In the latter project researchers and stakeholders jointly developed such a framework, which helps to analyze and advance the stakeholders' regular operations from a gender perspective. This means that specific activities and areas in their operations and organizations are pinpointed where gendered patterns are formed and reinforced. The stakeholders found that this makes it easier for them to identify manageable issues to address in their everyday work, instead of being overwhelmed by the comprehensiveness of the gender equality agenda. It also helps them to scrutinize and reform their established ways of thinking and doing, in a manner that improves the quality of their everyday work.

In order to make practical use of the framework, a digital tool – named Richer Business[5] – was developed as part of the project. The tool helps guide gender equality measures in SMEs and other organizations by presenting a number of practical scenarios of gender inequality in various parts of the organization, as well as reflective queries for relating each scenario to the user's own organization. It also provides links to measures, examples and literature related to each scenario. The tool was developed in cooperation with a professional communication agency, specialized in digital formats with a gender equality perspective. It differs from pre-existing tools in that it offers a solid academic knowledge base and a design that matches the needs and preconditions of SMEs and other organizations with limited internal resources.

A continuous challenge has been to schedule joint meetings and workshops, due to calendar mismatches and the participants' prioritization of regular operations, according to participatory observations of team meetings and stakeholder workshops. This has postponed several planned activities, which means that the joint process has been slower and less participatory than anticipated. The participation has been further delimited by difficulties to engage men and women to an equal extent, resulting in a female-dominated representation from both the stakeholders and the university. This challenge has been addressed by initiating cooperation with other industrial networks and projects, where more men are involved. Another challenge has been to reconcile the stakeholders' main interest in improved competitiveness and attractiveness and the researchers' main interest in improved insights into gendered patterns and practices. When meeting, the participants have nevertheless appreciated the mutual exchange of knowledge and experiences, engendering continuous insights that they can apply in their everyday work. In order to further extend this exchange, knowledge exchange and results dissemination to a wider national and international audience has been prioritized by the university's team.

Analysis

Co-creative forms and forums

Gender Contact Point and The Gender Academy share the ambition to establish permanent platforms for academia-society cooperation on knowledge-based gender equality practices, primarily in industrial companies. Their involvement of researchers from the university as well as managers and employees from companies and public organizations aligns with the multi-actor and multi-level mobilization of various societal sectors, organizations and communities that is a key component of co-creative platforms (cf. Mauser et al, 2013; Owen et al, 2013; Reypens et al, 2016). Their social configuration is also similar to other such platforms, with a variety of co-creative measures for jointly identifying, exploring and solving organizational and societal challenges. Another similarity is that the platform activities have ambulated between different locations, while the platforms themselves have been formally located at the universities. The physical configuration has not been a prominent feature of the platforms' co-creation, however, in contrast with similar platforms where open areas, flexible furnishing and art materials are used to enhance creativity and interaction. In regard to their organizational forms, the platforms have been established and managed based on several individual, time-limited projects that have served as a springboard for joint networks, events and labs (called workshops) that are common forms for co-creative platforms (cf. Dutilleul et al, 2010; Beunen et al, 2012; Mauser et al, 2013; Nevens et al, 2013; Owen et al, 2013; Baraldi et al, 2016; Reypens et al, 2016).

Gender Contact Point and The Gender Academy also share similarities with the co-creative forums and forms highlighted in studies of social innovation, where new solutions to societal and organizational challenges are developed through and for social inclusion (cf. Moulaert et al, 2013; Nicholls et al, 2015). Since the social inclusion in the platforms regards gender-focussed processes in regional networks of stakeholders, it is also similar to previous research on gender in regional innovation systems (cf. Andersson et al, 2012; Alsos et al, 2016). And since the platforms aim at improved knowledge and practices on gender equality, they also reflect previous research on 'gendered social innovation' (cf. Lindberg et al, 2015; Lindberg and Berglund, 2016). Specific forms of social innovation, perceivable in The Gender Academy and Gender Contact Point, are new cooperations in terms of researcher and stakeholder networks, new processes in terms of the joint development of new knowledge and measures, new methods in terms of knowledge-based gender equality measures, as well as new services in terms of digital tools for guiding gender equality measures (cf. Moulaert et al, 2013; Nicholls et al, 2015).

Mediating interests

In contrast to the most common co-creative constellations in social innovation – that include civil society organizations and public authorities – The Gender Academy and Gender Contact Point primarily involve universities and companies, and to some extent local and regional authorities (cf. Howaldt et al, 2018). The platforms nevertheless differ from each other in their stakeholder involvement, since Gender Contact Point involves the public sector actors more actively and The Gender Academy involves the companies more in-depth. Mediation of conflicting interests among the involved actors has been required in both platforms, as is common in social innovation (Howaldt et al, 2018). This has primarily concerned the stakeholders' interest of gaining access to useful knowledge and measures for improving their competitiveness and attractiveness through gender-equal operations and organizations, on the one hand, and the researchers' interest of gaining access to useful data and critically reflecting on the preconditions and potentials among the stakeholders in regard to gendered patterns and gendered transformation, on the other. These differences in the prioritization of practical or theoretical advancement manifested themselves in various ways, for example in mismatching calendar priorities, stakeholders' prioritization of regular operations and their resistance towards the applied measures and anticipated results.

These conflicting interests were mediated in Gender Contact Point and The Gender Academy by framing the academic scrutiny of the stakeholders' preconditions and potentials as a way to help improve the soundness and effectiveness of the applied measures for gender equality, and thus improve the stakeholders' competitiveness and attractiveness. The need among stakeholders for external support and practical tools to guide their gender equality measures – especially among SMEs due to their limited internal resources – may have enhanced the mediation. The digital tools, developed in both The Gender Academy and Gender Contact Point, manifest this mediation by compiling and communicating the developed knowledge, measures and examples in a manner that is easily accessible and useful for SMEs and other organizations. This mediation reflects the participatory research approach applied in both platforms, which emphasizes the mutual reinforcement of societal impact and societal relevance of science and innovation, here in the form of research on knowledge-based gender equality measures (cf. Aagaard Nielsen and Svensson, 2006; Gunnarsson et al, 2015).

Societal impact and relevance of research on gender issues

Gender Contact Point and The Gender Academy both aspire to improve the societal impact and the societal relevance of science and innovation, by establishing permanent platforms for university-society cooperation on knowledge-based gender equality practices. Previous studies of social innovation help distinguish the platforms' potentials and challenges for structural transformation in organizations and society (cf. Haxeltine et al, 2017; Westley et al, 2017). The joint development of new knowledge and measures in the platforms, through co-creative forms and forums, has the potential to challenge, change or replace existing understandings, solutions and institutions among the involved actors, in line with previous findings on how to achieve structural transformation (cf. Haxeltine et al, 2017; Westley et al, 2017). This is most evidently achieved through the joint management of gender equality measures by researchers and stakeholders in The Gender Academy and the joint development of a framework for gender-equal business models by researchers and stakeholders in Gender Contact Point. It may be further reinforced by the development of digital tools in both platforms, in order to guide knowledge-based gender equality measures in industrial SMEs and other types of organizations.

The transformative potential of The Gender Academy and Gender Contact Point share similarities with the previously discussed potential of gendered transformation in regional innovation systems (cf. Andersson et al, 2012; Alsos et al, 2016). The similarities primarily regard the potential to expand the range of actors, industries and innovations involved in co-creative platforms for societal impact and societal relevance of science and innovation, in a way that challenges, changes or replaces prevalent gendered patterns of segregation and hierarchy between women and men. There are also similarities with the previously highlighted potential of 'gendered social innovation' to develop innovative solutions that counteract segregating and hierarchical patterns of gender in various areas (cf. Lindberg et al, 2015; Lindberg and Berglund, 2016). The realization of these transformative potentials of Gender Contact Point and The Gender Academy is, according to studies of social innovation, dependent on simultaneous changes on the individual, organizational and societal levels (cf. Haxeltine et al, 2017; Westley et al, 2017).

On the individual level, transformative potential in The Gender Academy and Gender Contact Point might be distinguished in the form of increased use of academic knowledge on gendered patterns and gendered transformation among stakeholder employees, on the one hand, and increased know-how among researchers on how to collect, compile and communicate insights on these patterns and potentials, on the other. On the organizational level, a similar potential might be distinguished in the form of long-term commitment among the universities, companies and public authorities to promote and participate in the platforms and their co-creative processes, as well as improved gender equality in the stakeholders' organizations as a result of their participation. On the societal level, such potential might be distinguished in the form of an improved ability of these and other regional innovation systems to address complex societal and organizational challenges, by reinforcing the societal impact and the societal relevance of research on gender issues. There are, however, currently no plans for continued measurement of the platforms' long-term impact on these levels.

These multi-level potentials of Gender Contact Point and The Gender Academy are, in the light of social innovation studies, determined by complex interactions between the societal institutions that frame and regulate forms and forums for societal impact and relevance of science and innovation, and the societal actors trying to change these institutions (cf. Haxeltine et al, 2017; Westley et al, 2017). The time-limited project format used for developing and establishing the platforms contrasts, for example, with the extensive time required to achieve structural transformation in social innovation, according to previous studies (cf. Edvik and Björk, 2016). Even if both The Gender Academy and Gender Contact Point have hitherto succeeded in financing a string of individual projects on similar topics, their ambition to establish permanent platforms for university-society cooperation may require more resilient forms and forums in order to ensure long-term commitment and stakeholder alliances. This might be enhanced by the existing alliance between several university departments in Gender Contact Point and the regional declaration for university-society cooperation in The Gender Academy.

Taken together, the comparative case study of The Gender Academy and Gender Contact Point presented in this chapter shows that they largely align with the tradition of co-creation in the design field and other fields, where new insights and solutions are jointly developed by experts, users and other stakeholders for innovative transformation of gendered structures in organizations and society (cf. Sanders and Stappers, 2008). By establishing co-creative platforms, they have the potential to reinforce the societal impact and the societal relevance of research on gender issues, based on their similar and different aims, organization, strategies and challenges. This is in line with the highlighted trend of using such platforms to improve the societal impact and relevance of science and innovation in general (cf. Mauser et al, 2013; Owen et al, 2013; Reypens et al, 2016).

Acknowledgements

The research presented in this chapter was funded by The European Regional Development Fund and the subject of Design at Luleå University of Technology, Sweden.

Notes

1 www.kau.se/genusakademin
2 www.kau.se/genusakademin
3 www.ltu.se/centres/cdt/Gender-Contact-Point
4 www.ltu.se/centres/cdt/Gender-Contact-Point/Projekt/Gender-Smart-Arena-1.183822
5 https://richerbusiness.eu/

References

Aagaard Nielsen, K. and Svensson, L. (eds) (2006) *Action Research and Participatory Research*, Maastricht: Shaker Publishing.

Alsos, G.A., Hytti, U. and Ljunggren, E. (eds) (2016) *Research Handbook on Gender and Innovation*, Cheltenham: Edward Elgar Publishing.

Andersson, S., Berglund, K., Gunnarsson, E. and Sundin, E. (eds) (2012) *Promoting Innovation: Policies, Practices and Procedures*, Stockholm: VINNOVA.

Baraldi, E., Lindahl, M. and Severinsson, K. (2016) 'A proactive approach to the utilization of academic research: the case of Uppsala University's AIMday', *Science and Public Policy*, 43(5): 613–21.

Beunen, R., Duineveld, M., During, R., Straver, G. and Aalvanger, A. (2012) 'Reflexivity in performative science shop projects', *Gateways: International Journal of Community Research and Engagement*, 5: 135–51.

Dutilleul, B., Birrer, F.A.J. and Mensink, W. (2010) 'Unpacking European living labs: analysing innovation's social dimensions', *Central European Journal of Public Policy*, 4(1): 60–85.

Edvik, A. and Björk, F. (2016) 'Social change through temporary, short-term interventions: the role of legitimacy in organizing social innovations', in L. Andersen, M. Gawell and R. Spear (eds) *Social Entrepreneurship and Social Enterprises: Nordic Perspectives*, New York: Routledge.

European Union (2016) *Open Innovation, Open Science, Open to the World*, Brussels: European Commission.

Guest, G., MacQueen, K.M. and Namey, E.E. (2012) *Applied Thematic Analysis*, Thousand Oaks, CA: Sage.

Gunnarsson, E., Hansen, H.P., Steen Nielsen, B. and Sriskandarajah, N. (eds) (2015) *Action Research for Democracy: New Ideas and Perspectives from Scandinavia*, New York: Routledge.

Haxeltine, A., Pel, B., Dumitru, A., Avelino, F., Kemp, R., Bauler, T., Kunze, I., Dorland, J., Wittmayer, J. and Jørgensen, M.S. (2017) *Towards a TSI Theory: A Relational Framework and 12 Propositions*, working paper from The TRANSIT project, EU SSH.2013.3.2-1.

Howaldt, J., Kaletka, C., Schröder, A. and Zirngiebl, M. (eds) (2018) *Atlas of Social Innovation: New Practices for a Better Future*, Dortmund: TU Dortmund University.

Lindberg, M. and Berglund, K.-E. (2016) 'Gendered social innovation: a new research stream for gender inclusive innovation policy, research and practice', in G.A. Alsos, U. Hytti and E. Ljunggren (eds) *Research Handbook on Gender and Innovation*, Cheltenham: Edward Elgar Publishing, pp 214–28.

Lindberg, M., Forsberg, L. and Karlberg, H. (2015) 'Gendered social innovation: a theoretical lens for analysing structural transformation in organisations and society', *International Journal of Social Entrepreneurship and Innovation*, 3(6): 472–83.

Mauser, W., Klepper, G., Rice, M., Schmalzbauer, B.M., Hackmann, H., Leemans, R. and Moore, H. (2013) 'Transdisciplinary global change research: the co-creation of knowledge for sustainability', *Current Opinion in Environmental Sustainability*, 5: 420–31.

Moulaert, F., MacCallum, D., Mehmood, A. and Hamdouch, A. (eds) (2013) *The International Handbook on Social Innovation*, Cheltenham: Edward Elgar Publishing.

Nevens, F., Frantzeskaki, N., Gorissen, L. and Loorbach, D. (2013) 'Urban transition labs: co-creating transformative action for sustainable cities', *Journal of Cleaner Production*, 50: 111–22.

Nicholls, A., Simon, J. and Gabriel, M. (eds) (2015) *New Frontiers in Social Innovation Research*, New York: Palgrave Macmillan.

Owen, R., Bessant, J.R. and Heintz, M. (eds) (2013) *Responsible Innovation: Managing the Responsible Emergence of Science and Innovation in Society*, Chichester: John Wiley & Sons.

Reypens, C., Lievens, A. and Blazevicc, V. (2016) 'Leveraging value in multi-stakeholder innovation networks: a process framework for value co-creation and capture', *Industrial Marketing Management*, 56: 40–50.

Sanders, E.B.N. and Stappers, P.J. (2008) 'Co-creation and the new landscapes of design', *CoDesign International Codesign*, 4(1): 5–18.

Swedish Law of Ethical Review (2003) *Lag (2003:460) om etikprövning av forskning som avser människor* [*About Ethics Reviews of Research Involving Humans*], Stockholm: Utbildningsdepartementet.

The Knowledge Coalition (2016) *Portfolio for Research and Innovation: Cooperation, Creativity, Game Changers*, Amsterdam: The Knowledge Coalition.

Vetenskapsrådet (2017) *God forskningssed* [*Good Research Practice*], Stockholm: Vetenskapsrådet.

Westley, F., McGowan, K. and Tjörnbo, O. (eds) (2017) *The Evolution of Social Innovation: Building Resilience Through Transitions*, Cheltenham: Edward Elgar Publishing.

Wiebe, E., Mills, A.J. and Durepos, G. (2010) *Encyclopedia of Case Study Research*, Los Angeles: Sage.

Yin, R.K. (2009) *Case Study Research: Design and Methods*, London: Sage.

11

The Discourse of Rurality in Women's Professional-life Narratives: Gender and ICT in Rural Norway

Hilde G. Corneliussen, Gilda Seddighi and Carol Azungi Dralega

Introduction

This chapter explores how women experience ICT work in a particular rural context in Norway. While the global trend of digitalization is recognized as a driver for transforming working life and for supporting the development of more competitive economies, women are still under-represented in ICT education and work in Europe and in Norway (Eurostat, 2019; Barbieri et al, 2020). Women in ICT work more than women in many other occupations (EIGE, 2018), reflecting a feeling of pressure to submit to a 'greedy' male-dominated work culture of long hours (Watts, 2009). Similar tendencies have been found in Norway; women in ICT work full-time *or more*, depending on care responsibilities and support from partners (Seddighi and Corneliussen, 2021; see Chapter 9, this volume). While national gender equality norms and regulations are widely recognized and accepted, initiatives to achieve gender equality are left to each employer and organization, making the resulting gender structures of ICT highly dependent on the organizational culture (Corneliussen and Seddighi, 2020) and local enactments of gender (Pristed Nielsen et al, 2020: 14). Here we add another factor to the analysis of women's experiences in ICT work: rurality.

Rural communities have frequently been associated with traditional and conservative gender norms, as opposed to progressive urban areas (Little, 2002). The often static image of the rural emanating from these polarized narratives contributes to a notion of gender as universal and stable in rural areas (Little, 2014). Gender relations and gender roles are, however, constantly negotiated and changing, including in rural communities (Pristed Nielsen et al, 2020). Although details of 'rurality' include different features globally, the rural region in focus here, western Norway, shares some general features of western rural communities such as low density in population, small settlements and long internal regional distances. The region is recognized for its impressive alpine outdoor opportunities, but also for a typical rural organizational thinness with few and small private businesses, however, with the public sector as a major player as the largest employer in Norway (Larsen and Nesse, 2017). Although the region does not score very highly in terms of research and innovation, the development of ICT services and the ICT industry has been extensive; ICT workplaces have quadrupled since 2000 (Vareide et al, 2019: 12).

Within this context we explore how experiences of rurality are entangled in the professional-life narratives of 25 women working in ICT in this region. The analysis is based on a notion of gender as a social construction and entangled with ICT, work and rurality, combined with a perspective emphasizing the importance of material as well as immaterial factors for understanding development in rural regions (Bryden and Hart, 2004; Pristed Nielsen et al, 2020).

Literature review

Rurality has often been described in dualistic terms, associated with a strong gender divide in primary industries (Brandth, 2016) and traditional and 'patriarchal' gender norms (Forsberg, 2001), different from urban communities associated with more progressive gender norms (Pristed Nielsen et al, 2020). Rurality is, however, not a uniform concept, and diversification of livelihoods can be found in advanced rural regions (Vidickienė, 2017). Large geographic areas with low population density characterize Norway, Sweden and Finland as different from other European countries (NOU, 2020: 15). ICT and digitalization are considered important catalysts for innovation and economic growth in such regions, often tied to an assumption that increased use of ICT will reduce the significance of geography (Grip, 2020). Rural regions in Norway have high out-migration (Heleniak and Gassen, 2020) reflecting the 'mobility imperative for rural youth' (Farrugia, 2016: 836): young people's rural to urban migration in search of education and work opportunities (Pristed Nielsen et al, 2020). In some places, young women leave at a higher rate than men. Although this might suggest that a predominance of traditional, male-dominated workplaces makes the rural labour market challenging for young women, it has also been interpreted as reflecting the higher educational ambition of women (Pristed Nielsen et al, 2020). Women's higher out-migration from rural regions has also been seen as an escape from a society characterized by a traditional gender contract

(Forsberg, 2001), different from an urban 'modern gender contract' of more gender-equal practices in labour and politics (Grimsrud, 2011: 6). Gender patterns of working life affect in-migration too (Walsh and Gerrard, 2018), for instance making it less likely for women and men with a gender atypical education to return to rural regions (Haley, 2018). Mobility both in and out of rural regions can, however, represent a kind of empowerment: the ability to pursue interesting work opportunities (Hanson, 2010). As we will show here, the increase of ICT workplaces in the region of our study has provided opportunities for women to find less traditional work when deciding to return to the region.

An important aspect for understanding rural communities is the sense of belonging as 'place-belongingness', reflecting a 'personal, intimate, feeling of being "at home" in a place' (Antonsich, 2010: 645). 'Being rooted' in and feeling belonging for a place has been associated with empowerment because it gives access to social resources and networks (Pristed Nielsen et al, 2020: 18). This points to the importance of not only looking at labour and economic activities when studying women's experience of ICT work in a rural region, but also being aware of how other factors affect their work experience (Bryden and Hart, 2004; Pristed Nielsen et al, 2020).

Rurality is not only perceived as an opposite to urbanity, but also entails internal contradictions. Cruickshank et al suggest that there has been a competition between 'rural values as intrinsic', emphasizing the value of traditional rural culture, and the rural as an important site for national economic growth (2009: 73). The latter discourse has gained importance with intensified globalization and the growth of neoliberalism (Cruickshank et al, 2009), evident for instance in the increase of ICT workplaces in the rural region analyzed here (Vareide et al, 2019). The discourse of rural values includes images of rurality as idyllic, often associated with nature and family values. The assumptions that rural areas are a good place for children to grow up in (Grimsrud, 2011) and that living in the countryside produces a better quality of life have made in-migration into rural areas a life phase strategy related to expanding families (Villa, 2000). For some, nature as a prized asset has transformed rural 'remoteness' from being seen as a weakness to making its 'outstanding environmental quality' increase its attractiveness (Vidickienė, 2017: 176). Rural nature has, however, also been described as a masculine domain rooted in traditional gender structures, handled by men with large machines (Little and Panelli, 2003).

Research in Nordic rural areas indicates that local gender arrangements are affected by rural conditions: they are 'contingent upon and evolve from practices in space and place' (Pristed Nielsen et al, 2020: 15). However, different from assumptions of static gender patterns in rural areas, Pristed Nielsen et al reject the idea of a sharp dichotomy of gender roles as expressed in a traditional rural vs. a progressive urban version. Rather, they find many coexisting varieties of femininities and masculinities in their studies of remote communities in the Nordic countries (Pristed Nielsen et al, 2020). Making space for such diversity is vital for the success of the European policy goal of making rural regions attractive for women, as young women's higher out-migration rate threatens rural regions' viability and sustainability (Shortall and Bock, 2015). Our study adds important insights to this literature by analyzing the entanglements of the global trend of digitalization with the locally enacted structures of gendered working and living in a rural region of western Norway.

Theoretical framework

An underlying premise for this study is that social development, including of the gender structures of work and family life in rural regions, can be understood as changeable rather than fixed (Little, 2014; Pristed Nielsen et al, 2020). Our analysis builds on Bryden and Hart's (2004) theory emphasizing that the dynamics in rural regions rely not only on economic relations, but on a wider spectrum of material as well as immaterial and intangible factors such as traditions, values, beliefs, attitudes and more. The rural itself has been identified as an actor adding meaning to life in such regions, for instance through 'place-belongingness' (Antonsich, 2010: 645). In contrast to perspectives suggesting that the rural produces a specific social order including in gender relations (Forsberg, 2001), our analysis takes as a starting point that gender is a co-construction of work and rurality. Gender is developed in social situations and cultural contexts (West and Zimmerman, 1987) and is, for instance, reflected in the Norwegian labour market through horizontal and vertical gender segregation (Statistics Norway, 2018). These gender patterns of work are particularly notable in fields of ICT. However, when ICT work appears in new contexts, like new workplaces developed through increased digitalization in rural regions, this might also affect the gendering of ICT work. Our theoretical framework therefore aims to explore how the rural setting enters into women's experiences of working in ICT in a rural context. In previous studies we have shown that national gender norms promoting gender equality are widely accepted in the region (Corneliussen and Seddighi, 2020), but also that local enactments of gender represented by women working in ICT rely on employers' attitudes and private resources such as supportive partners and family, as much as family-friendly policies (Seddighi and Corneliussen, 2021; see Chapter 9 in this volume). Our analysis thus aims to identify how gender, ICT work and rurality are entangled and co-constructed as they structure the meaning of the women's work experiences.

Methodology

Interviews

The sample in this chapter consists of 25 women aged 24 to 59 who worked and lived in the rural region of western Norway at the time of the interviews in 2017–18. The women were recruited through research and innovation institutions and funders, ICT companies, and networks for women working with technology. About half the group had a university degree in computing. The others had degrees in non-technological disciplines, including fields such as social science, health care, law and economics. However, they worked with ICT and digialization. Some of the women in this latter group had also returned to university for a course or degree in ICT, while others had received formal or informal training in ICT through their work (see Chapter 4, this volume). Their workplaces were spread across the public and private sector, reflecting the global trend towards digitalization that is increasing the need for ICT experts far beyond traditional ICT industries (Ekeland et al, 2015). Their jobs included tasks ranging from hands-on programming to designing, building and implementing new technology. The women's different relations to the region affected their experiences, as 16 of the women grew up in the region, three came from other parts of Norway, while six had an immigrant background.

The individual interviews lasted approximately one hour and followed a professional-life history perspective, including questions about education and occupational history as well as an invitation to reflect more widely (Kvale and Brinkmann, 2009) on experiences related to ICT work, family life and rural living. All informants were anonymized and are identified with a capital letter from A to J following direct quotes. The study was approved by the Norwegian Centre for Research Data.

Analytical methods

The interview transcripts were initially analyzed using a grounded theory approach in order to allow for new perspectives to emerge (Strauss and Corbin, 1998). After reading and coding the transcripts, codes were extracted and organized in groups before categories were developed through writing memos, following Charmaz's guidelines (2006). Categories that were further developed for this chapter include the 'moving back'-storyline and 'our people', pointing to a 'place-belongingness', and the 'rural idyllic' images of nature and quality of life. We also draw on Laclau and Mouffe's (1985) discourse theory and their notion of meaning understood as a social process. Discourses consist of a web of signs that are placed into a specific relation to other signs and thereby create meaning (Winther Jørgensen and Phillips, 1999). In addition to ICT and gender discourses expounded in the theoretical framework, the analysis explores how narratives of the rural as a place of living and working involve several signs that together and through their specific constellations construct discourses about rurality.

Rurality in women's experiences of ICT work

The rural region of western Norway has developed beyond traditional rural economic activities, visible in the notable growth in the ICT industry (Vareide et al, 2019). We start by exploring the types of ICT workplaces the women found and the characteristics of working life in the region, before exploring 'place-belongingness' (Antonsich, 2010) and 'idyllic rurality' (Little, 2014).

Gendering of ICT work

Nearly half the women had been working in a city before deciding to move back home to the rural region. Many of the women had been looking for appropriate jobs for a while, indicating a shortage of ICT jobs relevant to them in the region. One of them had nearly given up hope: "I was thinking that 'well, then I just have to settle for a position in IT operations', give authorization, add new users, update Windows, and stuff like that, right. Which is a very important job as well, but you don't need a degree in civil engineering to do that" (F). Finally she had found a job in the region in a non-tech company expanding its ICT department to keep up with the requirements for digitalizing their services. This trend was notable for all the women in our sample, suggesting that the ongoing digitalization across sectors has opened up a particular type of ICT work opportunity that attracts women. This contributes to a new gendering of ICT work: first, the nine women in academic positions did not work in ICT departments, but rather in other and less male-dominated disciplines. Second, the public sector is a female-dominated workplace in Norway (Statistics Norway, 2018). The six women working with ICT in the public sector described their work experience as combining ICT as a masculine field with more gender-equal, even female-dominated, work environments such as health care services. Third, the rest of the group worked in the private sector, but none of them had positions as ICT experts in a private ICT company. Instead, they had found ICT jobs in organizations where ICT was secondary, but increasingly important due to the digitalization of systems, services and work processes. This suggests that increased digitalization opens up new opportunities for working with ICT in less male-dominated workplaces, and in organizations and industries where ICT expertise is not already occupied by men or images of masculinity.

The women's stories were not free from gender discrimination, for instance being belittled as a 'clever little girl' rather than a competent ICT expert, and other types of discrimination recognized from other studies of women in ICT work (Corneliussen et al, 2019: 385). However, other aspects of their work experiences appeared to be directly related to issues of rurality, such as the low population density, organizational thinness and a trend towards small businesses (Larsen and Nesse, 2017): "Perhaps you become a bit more visible and get more responsibility at a smaller workplace, because there are not many here with the same background as me, in fact almost no one, so you are sort of unique" (F). Several of the women had experienced high visibility in typically small companies with "one-person ICT departments". On the one hand, there were "fewer people to compete with" (C), but on the other, each employee might have to serve many different roles: "You get more interesting tasks because they need to use what they have" (E). One of the women who served in such a small company described her responsibility as literally everything to do with the company's ICT system; from design to implementing as well as training the users. The low density of people also affected how the employers cared for the employees: "They can't just throw you out and put someone else in. And that means that people are being taken care of in a very different way" (E). These experiences differed from the women's urban work experiences where there was higher competition. The scarcity of human resources in the rural region encouraged an attitude of taking care of and supporting employees: "I have had opportunities and challenges that I probably would not have had if there were more available candidates" (H). Managers above her had acted as mentors and pushed her into promotions including taking on a leader role in a process of digital innovation. Other women told similar stories of varied and interesting work tasks in the fields of ICT and digitalization, promotions and career opportunities coming their way, partly due to the shortage of human resources in the region. The flip side of the rich variety of opportunities within one company was the limited number of employers to choose from for ICT experts:

> 'There are perhaps two companies where you can work, and if you don't want to work in any of them you have to commute, … so that is what I've done; first I worked in one company, then I was commuting, and then I worked in the other company. If it doesn't work out here … it means going back to number one or starting to commute again.' (B)

The women's narratives suggest that the rural context added certain dimensions to their work experiences in fields of ICT and digitalization by making them visible and opening up career opportunities that they did not think they would have found in urban ICT workplaces.

Place-belongingness

The opportunities and support that the women found in ICT jobs, however, co-existed with a shortage of relevant jobs and companies to choose from. The importance of interesting work made many of the women willing to commute to work because living in the region also had a special value for them due to their 'place-belongingness' (Antonsich, 2010). This was highlighted in the narratives of 12 women who shared a 'moving back'-storyline: they had grown up in the region, moved out to undertake higher education, stayed away for work reasons, before finding a relevant job and moving back to the region. It was their original place-belongingness that made them search for work in the region. However, many had waited a long time before finding a relevant job as an ICT expert: "I have lived away since I started at university. I have been in [the city] the last 20-something years. I moved back home because an exciting job opportunity turned up. That does not happen every day, so that was not a difficult decision" (E).

Finding a relevant job was the trigger that made them return: "The main reason that I moved back was work. I have a very interesting and exciting job here, and it is obvious that I wouldn't have moved back home if I hadn't found a job that was at least as good as the one that I already had" (D). This justification for moving back and for staying in the region illustrates the entanglements of working and living in the rural region where differences between the urban and the rural also come into view. One of the women remembered her daily commute to the city, at least one hour each way, and the huge difference not having to do this made after she and her partner both found work as ICT experts in the region:

> 'It was mostly working and sleeping, and that's all you got to do. Thus, we didn't really see each other much. By moving here, we save a lot of time, we have shorter days and more flexible solutions. … There is a very good social network for outdoor activities here, for walking, biking, Alpine skiing, and more. We don't have to spend the weekends travelling far away. Now we can just spend an evening; have a short day at work and get out there. We have much more time for our own interests and for the children.' (J)

The 'moving back'-storyline highlights how rural life has certain qualities of life, and the idea of the rural idyll includes material and immaterial values (Bryden and Hart, 2004): "I think that some of the values we have here are values that you probably won't find in the big cities; that has to do with a feeling of unity, having good friends and to be close to family" (G). Important values refer to friends and family, suggesting that the women's return to the region also included a life phase strategy related to children (Grimsrud,

2011): "I want to live in a place with good conditions for bringing up my children, where I can have an exciting, demanding job, and I can have good experiences with nature in my everyday life without having to spend a lot of time moving from A to B" (H).

Furthermore, the 'moving back'-storyline describes the entanglements of place with work and life, illustrated by this lengthy quote from a woman who had experienced someone dying in her social circles:

> 'then he died, and that put my life into perspective. Suddenly I started thinking, "What are we doing all the way here in the eastern part of Norway with all our family so far away? This is so far away from our people". … Moving back was not about getting a babysitter, like many people think. It was about growing the real relationships, in particular between our parents and our children. That was what drew us. And I really love [the rural area]. I missed nature, and the various advantages were not difficult to think of. For instance, cottages that we can borrow [from our parents]; things we didn't have access to in the eastern part of Norway.' (F)

This woman's list of rural values and qualities was long, starting with "our people" and place-belongingness that both she and her partner felt for the region. While a condition for moving back was finding a relevant ICT job, the justification for moving was also tied to family bonds, social relations and nature.

The rural idyll and its threats

The western region of Norway is recognized for its spectacular nature including high mountains and deep fjords, two of which have even been added to the list of UNESCO World Heritage sites. This nature which makes the region a target for outdoor activities holds a special place in the 'moving back'-storyline: "I enjoy being outside, like outdoor activities and nature, and perhaps the main reason for moving back home was that I missed the mountains. Proper mountains" (D). While many of the values relating to place-belongingness were shared only by the women originating from the region, the values of nature and other aspects of the rural idyll were also expressed by women with a weaker sense of place-belongingness, including this immigrant woman:

> 'I walk to work in 15 minutes. It's a pleasure to walk and already that short time, twice a day, helps you to get a clean brain, get loose. … The biggest advantage of working as a researcher in [place] is that you save a lot of time that you waste in big cities in transport and organization of your work.' (I)

Logistics and transport are quite different in sparsely populated regions compared to urban traffic. This can produce an impression of time efficiency if one lives close to one's work in a rural area and does not have to rely on public transport, illustrating the inseparable character of working and living.

The image of the rural idyll was, however, also threatened, for instance by an urban-rural power structure including what the women experienced as urban ignorance, as this outburst by a female leader in digital innovation illustrates:

> 'It is not like we are a random group of peasants sitting here, trying to produce something. We have competences that are no less than in any other place. I'm so sick and tired of having to prove that we can manage things in this region … and that attitude where we have to prove ourselves. Twice.' (C)

Women working in ICT in the rural region, she suggested, not only had to prove themselves within a male-dominated occupation, but also against an urban elitist attitude.

A more problematic threat for the region considering the importance of making people want to live and work there, was the double-edged effect of place-belongingness. The 'moving back'-storyline illustrates that many rural values are tied to place-belongingness which was more available to women with family roots in the region. Even the women who had returned after living away for a long time benefited from their old social networks, old friends and people whom they recognized from school. For many, this type of network was important, not only on a private level, but also for support and confidence at work. But for the women who did not share this type of place-belongingness, the exact same values that were celebrated in the 'moving back'-storyline could become barriers. One of the youngest women in our sample, for instance, had moved to the region with her boyfriend, and at the time of the interview she was contemplating moving out again because she did not have a social network. This was even more tricky for women who were also immigrants to Norway, for whom both language and local traditions could become barriers for their social inclusion. One of these women described how she felt ignored and left out of small talk among her peers because she did not share their relation to nature: "Then I realized that I am not a skiing buddy" (A), reflecting the importance that outdoor sports activities can have for work relations in a region where such activities are highly valued.

Discussion

The analysis of women's experiences of ICT work in the rural context of western Norway does not support the notion of rurality as entailing static and traditional gender structures, but rather indicates a labour market in transition, partly as a result of digitalization across sectors. A previous study found that rural ICT employers still relied on gender stereotypical notions of ICT competence when recruiting to ICT jobs, and that few women applied for these jobs (Corneliussen and Seddighi, 2020). The patterns uncovered here indicate that women find workplaces responding to new processes of digitalization that are situated in less male-dominated organizations more attractive – perhaps also more available – than jobs in the private and highly male-dominated ICT industry. While previous research found that it is less likely for women with an atypical education to return to rural regions (Haley, 2018), the atypical female ICT experts in our sample disprove this trend. However, simultaneously it is the more gender-typical workplaces such as the female-dominated public sector that trigger their return to the rural region. Many of these women returned to the region after spending up to 20 years away. Thus, while young women might still be under the spell of the 'mobility imperative' (Farrugia, 2016: 836), this group of middle-aged women wishing to return or move to the rural region could be a potential target group for ICT employers seeking to recruit. However, so far it seems that only certain sectors are successful in this.

The women's constructions of rurality often included a comparison to urban environments. In-migration narratives intensified this as the women emphasized how the rural shaped their work and career. Thus, the sparsely populated region with its attendant effects on the labour market made them stand out, become visible as resources and therefore have interesting career opportunities. They were encouraged to take new responsibilities, but were also supported by employers who realized that they needed to take care of the existing human resources. Previous research suggests that support is particularly important for women engaging in occupational fields associated with men (Holtzblatt and Marsden, 2018). Thus, the support that the women identified as a quality of the rural region might have been highly valuable for making women feel more welcome in ICT jobs. The downside of being in a rural area was the thinness of organizations: the few relevant employers made job switching more difficult. In the end it was the strength of place-belongingness that affected many of the women's decision to stay or leave if the current job did not work out.

Place-belongingness also had a flip side, making the region attractive for some while producing challenges for others. In the 'moving back'-storyline it was finding a relevant job that was the main trigger for making women return to the region. However, it was their place-belongingness and the discourse of the idyllic rurality that justified the move. This rural idyll included values associated with closeness to nature, quality of life and more time for children, closeness to supportive grandparents, and more. Many women with family struggle to find a balance between time for work and family, including in this rural context (see Chapter 9, this volume). The values and qualities of the rural region emphasized by the women illustrate how place took an active role as the women negotiated their balance between work and family: most found it is easier to retain a good balance in the rural region rather than in the city. An important aspect of this was their sense of belonging as reflected in family and social relations.

But the same features that provided advantages for women with roots in the region created disadvantages for those without such roots. That the entanglement of working and living offered both prospects and challenges is a critical point to note: the rural as a good place for children is a selling point only for women with children; closeness to family only counts for those with roots in the region, and having access to social networks does not come automatically for newcomers. Nature was a major attraction for many, but not everybody became a "skiing buddy". Immigrant women were the majority of those who did not draw on the discourse of the rural idyll, especially in relation to family and social relations. Thus, although digitalization and the growth of ICT workplaces attracted the female ICT experts to jobs less traditional in a rural setting, the narratives of rurality were still tightly connected to making sense of 'a traditional way of life' and belonging (Grimsrud, 2011).

Conclusion

In this chapter we have shown how the discourse of the rural appears and is represented in narratives about living and working in the rural region of western Norway among women working with ICT. Digitalization has been launched as a solution securing a sustainable future across industries and sectors, and also as important for rural regions (Ekeland et al, 2015). Making remote rural regions attractive for young women is vital for sustainable population development in these areas (Vidickienė, 2017). Identifying how the rural enters women's work experiences, our findings suggest that a combination of a rural idyll discourse and the discourse of the rural as an actor in economic growth (Cruickshank et al, 2009) can be utilized to make the rural appear attractive to women. It is also necessary to recognize that women are not a uniform group, and we have shown how place-belongingness (Antonsich, 2010) is limited to women with roots in the region, while other rural values such as nature and quality of life make the region attractive for a more diverse group of women. We also recognize that the women contributed to discourses of rurality in at least two ways. First, they emphasized differences between the rural and the urban and promoted discourses of the rural idyll, quality of life and place-belongingness. Second, they also emphasized similarities, demonstrating the rural as a place of high competence in ICT development and innovation and claiming their equal worth compared to their urban collaborators. The rural as a place for digital innovation was, after all, the door opener for these women to enter the still highly male-dominated field of ICT research and innovation. Their choice of workplaces suggests a new co-construction of gender and ICT in which women not only participate, but also experience a work environment that is less male-dominated than women in the more traditional ICT industries have reported (Watts, 2009).

Support and networks are important for women in male-dominated fields (Holtzblatt and Marsden, 2018). Our findings suggest that further improvements can be made to women's experience of ICT work by recognizing that different groups of women have different senses of being included and excluded from social and professional networks in ICT and in rural regions. While certain gender structures appear to be more stable than others, our study contributes to the critique of seeing rural gender structures as unchangeable (Little, 2014) by providing a more nuanced image of women's work experiences entangled with rurality. More empirical studies are needed to further develop our knowledge about how the gendering of different workplaces and industries develops in rural regions, and more importantly, to learn how the private ICT sector and female ICT experts can become better aligned for the future.

References

Antonsich, M. (2010) 'Searching for belonging: an analytical framework', *Geography Compass*, 4(6): 644–59.

Barbieri, D., Caisl, J., Karu, M., Lanfredi, G., Mollard, B., Peciukonis, V., La Hoz, M.B.P., Reingardė, J. and Salanauskaitė, L. (2020) *Gender Equality Index 2020: Digitalisation and the Future of Work*, Luxembourg: EIGE: European Institute for Gender Equality.

Brandth, B. (2016) 'Rural masculinities and fathering practices', *Gender, Place & Culture*, 23(3): 435–50.

Bryden, J.M. and Hart, K. (2004) *A New Approach to Rural Development in Europe: Germany, Greece, Scotland, and Sweden*, Lewiston, NY: Edwin Mellen Press.

Charmaz, K. (2006) *Constructing Grounded Theory: A Practical Guide through Qualitative Research*, London: Sage.

Corneliussen, H.G. and Seddighi, G. (2020) 'Employers' mixed signals to women in IT: uncovering how gender equality ideals are challenged by organizational context', in P. Kommers and G.C. Peng (eds) *Proceedings for the International Conference ICT, Society, and Human Beings 2020*, IADIS Press, pp 41–8.

Corneliussen, H.G., Seddighi, G. and Dralega, C.A. (2019) 'Women's experience of role models in IT: landmark women, substitutes, and supporters', in Ø. Helgesen, E. Nesset, G. Mustafa, P. Rice and R. Glavee-Geo (eds) *Modeller: Fjordantologien 2019*, Oslo: Universitetsforlaget, pp 375–95.

Cruickshank, J., Lysgård, H.K. and Magnussen, M.I. (2009) 'The logic of the construction of rural politics: political discourses on rurality in Norway', *Geografiska Annaler: Series B, Human Geography*, 91(1): 73–89.

EIGE (2018) *Women and Men in ICT: A Chance for Better Work–Life Balance: Research Note*, Luxembourg: European Institute for Gender Equality, Publications Office of the European Union.

Ekeland, A., Pajarinen, M. and Rouvinen, P. (2015) *Computerization and the Future of Jobs in Norway*, Oslo: Statistics Norway.

Eurostat (2019) *ICT specialists in employment: statistics explained*. Available at: https://ec.europa.eu/eurostat/statistics-explained/index.php/ICT_specialists_in_employment, accessed 10 May 2021.

Farrugia, D. (2016) 'The mobility imperative for rural youth: the structural, symbolic and non-representational dimensions rural youth mobilities', *Journal of Youth Studies*, 19(6): 836–51.

Forsberg, G. (2001) 'The difference that space makes: a way to describe the construction of local and regional gender contracts', *Norsk Geografisk Tidsskrift* [*Norwegian Journal of Geography*], 55(3): 161–5.

Grimsrud, G.M. (2011) 'Gendered spaces on trial: the influence of regional gender contracts on in-migration of women to rural Norway', *Geografiska Annaler: Series B, Human Geography*, 93(1): 3–20.

Grip, L. (2020) *Genusperspektiv på regionala utmaningar, regionalpolitik och demografisk utveckling i en nordisk kontext*, Gøteborg: NIKK, for the Nordic Council of Ministers.

Haley, A. (2018) 'Returning to rural origins after higher education: gendered social space', *Journal of Education and Work*, 31(4): 418–32.

Hanson, S. (2010) 'Gender and mobility: new approaches for informing sustainability', *Gender, Place & Culture*, 17(1): 5–23.

Heleniak, T. and Gassen, N.S. (2020) 'The demise of the rural Nordic region? Analysis of regional population trends in the Nordic countries, 1990 to 2040', *Nordisk välfärdsforskning* [*Nordic Welfare Research*], 5(1): 40–57.

Holtzblatt, K. and Marsden, N. (2018) 'Retaining women in technology: uncovering and measuring key dimensions of daily work experiences', *Proceedings from the 2018 IEEE International Conference on Engineering, Technology and Innovation (ICE/ITMC)*, pp 148–55.

Kvale, S. and Brinkmann, S. (2009) *Det kvalitative forskningsintervju*, Oslo: Gyldendal akademisk.

Laclau, E. and Mouffe, C. (1985) *Hegemony and Socialist Strategy: Towards a Radical Democratic Politics*, London: Verso.

Larsen, Ø.H. and Nesse, J.G. (2017) 'Den immaterielle sida av nettverkssamarbeid', in J.R. Andersen, E. Bjørhusdal, J.G. Nesse and T. Årethun (eds) *Immateriell kapital: Fjordantologien 2017*, Oslo: Universitetsforlaget, pp 362–97.

Little, J. (2002) *Gender and Rural Geography*, London: Routledge.

Little, J. (2014) 'The development of feminist perspectives in rural gender studies', in B. Pini, B. Brandth and J. Little (eds) *Feminisms and Ruralities*, London: Lexington Books, pp 107–18.

Little, J. and Panelli, R. (2003) 'Gender research in rural geography', *Gender, Place and Culture: A Journal of Feminist Geography*, 10(3): 281–9.

NOU (2020: 15) *Det handler om Norge: utredning om konsekvenser av demografiutfordringer i distriktene*, Oslo: Kommunal- og moderniseringsdepartementet.

Pristed Nielsen, H., Hayfield, E.A. and Arnfjord, S. (2020) *Equal Opportunities for Men and Women in Geographically Isolated Labour Markets in Læsø (Dk), Suðuroy (Fo), and Narsaq (Gl)*, København: TemaNord 2020: 522, Nordic Council of Ministers.

Seddighi, G. and Corneliussen, H.G. (2021) 'The illusion of balance: women in ICT working full-time and still having a feeling of opting out', *Feminist Encounters*, 5(2): art. No. 26.

Shortall, S. and Bock, B. (2015) 'Introduction: rural women in Europe: the impact of place and culture on gender mainstreaming the European rural development programme', *Gender, Place & Culture*, 22(5): 662–9.

Statistics Norway (2018) *Women and Men in Norway*, Oslo: Statistics Norway.

Strauss, A. and Corbin, J. (1998) *Basics of Qualitative Research: Techniques and Procedures for Developing Grounded Theory*, London: Sage.

Vareide, K., Vareide, D. and Persdatter Miland, K. (2019) *Regional analyse for Sogn og Fjordane 2019: næringsutvikling, befolkningsutvikling, attraktivitet og scenarier*, Bø: Telemarksforsking.

Vidickienė, D. (2017) 'Attractiveness of rural areas for young, educated women in post-industrial society', *Eastern European Countryside*, 23(1): 171–90.

Villa, M. (2000) 'Rural life courses in Norway', *The History of the Family*, 5(4): 473–90.

Walsh, D. and Gerrard, S. (2018) 'Gender, mobilities and transformation in Loppa, a rural municipality of Norway's high north', *Gender, Place & Culture*, 25(8): 1154–74.

Watts, J.H. (2009) '"Allowed into a man's world": meanings of work–life balance: perspectives of women civil engineers as "minority" workers in construction', *Gender, Work & Organization*, 16(1): 37–57.

West, C. and Zimmerman, D.H. (1987) 'Doing gender', *Gender & Society*, 1(2): 125–51.

Winther Jørgensen, M. and Phillips, L. (1999) *Diskursanalyse som teori og metode*, Frederiksberg: Roskilde Universitetsforlag Samfundslitteratur.

Index

Q

R

S

V

W

Y